THE GREATEST FIGHTS
THAT NEVER WERE

This book is dedicated to Great Uncle Reg,

who has been watching boxing for nine decades.

First published in 2014 by New Holland Publishers Pty Ltd
London • Sydney • Auckland

The Chandlery Unit 114 50 Westminster Bridge Road London SE1 7QY United Kingdom
1/66 Gibbes Street Chatswood NSW 2067 Australia
218 Lake Road Northcote Auckland New Zealand

www.newhollandpublishers.com

A record of this book is held at the British Library and the National Library of Australia.

ISBN 9781742575582

Managing Director: Fiona Schultz
Publisher: Alan Whiticker
Project Editor: Emily Carryer
Designer: Andrew Quinlan
Photographs: Getty Images, Clay Moyle, Kyle David and Harry Otty
Proofreader: Julie King
Production Director: Olga Dementiev
Printer: Toppan Leefung Printing Ltd (China)

10 9 8 7 6 5 4 3 2 1

Keep up with New Holland Publishers on Facebook
www.facebook.com/NewHollandPublishers

THE GREATEST
FIGHTS
THAT NEVER WERE

★ ★ ★ ★ ★ ★ ★ ★ ★ ★ ★ ★ ★

Matthew Bazell

NEW
HOLLAND

Author's Note

Over the decades there have been countless lost bouts which could be considered great fights that never were. So much so, that I'm not aiming to bring the reader a definitive account that cites even near to every single one. There will be lost bouts not included in this book, which some people will feel should be. However, the chapters chosen are simply some personal favourites and I hope that they resonate with you

A massive thanks to Steve Bunce for writing the foreword. Much appreciation as well to Herol Graham and Barry Hearn for taking the time to meet me for a sit-down interview.

I'd also like to say thank you to Clay Moyle, Miles Templeton, Harry Otty, Joe Egan, Donald McRea, Greg Smith, Alan Whiticker, Emily Carryer, Jim Delany, Catherine Bazell and all the family.

Contents

FOREWORD   **9**

By Steve Bunce

ROUND 1   **11**

It Ain't Showtime. . .Ducking and Diving

ROUND 2   **25**

Tyson and the 'Terrible' Lost Heavyweight

ROUND 3   **49**

'Lights Out' for Title Unifications

ROUND 4   **75**

Schmeling Is Denied a Date with Cinderella

INTERLUDE   **93**

The 'Hawk' Falls Off the 'Money Tree'

ROUND 5   **96**

Don't Let Me Call You Chicken, Bowe!

ROUND 6   **117**

Dodging the 'Bomber': Herol 'Bomber'

ROUND 7   **134**

Sam Langford: Too Black, Too Dodged

ROUND 8   159
When Larry Didn't Meet George

INTERLUDE   177
The Wasted One

ROUND 9   180
Fights That Should Never Have Happened

ROUND 10   208
Ten Crackers Not to Go Off

ROUND 11   258
Benn, Hearns, Jones: The Lost Wars

INTERLUDE   276
The Wasted Ones

ROUND 12   282
The Cubans Are Not Coming

ROUND 13   300
Friendship and Brotherhood

ROUND 14   316
Rematches and the 'Fight' That Thankfully Didn't Happen

ROUND 15   338
No Grand Daddy at the MGM Grand?

FOREWORD

by Steve Bunce

Boxing has a glorious history of lost fights; it is nothing new and it will not end anytime soon. Some of the best fights in history never happened. Some of the greatest boxers in the sport's rich history never had the one defining fight, the one night that would have forever changed their legacy.

As fans we usually take the process one-step further and create fantasy fights, matching boxers from different weight classes and decades in mad fights that have no outcome. We put the Sugar Men together and ask what Sugar Ray Robinson beats what Sugar Ray Leonard? People argue about Robinson at welter against the best Tommy Hearns. It goes on and on and it is fun. It is fun because time, a genuine excuse, denied us all the fight.

This book is not about genuine excuses, not about the fantasy fights that illuminate our late-night viewing of imported fights and the nights in bars debating endless pointless crazy fights. No, this book deals in facts and fights that should have taken place and could have taken place. This book highlights what is wrong with the boxing business and it is, trust me, not a new phenomenon.

Why has Floyd Mayweather not met Manny Pacquiao, what about Lennox Lewis v Riddick Bowe, Roy Jones v Nigel Benn and dozens of other ancient and modern fights that fell through holes? All of the biggest names are here; nobody, it seems, is free from scrutiny.

This book takes the fantasy fight one stage further, smashes the illusion and shatters the idea that great fights are pure fantasy—this book is about great fights that should have happened and could have happened. This is not a book of fantasy fights, it is a long-overdue book of lost fights and reading about them is as good as it will ever get.

ROUND 1

IT AIN'T SHOWTIME... DUCKING AND DIVING!

'Boxing is like no other sport. It has no national commissioner to set standards for health and safety. In boxing there are no leagues or schedules. Every match is a separate deal. There is no rational structure. The chaos itself is an impediment to reform. The casual fan does not understand how the sport is run. In baseball, the standards reflect a quantifiable reality.'

Jack Newfield, author of *The Life and Crimes of Don King*

'Boxing fans play the what-if game a lot. What if…Muhammad Ali fought Jack Johnson? What if…Oscar De La Hoya fought Sugar Ray Leonard? Alas they are often forced to play it in the present.'

Dan Jones, *Evening Standard*, 2014

Throughout a successful and glittering career Tiger Woods has had to play all the best golfers of his generation. The structure of the sport meant that there was no other route for him to win the major honours and become an undisputed golfing legend. In the world of football you will never hear a phrase such as, 'Man United wouldn't be league champions if they hadn't ducked playing Chelsea'.

How different things would be if the weird and unstructured world of boxing was universally applied in other sports. Imagine if Roger Federer ended his career with question marks hanging over him regarding whether or not he had faced the best opponent of his generation. 'That Federer was one hell of a player, but he never faced Nadal, that would have been a classic'. You may hear people remark, 'I wonder what would have happened if Pete Sampras had played Bjorn Borg'. But that's a different scenario, as two careers were separated by different generations. So let's be clear: this book will not speculate on what would have happened if Mike Tyson had fought Muhammad Ali. Those two men peaked around twenty years apart from one another. Ali's undisputed prime was around 1964 to 1967, while Mike Tyson was born in 1966. There was no possibility of that fight ever happening and no chapter in this book will concentrate on 'dream matches' that couldn't feasibly have happened. As Harry Carpenter once said, 'People always want to compare someone from the past to today…it doesn't matter. All you have to be is the best in your own time, that's all you can ever ask'.

The subject of opponents not competing against one another is a discussion commonplace to boxing. A breakdown of a fighter's legacy will not pass without the inevitable cross-examination of what didn't happen, as opposed to what did. 'If he'd fought that guy he wouldn't have remained undefeated. If he'd fought that chap his legacy would have had more credibility'. The debates on what failed to transpire are an obsession, and we just don't have comparable conversations when talking about other sports.

Whether it be politics, friendship, corruption, racial prejudice, organised crime or, in the Klitschkos' case, family ties, a combat sport like professional boxing can uniquely allow its performers to be able to avoid a top-quality opponent through their, or their management's, own choice. 'Don't want to fight that man? No problem. Let's hold talks with the other guy'. Titles can be taken away from boxers for ducking an opponent, but it's not in the public eye and very little kudos is lost. The most well known example of this was when Riddick Bowe was stripped of his WBC title after avoiding the number-one contender Lennox Lewis. Upset at the decision of the World Boxing Council, Bowe literally dropped his title belt into the garbage in front of the world's media. His statement was simple: Lennox, if you want the belt then you can pick it out from the trash. That incident aside, the casual boxing fan will probably struggle to recall other moments where titles have been stripped for not facing a number-one contender, despite such a scenario being very common.

The paradox of boxing is that it's a sport, which is more intense, brutal, cruel and sacrificial than any other, yet performers of other sports don't have the same luxury of being able to pick and choose opposition that suits their style. Let's suppose that Barcelona beats Bayern Munich in the semi-final of the Champions League. In the other semi-final Real Madrid beats AC Milan. However, Madrid decide that they don't like the terms of the Barcelona final, therefore they go off and play Ajax instead—it would be farcical.

In 2013, it was reported that Bernard Hopkins would like a shot at the super middleweight king Andre Ward, but that the fight was unlikely to happen because Hopkins was contracted to the cable network, Showtime, while Ward was with HBO. Once again, such broadcasting politics is a unique scenario that sets boxing apart from other sports and gets in the way of the best possible scheduling for the paying fan. In other sports, TV networks bid for the right to show previously agreed fixtures, while with boxing, the opposite scenario occurs. Imagine the Super Bowl not going ahead because the Dallas Cowboys and the New York Giants had separate broadcasting contracts.

In recent years, promoter and cable network rivalry has become a major reason that fights have not happened. Top Rank promotions, whose main star has been Manny Pacquiao, have a relationship with the broadcaster HBO. While their rival, Golden Boy Promotions, work with Showtime and have the rights to the fights of Floyd Mayweather. The two rival promoters don't like to work with one another and will keep their events within the stable, or seek opponents who are independent of their rival. In late 2013, a natural match that would have pitted form against form would have been Floyd Mayweather against Timothy Bradley, in a fight in which one man would lose their unbeaten record. Such matchmaking, however, depended on Top Rank's Bradley becoming freelance or moving to Golden Boy Promotions. Mayweather's close working association with GBP and his contract with Showtime meant that fighting an opponent contracted to Top Rank was out of the question. Golden Boy's CEO Richard Schaefer made it clear that while with Top Rank, his stable of star names would not be fighting Bradley, and said, 'Remember what Bob Arum [Top Rank's boss] told Shane Mosley when he wanted Pacquiao, or remember what Arum told Juan Manuel Marquez when he wanted to fight Pacquiao? He told them that they would get the fight but only if they would be free agents [free of Golden Boy]'. Schaefer added, 'Well what goes around comes around. Once Tim [Bradley] is a free agent we would be happy to have him in the mix with all the great fighters we have'.

As it stands, Bradley could not be matched up with other Golden Boy fighters such as Amir Khan, Danny Garcia and Adrian Broner. This led *Boxing News* editor Tris Dixon to describe Bradley as the most effected fighter in a long-standing promotional cold war. The feud between the promoters went back to when the 'Golden Boy' himself, Oscar De La Hoya, left Top Rank to create GBP with Richard Schaefer. Then Floyd Mayweather moved from HBO to Showtime, which intensified a bitter relationship between the two cable networks. The promoters and cable networks became tribal and formed alliances. Boxing's biggest feud became Top Rank/HBO versus Golden Boy/Showtime. This was a rivalry that fans were not interested in and mostly came to resent for getting in the way of the best matches being made.

When asked by *Boxing News* if such a feud was good for the sport, the British promoter Frank Warren said that at least it wasn't a monopoly, but it would mean that fights will be prevented from happening.

The trainer Eddie M. Muhammad responded to the same question by saying, 'You're not going to have the quality fights that people want to see because the two sides are always feuding'.

The manager Cameron Dunkin added, 'I don't think it's good for boxing because the fans want to see everybody fight everybody'.

If a Top Rank star loses to a GBP star, or vice versa, one promoter becomes perceived to be the sport's leader. At the time of writing, the most intriguing and unpredictable match that boxing could make would be Floyd Mayweather against the formidable Gennady Golovkin from Kazakhstan, a man described as so dangerous he can't get a shot. Even if Mayweather was willing to fight Golovkin, the spanner in the works once again would be that one is contracted to HBO and the other contracted to Showtime. So, instead, most of the talk revolved instead around Mayweather fighting Golden Boy talent such as Amir Khan and Danny Garcia. Promoter Dan Goossen told *Boxing News*, 'It's never good, if a rift, for whatever reason, between promoters, prevents good fights from being made. All one has to do is look at Mayweather-Pacquiao not being made'. He added, 'Any promoter that doesn't do everything in their power to deliver the biggest and best fights for their fighter and the fans should be suspended or fired by that fighter'.

Danny Flexon of *Boxing News* was also sceptical of such promoter and broadcaster feuds being any good for the scheduling of the sport. 'It's bad. We, as fans and pundits, are being robbed of some great fights. The Mayweather situation exemplifies this issue in microcosm. Few knowledgeable boxing observers believe Amir Khan deserves the next shot at Floyd, but when speculation begins regarding "Money's" next opponent twice each year, one can immediately rule out any non-GBP and non-Showtime fighters. So no Tim Bradley (TR), Sergio Martinez or Gennady Golovkin (both HBO), all of whom are more deserving than Khan and would, in my view, give Mayweather a sterner challenge'.

The people with the power to stop the Cold War are the paying fans. If buying and viewing figures for both sides go down because the best fights are not being made then it would force Top Rank/HBO and GBP/Showtime to work together in order to pick up business. One factor that doesn't help ratings in boxing is when HBO and Showtime put on events at the same time, forcing fans to choose one or the other. A similar thing happened in wrestling in the late 1990s when the two big companies, WCW and WWF, went head to head in a Monday night ratings war. Wrestling fans would have watched both programmes if they were aired on different nights, but they were forced to make a choice on Mondays. WCW lost the unnecessary war that they started and went bust in 2001 due to low ratings. If Top Rank/HBO and GBP/Showtime worked together to put on the best possible scheduling, then the chances are that fans would be happier and the fighting stables for all sides would become even stronger.

In the modern era, another factor that has got in the way of fights happening, and ducking being made easier, is the quantity of world championship belts. I was at a small boxing event in Bethnal Green, London, recently and, to my surprise, there was a world title up for grabs— some intercontinental belt that nobody had heard of or remotely cared about (no disrespect intended, but that also goes for the two fighters involved in this 'world title' bout). Joe Calzaghe once noted, 'All these intercontinental titles. What are they and who cares? The only Inter I knew growing up was a football team in Milan and I never liked them either'.

Then we have the four recognised world championship bodies, two of which were created as early as the 1980s. The World Boxing Association, formally known as the NBA, was first and came about in 1962, shortly followed by the World Boxing Council a year later. Then in 1983, along came the International Boxing Federation, and if three organisations were not enough to devalue the words 'world champion', the World Boxing Organisation was formed in 1988. In the 1990s the WBO and WBC super middleweight titles were held by Brits and defended mostly on their shores. At the same time, the IBF and WBA counterparts were being fought over on the other side of the Atlantic. Although it was a great era for middleweight boxing, it somehow feels incomplete because we didn't see the collisions and unifications that would have given total clarity to reputations and to the sport. It was far easier for the four titleholders to remain champions by not fighting one another.

Other sports do not have four world governing bodies; and how weird and absurd it would be if the nature of boxing scheduling was universal. Going back to the hypothetical football example I used. Real Madrid go off to play Ajax because they don't fancy mixing it with Barcelona, well that game against Ajax is another version of the Champions League Final. But it isn't sanctioned by UEFA, it is sanctioned by CEFA, the Confederation of European Football Associations. And Madrid beat Ajax to become champions of Europe. Barcelona also win their UEFA sanctioned final and claim to be European champions. But Madrid and Barca don't have to face each other because it's fairly convenient for them to play it safe and both reign as champs at the same time. Meanwhile, Manchester United beats Juventus in the other Champions League final that is sanctioned by AEFA, the Association of European Football Associations. The month before that, Inter Milan beat Manchester City in the Champions League final sanctioned by IAFF, the International Association of Football Federations. In the following months, Inter Milan put out a challenge to play Manchester United. This was a matchup

that the football world was eager to see happen, but unfortunately talks
fell through over money, broadcasting rights and the choice of venue.
So instead, Manchester United played Millwall in a one-sided farce.
They used a mass brawl between supporters of the two clubs to drum up
hype for a contest, which, beforehand, no one was really interested in.
The promotional manipulation of the brawl between the hooligans was
condemned strongly by the media. However, when the time came for the
game, hype took over and the pay-per-view sales were solid.

Just as there are a high quantity of belts there are also a high number
of weight divisions, which make it easier to duck tricky things that may
not suit your style. In the black and white TV era before the 1970s there
was one world championship in eight weight divisions. Today, there are
world champions in 17 divisions in which the weight disparity is hardly like
comparing Laurel to Hardy. There are now four flyweight divisions alone
that range from 108 lbs (49 kg) and 115 lbs (52 kg). The range of the three
featherweight divisions is a mere 6 lbs (2.7 kg) and one small Mars Bars
binge can push you up from a junior to a super. The three welterweight
divisions are within just 14l bs (6.3 kg) of one another, whereas years earlier
there was just one welterweight division which had a weight limit of 147 lbs
(66.7 kg). The next step up to middleweight was 13 lbs (5.9 kg) , which was
a significant difference in weight.

To highlight a recent example of ducking accusations levelled at
someone for moving weights: in 2012 the emerging star Adrian Broner and
his management accused the WBO champion Ricky Burns of moving up
from the 130 lbs (59 kg) weight class by 7 lbs (3 kg), just so he could avoid
fighting him. Broner said, 'This is a career where you can guide yourself

through things, and if you see something that don't look right, you can duck or jump over and that's what he did'.

Quantity of contests for a fighter, or in this case the lack of, will also play a part in whether or not careers are finished without lots of question marks regarding lost matchups. The modern boxing superstar tends to fight once or twice a year, therefore it's inevitable that many potential bouts that seem well matched and worthy will not go ahead. In the first half of the twentieth century it was normal for a boxer to have a fight tally record of 100 bouts or more.[1] Sugar Ray Robinson, whose career spanned 1940 to 1965, competed in over 200 professional bouts and 85 amateur contests. In 1941 alone Robinson fought 20 times, and in the final year of his career he still had 14 fights left in him—and we're not talking about tickling contests here either. This book will not have any chapters that heavily feature Sugar Ray Robinson. I'd say that man had more than enough punch-ups. But it does not conclusively mean that having lots of fights indicates that a career can totally end without a few *what ifs*. The legendary and flamboyant light heavyweight champion Maxie Rosenbloom finished his career with 299 bouts, and there are experts who insist that he was sidestepped by Joe Louis for the heavyweight title in the 1930s.

In general terms, however, the high pay of a big-name fighter means they're not required to compete very often and this, of course, rightly or wrongly, limits possibilities.[2]

The 1960s and 1970s were when TV audiences got bigger, earnings more lucrative and schedules relatively less demanding. A top-name boxer didn't need to have more than one or two fights a year in order to live the good life. In the 1970s Joe Frazier would fight an average of twice a year, which is similar to today's heavyweight champion Wladimir Klitschko. A big-money fight against David Haye was Wladimir's only contest in 2011, while he fought three very beatable non-box office names in 2012. David Haye's average became just one fight a year and he looks set to retire on less than 30 professional contests. In 2012, the year when a lot of people felt that Haye should have fought Vitali Klitschko, he spent his time in the jungle for *I'm a Celebrity Get Me Out of Here*, or as comedian Paul Merton appropriately calls it, 'I'm not a celebrity get me on this programme'.

There's certainly no sane or reasonable argument to say that boxers should fight to the schedules of Ray Robinson or Maxie Rosenbloom, and it's good for the health of the modern-day boxer that they don't have to put their lives on the line too often. Medical reports are clear in concluding that the more fights a boxer has, particularly at an older age, the more chance there is of brain damage. Ray Robinson himself was a victim of too many fights. In the final 15 years of his life he suffered from dementia as a direct result of boxing. His dementia was severe enough for the great man to not know how great he really was. An argument in this book will not be that someone like Chris Eubank should have had more than 48 fights, the tally which he finished his career with. In contrast, he should have had fewer fights and instead of going up against 'bum of the month', he could have fought one or two more legacy definers against the biggest names in his division.

'Ducking' is a factor which prevents fights from happening. As for diving, in the 1940s and 1950s, the mob, fronted by Frankie Carbo and Blinky Palermo (called 'Blinky', some say, because he couldn't look you in the eye) prevented matches that should have happened if anyone crossed their path. They unofficially ran the sport and if you challenged them or refused an instruction, you could be outcast in spite of your ability. Refusing an instruction usually meant saying no to taking a dive or being party to a fixed fight.

Immortalised by the Marlon Brando line, 'I could have been a contender, I could have been somebody', in the film *On the Waterfront*, match fixing by the mafia was common in boxing, and if you refused to do what you were told, then you would not get the matches that your talent may have warranted. They denied the sport some potentially classic matchups. One prime example is the heavyweight contender Coley Wallace who should have been given the chance to fight Rocky Marciano in the 1950s. After all, Coley had registered a win against The Rock from Brockton when the two competed as amateurs. Wallace claims to have won that fight easily, although there have been mixed reports, as some journalists said the decision to award Wallace the win was a travesty. One man was said to be so outraged at the decision that he quite literally fell off his chair. In contradiction to those protests, the boxing journalist Jim Breslin claims that the reporters who questioned the decision were 'Either lying or were not at the fight'. Breslin recalls an easy win for Wallace who knocked down Marciano twice in a three-round contest. In his professional career Wallace got himself on the wrong side of the mob by refusing to take a dive to Marciano. Looking back on his career Wallace recalled, 'They [the mob] wanted a white champion. Blinky told me if I wanted to fight Marciano, I would have to take a dive. I told him "No, forget it"'.

That refusal by Wallace to partake in diving made him an outcast and he had nowhere credible to turn in order to have a successful career. Fighters that fell out with the likes of Carbo and his partner Blinky didn't have other golden paths in the sport. It was the gangster's way or the highway and anyone who tried to run independent boxing promotions were dealt with brutally. Taken from Thomas Myler's excellent book *Boxing's Hall of Shame*, Wallace describes his predicament:

> That was the fight game in the 1950s. You kept quiet or you didn't fight. I just let it go. That was boxing. I didn't fight for the title, but I have my pride. Frankie Carbo controlled boxing. You had to go with him, and the way to Carbo was through Blinky. I could have gone to somebody else, but without Carbo, you didn't get the big money or the big fights. Carbo controlled all the champions…I get angry when I think about Blinky Palermo…he could have done better for me, he ruined boxing for me.

Carbo and Blinky also denied matches and ruined the career of an up-and-coming New Jersey welterweight called Vince Martinez who was a fighter full of promise in the late 1940s. He got himself on the wrong side of the mob by first protesting their deductions on his earnings, and then refusing a $20,000 incentive to lose a fight. Not only did Martinez refuse to be part of a fix but he reported their intentions to the sporting authorities. In reward for his admirable honesty, Martinez was effectively suspended from the sport. This was because Carbo controlled the corrupt Managers Guild. No worthy boxing manger, no worthy fight. To quote Thomas Myler: 'The message was clear: if you want to get the fights that matter, join the guild; otherwise, you're out'.

Martinez recalls: 'We ran into a stone wall every place we turned. At first we couldn't understand it. Here I was a top-ranked contender and not a promoter in the country would give me work. Then we found out, I was blacklisted'. Finally, in 1961, Blinky Palermo and Frankie Carbo were both sentenced to 15 and 20 years for the crimes in boxing of conspiracy and extortion. However, in the 1980s and 1990s the promoter Don King carried on the tradition where if boxers crossed the line they'd be outcast.

That leads us on nicely to Round 2 . . .

1. Of the olden day era, Rocky Marciano is the superstar whose fight tally is similar to what we're used to today, assuming a fighter doesn't go well beyond his prime. Marciano retried on 49 bouts, which is also the amount of fights that the legendary champion 'Homicide' Henry Armstrong had in the space of just three years—and these were his comeback fights after he initially retired! 'Homicide' once fought five title defences in the space of one month. Armstrong will not feature in this book. Like Robinson I'd say he had more than enough punch-ups. In the modern era, Mike Tyson is the heavyweight boxing superstar who fought at a rate of over once a month during the time of his prime. In 1986, Tyson boxed an incredible 13 bouts, ending that year with the knockout of Trevor Berbeck to become the youngest world heavyweight champion. Of those 13 fights, seven of them didn't go past the 2nd round—so it was more a case of Tyson beating a guy up once a month.

2. Not to mention the lesser round schedule, which was reduced from 15 to 12 in 1982. This measure was in reaction to Ray Mancini's lightweight championship fight, in which his South Korean opponent Duk Koo Kim died a few days later as a result of head injuries sustained. This was a horrific story all round as Kim's mother committed suicide, as did the match referee. On the subject of rounds being reduced from 15 to 12, Mancini commented, 'It just bothers me, the guys today, God bless them, but they get paid a whole lot more for doing a whole lot less!' Mancini, a warrior of the sport, fought 37 bouts in total, but was very much affected by the Kim fight, and many believe he was traumatised and lost his edge as a fighter.

ROUND 2

TYSON AND THE 'TERRIBLE' LOST HEAVYWEIGHT

'Boxing doesn't have a schedule, doesn't have a commissioner, doesn't have a series of teams, it's not a highly structured sport. Don [King] works within the non-structure or the disorganisation of the sport.'

Seth Abraham, boxing TV negotiator

'I like fighters and I hate injustice. I like fighters like Ali, Witherspoon and Mamby. I don't like what Don King did to them. They are decent people. We are on earth for a short time and we have to do good.'

Thomas Hauser, respected boxing author

It would be reasonable to say that Mike Tyson faced every credible opponent in the heavyweight division during his prime in the mid to late 1980s, with the exception of one stand out name. Although, when I jotted down the idea of Mike Tyson-Tim Witherspoon as a possible feature for this book, I didn't do so with 100 percent conviction. Mainly because an important consideration in highlighting fights that should have happened is a battle of two near equals—the irresistible force versus the immovable object. Iron Mike versus 'Terrible' Tim would have been more like the irresistible force versus the talented and experienced underdog. Especially considering that the two would most likely have met during Tyson's prime between 1986 and 1988, the time when the New Yorker from Brownsville built up a reputation as one of the most brutal knockout merchants in heavyweight history. Tim Witherspoon was not the immovable object, and you'd have to make a very good case for him in being able to beat an in-prime Mike Tyson. But when one delves into the career obstacles of Witherspoon, there is no doubt that this lost fight must not only be included, but should be considered a cornerstone of the entire subject of events that should have gone differently. Plus there are those who would say that a fit and positive-minded Tim Witherspoon would have represented one of Tyson's most formidable opponents. On Witherspoon's official website it states:

> Tim was regarded as one of the most promising heavyweight
> boxers of his era but the legal battles and time out of the ring due
> to his management cost Tim more glory when he was at the peak of
> his career. Tyson v Witherspoon would have been the best fight

on earth if they were both in their prime, many believe Tim had the style to trouble a young Tyson.

Even if Witherspoon had ended up a lamb to the Tyson slaughter, he had earned the chance for a big payday that would have come with fighting Iron Mike. Stoke City are not usually expected to win away at Chelsea, but it's not beyond the realms of possibility if they are focused and the opposition has an off day. Stoke still have the right to compete. They can't be denied that opportunity because a corrupt executive of the Premier League doesn't like them. To put it in very simple terms, the sabotage of Witherspoon's career and other heavyweights of the same era represents everything that's deplorable and immoral about those who have run boxing for their own ill-gotten gains.

The beginning of the end for Witherspoon had come in 1982 when he was an unknown and signed a long-term deal with the flamboyant Don King, the most successful promoter in boxing history. The signing of the contract came about after King tried to get Cleveland State Boxing Commission to revoke Witherspoon's licence. 'The commission is me, them guys ain't nothing. It's me. They do what I tell them', King is claimed to have said to Witherspoon, who he was angry with for pulling out of a fight due to an injury and the advice of his doctor. The little-known Witherspoon was so desperate for some income that he signed his career away for chicken feed. Part of the deal included a guaranteed world title shot, but it meant that Witherspoon was contractually obliged to have Don's stepson Carl King as his manager, who would go on to take 50 percent of all Witherspoon's earnings. In America, boxing laws stipulate that you cannot promote and manage the same fighter. The job of the manager is to be independent and negotiate as much money as possible from the promoter. This wasn't going to happen with Carl King and the idea that he was independent of his stepfather was absurd, though allowed to happen. Don King is claimed to have once said 'Carl is me. I'm Carl'. Deductions of Witherspoon's earnings in the name of Carl King would be the fundamental factor in the downfall of the fighter's peace of mind and ultimately his career. Author of the brilliant book *The Life and Crimes of Don King*, Jack Newfield concluded, 'By signing Witherspoon, King now controlled nine of the top ten heavyweights in the world. The vulture on the ring post had another meal'.

Tim Witherspoon learned his trade by trading with the best. He never got the chance to fight Tyson, but he did step in the ring with Muhammad Ali on a number of occasions. The two were sparring partners at Deer Lake in Witherspoon's home state of Pennsylvania. 'If everybody in the world was like him [Ali], we wouldn't have any problems in the world', was Witherspoon's assessment of his employer.

Nicknamed 'Terrible', he was born in Philadelphia in 1957 and started boxing professionally in 1979. Witherspoon's first title shot came about just 15 fights into his pro career in 1983, when he was pitted against the great Larry Holmes for the WBC belt. He nearly pulled off a huge upset and Holmes was awarded a close points decision which many people felt should have gone the other way. In his autobiography Holmes recalled, 'Witherspoon was, I thought, a talented fighter. I can tell you this. He gave me hell when we fought. . .I escaped with a split decision that night…' A year later, in 1984, Witherspoon did became a world champion by beating the Don King-controlled fighter Greg Page on points to win the WBA title which had been vacated by Michael Dokes, another Don King fighter and a man who developed a destructive cocaine habit. Later on that year Witherspoon lost the title on points to Pinklon Thomas. Then two years later in 1986 he would become only the third man in history to regain the heavyweight title when he beat Tony Tubbs on points in a contest considered so devoid of action that it made Audley Harrison-David Haye seem like the Thrilla in Manila.[1] The standard of 1980s championship heavyweight boxing had slipped badly and boxers with talent like Witherspoon were not fighting to their full potential. The Tim Witherspoon who won the title back against Tubbs in 1986 was not as good as the young and inexperienced Tim Witherspoon who narrowly lost a decision against Larry Holmes three years earlier. Issues relating to payments were affecting his state of mind, as aside from Carl King's large slice of the fight fee, deductions were also made on a whole miscellaneous list of questionable expenses. King's stable were becoming demoralised, and in later years they would be referred to as the 'lost generation' of heavyweights—such a contrast to the 1970s which became known as the golden years of heavyweight boxing. The journalist Jack Newfield who was a thorn in the side of King, said of the Witherspoon-Tubbs match and undercard, 'The whole evening turned out to be a grotesque farce, featuring almost seven of the self-destructive heavyweights of the lost generation. It was a seven-hour evening of dreadful performances by athletes who didn't train, didn't care, and knew their purses were getting attached by the IRS anyway'.

Witherspoon describes the stable of Don King fighters as 'like being back in the ghetto...Oh man did I hate that training camp. The mentality put most fighters back into an uncaring situation. The fighters didn't have no money. There wasn't 100 dollars between us. We knew that Don was charging us for staying there. The morale was real low. There was drugs floating all around the camp'.

Meanwhile, a kid called Mike Tyson, under the guidance of Cus D'Amato, was making huge waves in a lacklustre heavyweight division. D'Amato was an anti-greed, anti-Reagan socialist who told his young apprentice, 'Money is something to be thrown off trains. To me, the things that I value, I couldn't buy. I was never impressed with money. Too many of the wrong people have a lot of money so the association is not good. The truth was, I wasn't careless about money. I gave money to people in trouble. I don't consider that wasting it'.

From his days as an amateur, 'Kid Dynamite' was steamrolling over every fighter put in his way and after just a handful of professional fights, it was obvious that Mike Tyson was going to be the dominant force of heavyweight boxing. In 1985, Tyson boxed his first 13 bouts and won all by way of knockout. By 1986, his management team of Bill Cayton and Jim Jacobs were constantly being asked if their kid was already worthy of a title fight against one of the champions. Witherspoon was one of the world champions on the scene but was not fighting to his true potential. It's easy to be demoralised when you work hard on the promise of gold, only to end up with a bit of myrrh. When Witherspoon fought Larry Holmes in 1983 his purse was $150,000. He only received $52,750. When he fought James 'Quick' Tillis the same year his purse was $50,000, but the pay cheque read $22,500. Before that fight he had complained, 'I don't care anymore…If I don't get paid the way I should, why should I care?' When Witherspoon won the vacant WBA title against Greg Page in 1984 his purse was $250,000.

He only saw $44,640. Page himself was getting the same treatment from King, to which Jack Newfield said, 'Like so many of King's alienated fighters, Page let his anger turn to self loathing. He sulked and barely trained, virtually going on strike at the gym. He over ate, partied and lost his motivation. It was a syndrome that would damage a whole generation of King's heavyweights, including Witherspoon, Dokes, Tubbs and Tucker'.

When Witherspoon fought and lost a title defence against Pinklon Thomas in 1984, he was told he was getting $400,000. He ended up with $116,000. He told Jack Newfield, 'I wonder how Joe Montana would play in the Super Bowl if every season he knew in advance he was going to get robbed and be given less than half his pay for the game'.

As a result, Witherspoon left Don King to go solo as a freelance fighter. But where could he go when King had the monopoly of the heavyweight division? King's place on the board was Mayfair, while his fighters were stuck on the Old Kent Road. There was nobody credible to fight and so Witherspoon had no choice but to go back to Don King Promotions. He recalls, 'I was signed into slavery'. King hated rebellion and despite coming back, Witherspoon remained out of favour.

In 1986, Witherspoon won the title back against Tony 'TNT' Tubbs. After deductions he was paid $10,000, which was a staggeringly insulting reward for becoming only the third man in history to retain the heavyweight title.

After defeating Tubbs, Tim Witherspoon's first title defence embedded him into the psyche of many British boxing fans. He was the champion who was destined, they thought, to get beaten by Frank Bruno, who would then become the first British heavyweight champion since Bob Fitzsimmons in 1899. Bruno respected his opponent and in his autobiography recalls, 'I thought Witherspoon was underrated. Maybe he didn't look the part—he wasn't exactly slim line—but he was a skilful fighter, with a dangerous over-arm right. Not many boxers throw that one'.

The setting was Wembley Stadium in 1986, and Witherspoon was back and in good spirits. After all the money issues he had with King, the Bruno fight, finally and seemingly, got him the payday that he had worked so hard for. The problem, however, was he went into the fight not actually knowing how much he was earning. Reports from the time said the champion's fee for his defence in a foreign land was $900,000, leading Witherspoon to cheer, 'I'm going to be a millionaire!' The actual contract stated that along with training expenses the fee was half a million. It was still more than he had ever earned and the defending champion was in a good frame of mind going into the fight.

The crowd at Wembley Stadium were predominantly pro-Bruno, but also in attendance were ten American jurors who were being treated to a freebie by King as a thank you for a not-guilty verdict at his tax avoidance trial.

The fight kicked off at 1 a.m. local time and Bruno got the better of the early rounds and looked like championship material. Big Frank was aggressive and certainly more worthy of being a champion than many of the fighters on the heavyweight scene who had been world title holders. Bruno's major weakness was punch resilience, and in the seventh round Witherspoon rocked him a few times and gradually began taking control. By the end of the ninth round the TV commentator Harry Carpenter noted, 'For two big men this has been fought at tremendous pace'.

The match was proving a total contrast to the awful Tubbs-Witherspoon hold and slug-fest. In the tenth round Witherspoon dazed Bruno who staggered backwards to the corner of the ring. Witherspoon went in for the kill and Terry Lawless in Bruno's corner threw the towel in. 'I can come back, I'm a great champion, I'm never gonna quit, I'm a Capricorn like Ali, Frazier, all the great fighters', said the victorious 'Terrible' one.

Witherspoon celebrated the win in a limousine that passed the sights of the British capital and he partied through the night. He recalls the initial aftermath of the Bruno fight as the happiest moments of his life. The next day, the sun shone in London and Witherspoon had reasons to be cheerful. He had defended his title against a very tough opponent and was to be paid well for his efforts. Muhammad Ali gave him a warm hug in the hotel lobby. Years earlier Ali had looked at Witherspoon as a sparring partner, now he was looking at a successful defending world champion. Life was now fun despite the bruises. 'I was so happy that even my soreness felt good'.

This victory now put him in line for a big payday against Tyson, who by now was the biggest star in the division. On returning to the States, Witherspoon was about to come crashing back down from cloud nine once he realised how much he was really being paid for the Bruno fight. Don King had delivered a royal screw job in London and paid Witherspoon a mere $90,094 for his efforts. Less than one tenth of what a defending champion should be paid for a big fight, and, to quote Jack Newfield, 'An independent manager should have gotten Witherspoon $1 million for this fight'. Carl King was as independent from Don as Pinky is to Perky—and he received $275,000 for Witherspoon's sweat and sacrifice. The challenger to the title and loser of the fight Frank Bruno was paid $900,000 by Mickey Duff. In his autobiography Bruno acknowledges the injustice towards his opponent and describes the fee of just $90,000 for a defending champion as 'incredible'.

Despite Tyson-Witherspoon now being the natural matchup, the Bruno screw job destroyed Witherspoon's spirit and drive. His future manager Tom Moran told Jack Newfield, 'Tim's love for boxing as a sport died after the Bruno fight…he felt he lost his manhood by staying with King all those years'.

In December 1986, Witherspoon would defend his title against James 'Bonecrusher' Smith, who he had beaten on points the previous year. The plan was that whoever won the rematch would go on to face Mike Tyson, who was at ringside to study his next opponent. This was the most feasible moment in time when Tyson-Witherspoon could have happened. A contract had been officially signed, and either Witherspoon or Bonecrusher would get $1 million in what would be a title unification.[2] Unfortunately, Witherspoon was a demoralised shell of the man that beat Bruno at Wembley. There was no reason at all why a $1 million dangling carrot to fight Tyson would have been a motivation, because past experience proved the money would probably be far less. Witherspoon did not care and did not train in preparation to defend his title against Bonecrusher Smith. His fee was $400,000, though after deductions he was paid just $129,000. This time, Witherspoon wouldn't even have victory in the ring as a consolation. No sooner had the fight started than Witherspoon was down on the canvas. He got back up and was floored by Bonecrusher two more times. Witherspoon looked okay to carry on, but under the WBA three knockdown rule the fight was over and a new champion was crowned. Witherspoon, who had dug so deep to defend his title at Wembley Stadium, lost on a whimper. He later claimed that he didn't care and was happy to lose just so Don King would be out of his life. Mike Tyson at ringside, however, looked happy at the outcome. ITV's Jim Rosenthal asked him, 'Your advisers feel that maybe Bonecrusher Smith might suit you a bit better than Tim Witherspoon?' To which the superstar replied, 'I'm so satisfied that he won. It's going to be a tremendous fight between two brutal punchers'.

It wasn't. Tyson-Smith was an awful anticlimax. Bonecrusher's ambition was not to get knocked out. At the time there was kudos to be gained by losing to Tyson but going the distance. So for 12 boring rounds Bonecrusher played it negatively and lost on points. Smith in later years expressed regret for showing too much respect for Tyson and not fighting. He told *Ringside*, 'I fought a defensive fight. I didn't believe in my own abilities at the time…I think the media did more than Tyson. The media hyped him up more than what he was. I bought into it'.

Bonecrusher didn't know it at the time, but Tyson was fighting with a neck injury. In his autobiography Iron Mike expressed relief that his opponent didn't pressure him, as he was highly vulnerable. Had Tyson that night been fighting a man who wanted to win, things would have been very interesting.

1986 had started very well for Witherspoon and had ended very badly. His title had gone, his career was on the slide and he had little money to show for being a two-time heavyweight champion. He decided that the time had come to take on King in the courts. His focus went away from the ring and to politics and legal disputes. In 1987, Witherspoon, with the help of his new manager Tom Moran, filed a lawsuit against Don and Carl King in the region of $25 million. Lawsuits were no stranger to King who was used to settling out of court. Two years passed and in 1989 Witherspoon turned down a settlement of a mere $30,000. He demanded the case go to court despite intimidation, which included his trainer receiving a visit from none other than an ageing Blinky Palermo: the convicted mobster who was found guilty of match fixing in the 1940s and 1950s. Witherspoon stood by his convictions and the case would roll on for another four years before King agreed to pay out $1 million in a settlement.

The man Witherspoon beat for the title in 1986, Tony Tubbs himself was no stranger to being demoralised by his promoter Don King. Muhammad Ali was a fan and tipped Tubbs for great things, but 'TNT' became the embodiment of a good boxer who let his talent slide away. As a result his physique matched his surname. His title shot in 1988 against Tyson in Tokyo was a predictable happening that lasted just two rounds. Tubbs held his own in the first round but was horribly knocked out in the second. It was not a glorious moment as the unfit Tubbs wobbled backwards and fell against the ropes and onto the canvas after a Tyson left hook.

Witherspoon liked and admired Tony Tubbs and indentified with his predicament. 'Tony and I used to be stable mates and I love Tony like a brother', said Tim who was upset that Tubbs was ridiculed by commentators like HBO's Larry Merchant who referred to him as a 'Fat bug on Tyson's windshield', and joked, 'If whale hunting is outlawed in Japan then Tyson hasn't heard about it'. Witherspoon hit back, 'They kept talking about Tony like he was a dog'.

After Tyson's demolition of Tubbs, Robert Seltzer wrote in the *Chicago Tribune*:

Tim Witherspoon watched a horror movie on television Sunday night. It was called Mike Tyson vs. Tony Tubbs. Sure, it was short, with a running time of only 5 minutes 54 seconds. But it was no less horrifying for its brevity. Especially if, like Witherspoon, you are being mentioned as an opponent for the undisputed heavyweight champion. Not that Witherspoon is scared. It is just that he does not want to end up like Tubbs, doing a rumba in the corner and falling to the canvas, his eyes glazed, his senses apparently on an extended leave..

In 1988, a Don King-free Witherspoon was firmly in the mix to face Tyson and he was determined to get fit to face the seemingly unstoppable champion. He didn't want to be ridiculed in the way that the overweight Tubbs was and spoke of his desire to shed pounds in order to have any chance. He told Seltzer, 'My main objective now is to get into shape. I want to be in the best shape of my life when I meet Tyson…When the bell rings for Tyson I don't want him to jump all over me and embarrass me'.Robert Seltzer's article in the *Chicago Tribune* also noted, 'Tyson has four fights remaining in his six-fight, $26.5 million deal with HBO, and co-manager Bill Cayton wants to match the champion against Witherspoon for one of those bouts'. 'I know they want me', Witherspoon said. 'I'm a two-time world champion…this is my big chance. I want to be a three-time champion'.

Considering Don King's near monopoly on the heavyweight division and Witherspoon's ongoing lawsuit against him, the former two-time champion had no chance of a title shot against a Don King-controlled fighter, so his aim had to be Tyson. At the beginning of 1988 Mike Tyson was not part of King's empire. Witherspoon-Tyson for the undisputed title was likely to happen, but the catastrophe for Witherspoon was that Iron Mike would soon fall into the grasp of the persuasive and charismatic super promoter. The management and promotional team of Bill Cayton and Jim Jacobs were appointed managers of Tyson by his trainer and mentor Cus D'Amato who died in November 1985. History, however, does not shed either man in a heroic light as they are believed to have taken more than their fair share of Tyson's earnings. Iron Mike would go on to refer to Cayton and Jacobs as 'bloodsuckers', but at the time of Jim Jacob's death in 1988 Tyson saw him as one of his few close and trusted friends. When Tyson fought Tubbs in March 1988, Jim Jacobs was in hospital with a serious illness and would die shortly afterwards. This left Bill Cayton alone as Tyson's manager. He was a smart and astute man but no match for the brilliantly cunning King, who over the course of 1988 would cleverly lure Tyson into his stable. At Jim Jacob's funeral, King went to great lengths to impress and woo the grieving heavyweight superstar. According to Jack Newfield's biography of King, he somehow managed to become a pallbearer at Jim Jacob's funeral despite:

1. Not being invited to the funeral.
2. Not being liked by the person he was carrying in the coffin.

Over the coming months, King would slowly and cleverly bring Tyson in by acting as a father figure to the vulnerable champion, who, in the space of a few years, had lost his mother, Cus D'Amato and now his manager. Tyson had a degree of love and respect for Jim Jacobs, but not for Bill Cayton. Now, alone, Cayton was there for the taking and it was only a matter of time before he was dropped.

In winning the right to be his promoter, King used race as a reason for a black fighter to go with him. Jacobs and Cayton were portrayed by King as Jewish slave masters and that eventually got through to the heavyweight superstar who said in his autobiography, 'He was always spouting some bullshit that the white motherfuckers were no good and that they were out to kill us all. I actually started believing some of his shit. I played into that stuff. He contaminated my whole barometer'.

Race and playing on black unity was a tried and tested Don King tactic. In the mid 1980s Witherspoon had tried to organise a revolt with his stable mates over King's deductions on their payments. 'King the survivor' preached that the white man was trying to divide them. Witherspoon recalls, 'The next night Don had a big party in his house and it was all white people. None of us black fighters got invited'.

Of course the irony to King's claim on black unity was that he as much as anyone had a horrible history in exploiting and ripping off black fighters. In contrast, he was very generous to any fighter who he felt he could sell off as a real-life Rocky Balboa. If Tim Witherspoon was a white fighter from Boston, named 'Jim O'Witherspoon', and wore a Shamrock on his shorts, then Don King would have treated him like royalty and paid him accordingly. Jack Newfield pointed out, 'Don King has been a lousy promoter for good black fighters, but he has been an outstanding one for lousy white fighters'.

Witherspoon once noted that King's 'speciality is black-on-black crime'. But that didn't stop King from preaching black power, and in the 1980s he was a prominent member of Artists and Athletes Against Apartheid, a pressure group to help deter performers from going to apartheid-ruled

South Africa. In the 1980s the South African gambling resort Sun City was regularly bidding large sums of money to stage big heavyweight title bouts. Fighters who were being made these offers were lobbied by Artists and Athletes Against Apartheid, whose message was that any fight in Sun City legitimised South Africa and harmed the struggle for equality. Meanwhile, in 1984, King indirectly helped stage a WBA title fight at Sun City between the black American Greg Page and the white South African Gerry Coetzee. Both fighters were contracted to King who had encouraged and failed to get the heavyweight contender David Bey to go to Sun City and fight Coetzee. King had managed to persuade Page, but the flamboyant promoter knew that he could not be seen to have openly helped stage the fight. Therefore he quietly took a $1 million pay-off by a South African promoter. King's nemesis, Jack Newfield, once questioned him on this matter during a press conference in Las Vegas in 1991. King was on his high horse about the IBF's decision to allow black South Africans (who he did not hold contracts with) to be ranked, as long as the fights were staged outside of South Africa (which, when you think about it, is morally fine). He attacked the IBF President Bob Lee and preached, 'How can a black man work with apartheid. He's a traitor, an uncle Tom'. Newfield called out, 'What about the one million you took from Sun City?'

To say that question touched a nerve would be an understatement. What followed was a comical and aggressive verbal attack from King who approached Newfield and ranted, 'You ain't nothing but a scumbag…You are dirt…You are nothing…You are Goebbels!. . .You're prejudiced!. . .You are an SOB'.

King then told the surrounding reporters, 'Jack Newfield is the worst person who has ever lived'. Adolf Hitler, Pol Pot, Joseph Stalin and Genghis

Khan were all responsible for the murders of tens of millions of innocent human beings, but none were so deplorable as to ask a dodgy boxing promoter a legitimate question over double standards.

As King aggressively ranted at him, virtually nose to nose, Newfield recalls, 'Two thoughts raced through my mind: is my cameraman getting this? This guy has killed two people!'

For the first killing, King received no criminal charge as he reportedly shot back in self-defence during an attack on him at his home. The second killing was when he kicked a man to death on the streets on Cleveland in 1966. The victim, Sam Garret, owed money to King who at that time ran the numbers racket in Cleveland. Reports suggest that King attacked Garret in a bar, dragged the smaller man outside and viciously stamped on his head on numerous occasions. He got away with a manslaughter sentence and served just a few years. Such previous behaviour would harm his chances of working in other sports. But in boxing a serious crime record is no obstacle to involvement. Regarding King's history, the boxing author Thomas Hauser points out, 'He spent three and half years in prison for manslaughter. He was the largest numbers Czar in Cleveland. There's no way that Don King could buy a National Football League franchise. He couldn't do it. But he can go right into boxing. All he has to do is want to do it'.

Not only did a history of crime prove no obstacle to Don King being in boxing, but it also gave him a position of strength through notoriety. Fighters had every reason to believe and fear what might happen to them if they upset King. This was a man capable of killing. In the 1980s when Larry Holmes told King he was switching promoters, the promoter allegedly threatened violence and told the champion, 'If you do that I'll have your legs broken'. Similar threats were allegedly made towards Witherspoon during his lawsuit and were enough to make him carry a weapon. Speaking on the film, *Don King Unauthorised*, Witherspoon's manager Tom Moran said, 'He [King] threatened that if he [Witherspoon] didn't settle the lawsuit by the end of the week, he wasn't gonna have to worry about settling because he wouldn't be breathing'. If a man who had already killed someone said that to you, you'd take such a threat very seriously.

The capture of Mike Tyson was the icing on the cake for King's control of the heavyweight division and for Witherspoon it spelled the end. One big name Witherspoon could have fought was the brilliant Michael Spinks who was promoted by Butch Lewis. But Spinks decided to retire after his devastating loss to Tyson in 1988. There was nowhere to go and from this point on in 1988 the name Tim Witherspoon forever drifted out of the title picture. He would no longer be a marquee name or title contender. When he lost the belt to 'Bonecrusher' Smith in 1986 it turned out to be the last time he would ever fight for a world title. He had become what Don King warned would happen to anyone who challenged him—the needle in the haystack; 'hard to find'. Harder than any title fight was his six-year battle in the courts with King, for which Jack Newfield praises the ex-champion:

> Witherspoon stood up to King, and the whole boxing system, more courageously than any other fighter. He stuck to his lawsuit for almost six years so that young fighters in the future could have some measure of independence, some measure of dignity and honest accounting, some freedom of choice in a manager. Witherspoon was too flawed to lead a slave revolt. But he gave

it his best shot so that other fighters would not be exploited and demoralised as he was.

Witherspoon knew that his lawsuit would effectively end his career in the big time, especially considering that King's relationship with the governing bodies was key to his control over the fighters. For example, in 1983 when Larry Holmes decided to promote a fight of his own against Lucien Rodriguez, the WBC were straight on the phone to tell Holmes that he would be stripped of the title. So Holmes then came to an agreement with King that he would fight Rodriguez as a Holmes promotion, and then Tim Witherspoon as a Don King promotion. Holmes said of the issue, 'Once I did agree to that, the WBC rolled over again and quit their threats…King and the WBC—hell they were tighter than canned sardines!'

While Tyson was being provided with some 'bum of the month' opponents, 'Terrible' picked up his form and between August 1987 and March 1992 he went undefeated in 12 straight fights under the promotion of Bob Arum. A former two-time world champion on a 12-match unbeaten run would normally be in high demand; however, form did not count for anything in getting Witherspoon back in the title frame. His opponents were not huge names, because of course King had the monopoly of the division; but he still went five years with a perfect record. He carried on though the 1990s, winning some, losing some, and finally retired in 2003 at the age of forty-five with a record of 69 wins, 13 losses and one draw.

Today, Tim Witherspoon is probably the only black American ex-boxing heavyweight champion who lives in the English town of Surbiton. I was given the former champ's phone number and contacted him to explain the nature of my book and that I was doing a chapter featuring himself and Tyson. It immediately resonated with 'Terrible' who said, 'Man that was the one. You have to include that. And it wasn't just me, there was other fighters who got screwed'. Witherspoon was a really nice, genuine guy, and he wanted to talk to me more, but wasn't able to because he is currently writing an autobiography and therefore can't contribute to other books on similar subject matter. On talking about Don King, these days he doesn't forgive but he does try to forget. He wants to move on, because to dwell on how badly he was treated has the potential to mentally destroy anyone. Today Witherspoon attends many boxing functions and charity events to answer questions and sign autographs. In recent years, he and Tyson have held the same stage and toured together for fundraisers. The two share a mutual respect and Witherspoon talks about Tyson in complimentary terms as a human being, as well as being a boxing great.

As for King, his twisted and destructive nature probably ended up losing him money, considering that the boxers he demoralised lost the desire to maintain and improve their ability, resulting in them having no mass appeal to the public. Had he treated his fighters with respect and paid them accordingly then there's little doubt that many of the 'lost generation' of 1980s heavyweights would have fulfilled their potential and gone on to achieve fan-favourite status. Fan-favourite status means more money for the fighter and for whoever promotes them. Instead, talented boxers got demoralised and gave up. Larry Holmes doesn't fall into that category, but he was a classic example of a boxer who was consistently screwed over and treated like garbage by King, who he in turn describes as a 'lying sack of shit'. In looking for an answer as to why King has a history of demoralising

his prize assets, Holmes is quoted as saying of his former promoter/
manager:

> I've had lots of time in recent years to think about why Don does
> what he does to fighters. With Don it was making money from
> them, sure, but there was something more to it…I believe that deep
> down Don King hates fighters, is jealous of them, because we can
> do what a fat old bullshitter like him can't do—and that's fight.
> That is why he wanted to have such power over us, to humiliate us.

Holmes is on to something there. Don King's obsession with screwing
people over has to be more than just money. It's part of a game—an addiction
in which the aim is to get the better of someone. A bit like when you see the
worst example of a global corporation who will sack workers and move jobs
abroad, even when they've declared billions in profit. Ten billion dollars profit
wasn't enough—they had to get that handful more. Gaining that extra bit of
money makes no real difference to their lifestyle yet it devastates the lives of
the people losing their jobs, along with the wider community.

King would seem to be of the same mould as the character Gordon
Gecko from the film *Wall Street*. Gecko loved money, no doubt, but more
importantly his buzz seemed to be getting one over on people. Witherspoon
himself summed up King's nature by saying, 'Don King would rather put a
dishonest quarter in his pocket than an honest dollar'. If King had a happy
stable of fairly-paid fighters who were cared for, nurtured and treated with
dignity, then today he would be an even richer man. Mike Tyson's ex-
manager Bill Cayton said of King in the 1990s, 'He's a great con artist and

you have to give him credit for being the most successful boxing promoter of all time. But I think he would have been even more successful had he not been such a great con artist'.

In the early 1990s, Don King acquired the services of an up-and-coming light heavyweight national champion called William 'Chocolate' Guthrie who, like Witherspoon, was also a native of Philadelphia. King used his usual tricks on 'Chocolate', such as a questionable deduction on earnings, and Guthrie was frustrated with King's overall dirty tactics. Instead of helping Guthrie on his career path, King seemed more concerned with playing games against the light heavyweight prospect. These tactics included lying about who his upcoming opponents would be. Guthrie's opponents would be training for him, while he was training for someone else. Despite facing some seemingly unnecessary obstacles from his own promoter, Guthrie remained undefeated and told King he was moving to a rival promotional umbrella. True to form, Don King played the race card and said that the white man was trying to divide them: 'They always want to rob and steal from the black man'. King's argument seemed to imply that black fighters don't mind being screwed over as long as it's from a fellow brother. While trying to persuade Guthrie to stay with him, King then made a phone call to Bob Lee of the IBF. He put Lee on speakerphone and the implications to Guthrie were clear: leave me and you don't get an IBF title shot and the matches that you want. Bob Lee advised Guthrie to stay with King, but 'Chocolate' ignored those warnings and parted ways. Guthrie filed a lawsuit against the IBF and won. King filed a lawsuit against Guthrie and lost. 'Chocolate' then got to fight for the vacant IBF light heavyweight title in 1997, which he won via a third-round knockout against a fighter called Darrin Allen. For him it was a fight that should have happened, but only did so because of his own self-esteem and perseverance. Guthrie lost his first defence against Sweet Reggie Johnson in 1998 and, like Tim Witherspoon, he would never again fight for a major world title after being dethroned.

Tyson thought that he could be the snake charmer, but he was young and foolish and concedes in his autobiography, 'I thought I could handle somebody like King, but he outsmarted me. I was totally out of my league with that guy'.

His relationship with Don King collapsed fully in the 1990s when he accused his promoter of embezzling some of his earnings. Despite King's denial of the accusation, Tyson became judge, jury and punisher and beat King to the ground outside the Beverly Hills Hotel in Los Angeles. In the documentary feature film of his life he described his former promoter as a 'deplorable, slimy, reptilian piece of shit motherfucker who doesn't know how to love anybody and who would sell his own mother for a dollar'. William 'Chocolate' Guthrie seemed to imply the same thing with a poignant statement about his former promoter:

> I'll never forget, I was in his home. With his family, his wife, his children, his grandchildren. And the children would be running around the house and I never saw King smile. But at the mention of money, he laughed, he smiled. His wife walked in. His children walked in. His grandchildren walked in. And I never saw him smile. And that to me is a man that you should never ever trust.

1. Floyd Patterson was the first man to retain the heavyweight title. Muhammad Ali was the second.

2. This match was supposed to be a Witherspoon-Tubbs rematch. But Tubbs had his own issues with King and pulled out. 'Bonecrusher' had a lawsuit going against King and dropped it in order to get the title shot.

ROUND 3

LIGHTS OUT FOR TITLE UNIFICATIONS. . .

'I'd love to whoop some British ass—especially that fucking
Eubank. I don't like that guy. I hate him!'
James 'Light Out' Toney

In a country with a pioneering and rich history in the sport, two polar
opposites cemented a domestic rivalry which made them legends in
British boxing.

First there was Nigel Benn, the street-fighting, fast-living ex-soldier who
was a knockout specialist and generally loved by the public.

An eccentric counterpuncher, despised by many, was from the same
rough streets of London and, like Benn, also came from Caribbean
heritage, yet Chris Eubank wore tweed, carried a cane and spoke like he
was Prince Charles' long lost brother. Such a contrast of personality and
style made for a dynamite collision that would be part of British boxing

folklore. In 1990 an enthralling and full-on battle ended in the ninth round when the American referee Richard Steele retired a beaten Benn who instantly cried his eyes out in heartache that he'd lost his WBO title to his despised rival. Steele went on to describe the matchup as one of the best he'd ever been involved in.[1]

A rematch was three years in the making and became the most hyped and publicity-generating match in British boxing history. Eubank-Benn II in front of 40,000 fans at Old Trafford ended in a draw and was more methodical and less brutal than the first encounter. Benn had a point deducted which would have won him the bout, raising many to still believe that he had the beating of his most bitter enemy. Had Eubank won then he would have claimed total superiority in the rivalry, but the draw had left unanswered questions: minutes after the result was announced there were talks of another rematch. 'Let's do it again', said Eubank, to the agreement of Benn's trainer Jimmy Tibbs. Benn wasn't at ringside and was so pissed off at the decision that he went straight back to the locker room. Part III is perhaps a match that should have happened, and most of us would not have complained about a trilogy. But more intriguing than a third fight was the prospect of both British fighters taking on some of the best super middleweights America had to offer. By this point in time in 1993, it was too late for them to fight the previous generation of American middleweight superstars such as Hagler, Hearns and Leonard. Those legends were either retired or fighting way past their prime. However, a new generation of highly dangerous American middleweights had emerged and were viewed by most experts and fans as ahead of the British boys and the real champions in the super middleweight division.

The promotion and build-up for the Benn-Eubank rematch match gave the impression that the British boys were soon set for a collision with a couple of America's finest. Part of the hype included a one-hour ITV special involving both men in front of a studio celebrity audience in a show called *Best of Enemies*. Hosted by Jonathan Ross and aired on the same day as the fight, it was entertaining stuff, even if at times the whole thing descended into a bunch of D-list celebrities laughing at a couple of great boxers. Certainly, some of the disrespect shown to Eubank by the host and guest audience could be deemed as quite nauseating. 'Simply the Best' ended up on the end of a tirade of sneers about how he takes himself too seriously, even though by that point in time, many of his fans had accepted his sensitivity as an interesting aspect of his persona. The Chris Eubank 'Spitting Image' puppet (dressed as a nun from *The Sound of Music*) was a highlight, but by far the standout moment from this one-hour TV special was a surprise appearance from one of the most feared fighters in the world at that time. The IBF super middleweight champion James Toney was not in town but he was beamed in on satellite from LA for a chat with his division rivals. Ross started off by interviewing the actor Mickey Rourke, who was sitting beside a typically moody-looking Toney; his arms crossed and looking like the ultimate super middleweight assassin. A gleam in Toney's eye suggested that he was about to relish what was going to transpire. Ross introduced the 'rather imposing figure' of Toney as the middleweight who was the main man to beat, and asked his opinion on the upcoming fight between Eubank and Benn. 'Lights Out' responded by sitting on the fence, but not in the traditional polite sense. 'I don't care who wins. I'll fight either one of them. In fact I'll fight both of them on the same night if you want me to!'

Unlike the studio audience, the two British fighters didn't laugh and both carried composed expressions which hinted of anger, offence and ultimately trepidation.

Benn instantly hit back: 'I don't mind going over there and fighting him. I done it with Barkley, Robbie Simms, Doug DeWitt. I'm not scared of him'.

'Let me tell you something. I'm not Iran Barkley. I'm not Doug DeWitt, if you come over here I'll kick your ass'.

'That's cool. I'll see you soon!'

After that exchange between Benn and Toney, Jonathan Ross asked Chris Eubank for his response. The usually never short for words Eubank stayed silent, his fingers resting on his face looking too dignified to give a response.

'Chris what do you have to say', repeated Ross, but the WBO champion remained silent—unlike James Toney who piped up, 'I'm the best. When I see you I'm gonna beat you and your mama's ass!'

'You're full of mouth', chipped in Benn.

Ross then asked Toney for his opinion on Benn's WBC title and Eubank's WBO, to which the IBF king said, 'Well the WBC stands for "we be crooks" and the WBO we don't even count that. I'm the real champ. If you want to be a proud champion you got to fight me. The only way they're going to make some real money is by fighting James Toney'.

As Ross began to wrap things up Toney barked, 'No fighters in England, they're all bums. Bunch of women over there!' The studio audience laughed at first, and then remembered they were English, so then booed.

Benn smiled at the brashness of his verbal attacker, which, as usual, made him the opposite of Eubank. 'Chris is particularly keen to meet up with you', joked Ross, implying that Eubank was scared.

Not a man to ever allow anyone the last word, Eubank finally spoke to Toney as the crowd hushed: 'You seem like you are purely ignorant... and I'll give you a few lessons in the ring'. The crowd cheered and applauded as Benn added, 'You're as thick as two short planks of wood, mate'.

A furious Toney went on a rant which couldn't be heard because Ross quickly wrapped it up by saying how glad he was that they were separated by thousands of miles. Toney pulled out his earpiece and stormed off.

It didn't look for one second like Eubank would want to go near Toney, whereas with Benn it looked a little bit more likely. Directly after the on-air dispute, the Dark Destroyer gave his feelings on a possible showdown with the IBF champion: 'Very good fighter indeed. I don't know what it is, but he has a serious problem. But once I get the job done [against Eubank] I would love to go over there and fight him'.

When Ross asked if he fancied his chances, one could sense a doubt that was very unusual for Benn, and his response was short and cautious: 'It will be a hard fight yeah. . .I thrive on fear'. Toney was scary and intimidating to say the least, even for a warrior like Nigel Benn.

Throughout the whole segment 'Lights Out' looked like he had genuine dislike and contempt for both men and this was no pantomime act to try and create hype and publicity. During this period of time the writer Donald McRae was able to spend time with James Toney as research for his award-winning book *Dark Trade*. Toney expressed to McRae his disgust for Eubank, Benn and the UK in general: 'I hate the British...They're losers, Eubank, Benn, Bruno, Lewis. They lack guts, they lack style. Over there, the women are ugly, the men are fat, chubby looking!' He added, 'Chris Eubank is nothing but a bum! Chris Eubank and Nigel Benn are losers. They're scared of me. They're running from a whippin''.

During the broadcast Eubank complained to Ross that Toney had brought his mother into the exchange of insults. If Eubank was offended by what was aired on the programme, it was nothing compared to what Toney said off camera to McRae. 'Chris Eubank, it's true your mother — she's got no titties, the bitch is through…same goes for Nigel Benn — your mama she's just like the Loch Ness Monster'.

Toney sounded ready and willing to take on either man and in conversation with McRae vowed, 'I want Eubank and Benn to hear me. I'd fight them on a "winner takes all" basis, I'd fight them on the same night — I'd bust them up, I'd take their hearts away. Eubank first and then his mama can suck my dick!'

Toney seemed to have a particular distain for 'that fucking Eubank', along with an obsession with his mother, and asked McRae to pass on a personal message: 'You tell him I say he's a pussy…You tell him his mother is a bitch and a hoe…You getting this, man?'

When McRae asked how Toney would plan to fight someone as awkward in style as Chris Eubank he replied in a deadpan manner, 'Well, I'd plan to kill him', to which the writer laughed. 'Don't laugh. I ain't joking. I'm gonna kill that guy! I don't like the way he runs off at the mouth'.

Even though Toney mocked the belts that Benn and Eubank both held he still wanted the straps round his waist. 'It's their belts I want as much as the money…I'm a fighter from the old school; I'm a throwback to the great days of boxing. I want to unify these different 'world' titles. The IBF, the WBC, the WBA, the WBO, the W-whatever. Shit, I want to be the undisputed champion of the world! Who else is like that today?'

Luckily for Benn and Eubank, the volatile 'Lights Out' Toney was not in Manchester on the day of their rematch, but another American middleweight superstar was. The WBA champion Michael Nunn was at ringside with a smiling Don King who had dollar signs flashing in his eyes. The statement of Nunn being at ringside was clear—he would fight whoever won out of Eubank and Benn. 'Michael Nunn is anxious to challenge whoever the victor is tonight', beamed King to which Nunn added, 'Hello to everybody in the UK. I'm looking forward to coming over here to fight in front of these great fans…that's what boxing's all about, the best fighting the best. Let's put it together and let's do this'.

A couple of months earlier, Eubank, Benn and Nunn had been sat round a press conference table in New York to discuss future fights and title unifications. In the Benn-Eubank themed book *The Hate Game*, author Ben Dirs recalls:

> Eubank managed to steal the show while upsetting just about everyone present, except perhaps his promoters. First, Eubank grabbed the microphone and demanded all questions be directed at him under 'parliamentary practice', which triggered catcalls and jeers. Benn and Nunn stood up to confront Eubank, before Benn and Terry Norris, the WBC light middleweight champion, left the dais in disgust.

Michael Nunn, born in 1963 in Iowa, was a formidable force in the middleweight division in the late 1980s and 1990s, and a natural successor to Sugar Ray Leonard as the world's number-one middleweight. He had the good looks and the ability to be a star like Leonard, but not the out of ring charisma. He was certainly no match for Eubank, Benn and Toney in the intriguing personality department. In 1988, Nunn was named fighter of the year by *KO Magazine* and Progress of the Year by *The Ring* magazine. Today he has the honour of being the biggest boxing name in residence at the Federal Correctional Institution in Texas. Serving 24 years for drug trafficking in 2004, Nunn won't be taking part in a Hall of Fame induction any time soon. Nunn's earnings were enough to have set him up for life. Now he's got life.

Despite his personal mistakes, he was at one time a world-class fighter and one who many were more than happy to sidestep. He may be behind bars now but he claims to still have the personal satisfaction of being a former world champion and a legacy to look back on with pride. At the time of the Benn-Eubank rematch, Nunn had only suffered one defeat, which was in his hometown of Davenport in 1991, against the perceived underdog James Toney. Up to that point Nunn had a perfect record of 36-0 and was the favourite to win the fight known as the Rumble at the Riverside. Toney, without much effort or acting, cast himself as the bad guy and in the pre-match build-up the TV commentator noted, 'He's been the villain all week and he kind of likes this role'. 'Lights Out' claimed that his opponent would run like a deer from his punches and proclaimed himself the 'Deer hunter' who was 'ready to lay some deer traps!' In contrast, the hometown favourite Nunn had a clean-cut hero persona; a far cry away from the convicted drug trafficker he is now.

This open-air bout was for the IBF middleweight title, and Nunn and Toney were two world-class formidable opponents, both in their prime and both undefeated. However, the world didn't know this about Toney just yet, and the odds on him winning were long. The first round was lively and even, with both men showing good offense and defence. 'Second to Nunn', trained by Angelo Dundee, went on to dominate the fight with a mixture of right jabs and quick combinations with his hand speed living up to his nickname. Nunn's shots were not bombshells but they were clean and they were scoring. Nunn was noted to have good chin, even if in most of his previous fights his punch immunity hadn't been tested that much because he was so difficult to hit.

Toney finally caught Nunn with a hard right in the seventh round but the hometown hero took it well and ended the round strongly. In the eighth round Toney came out determined and more aggressive. Before the ninth round the commentator heeded that Toney could be more dangerous as the fight progressed because he had more match fitness than Nunn, who had been less active in the past year. In the ninth round things really heated up: Toney rocked Nunn again, only to wake up the Davenport native who replied with a series of combination shots. But Toney came back with more heavy bombs to hurt the champ and at the end of the round Nunn looked badly shaken. The tide was turning and in the tenth round Toney once again looked the stronger and more aggressive fighter. Before coming out in the eleventh, Angelo Dundee told his champion not to get sloppy in the final six minutes, while Toney's corner warned that he was running out of time. The crowd (who had been fairly quiet for most of the fight) started to chant Nunn's name, as they could sense that things were on the slide. They were right to be worried because, with little more than a minute of round 11 to go, Toney floored the champion with a devastating left. Nunn struggled to get back up and just about made the count, only to be finished off in ruthless fashion. An onslaught from Toney sent him crashing down front first on to the ropes. It was unclear whether the referee called a knock down or not, but Nunn who was still on his feet bounced off the ropes, and with no defence to cover his face got floored with a three-punch combination. A white towel was thrown in and a new IBF champion was crowned—James Toney the Dark Emperor.

It was a devastating defeat for Nunn but minutes after losing he declared, 'I'll be back'. He was true to his word; a year later he beat Victor Cordoba to obtain the WBA title. This meant that along with Toney, Eubank and Benn there were four great champions in the super middleweight division and it was time for some collisions and unifications. Well, so fans hoped; fans certainly had good reason to think that these four champs would all meet in the ring. With the James Toney TV confrontation against Eubank and Benn, and Nunn being at ringside for the rematch at Old Trafford, it all seemed to be pointing in the direction of the British boys against the Americans. By this point ITV were no longer willing to pay big money for Eubank's play-it-safe list of opponents and it was either fight the best or go somewhere else. Part of the reason that ITV put up big money for Eubank-Benn II was the expectation of a Nunn fight to follow for the winner. In contrast, Eubank, Nunn, Benn and Toney would not go on to face one another—either for the first time or in a rematch.

Eubank-Nunn was doomed because Eubank-Benn part II ended in a draw. Had Eubank won or lost that match then he would have been contractually tied to Don King, which in all likelihood would have led to a showdown with Michael Nunn. In a contract agreed between Barry Hearn and Don King, the possibility of a draw was not considered and therefore King had no legally binding right for Eubank's services. Hearn broke the news to King during a press conference the day after the fight. King was holding court and boasting of how he was now the number-one promoter in England. He was in a jovial spirit and referred to Hearn as the world's greatest boxing promoter. With great plans in mind for big money fights he told him, 'Don't worry Barry, there could well be a role in this for you'.

Hearn then revealed to King that he never had an option on the draw. A livid Don disputed the paperwork and kicked off, but the contract was clear in that a draw was not mentioned. This was an awful moment for the cunning king, as the rules with dealing with Don King were very clear—he was the one who was supposed to get one over you, not the other way around. Hearn told me that King's involvement in the Eubank-Benn promotion began when the American had paid him £2 million for the TV rights outside of the UK, in which Frank Warren played a third party role as a mediator. King had phoned up Hearn and told him, 'I'm going to be your partner in the fight'. To which Hearn inquired, 'Oh really, what makes you think that?' King's money talked louder than words and in return for his £2 million investment he would get future promotional rights to both fighters, 'win or lose'. Hearn discussed it with Eubank and Benn and they both agreed to go with King after the fight.

The draw was a Godsend for the Essex promoter, who not only ended up with King's money for the TV rights, but also the right to still promote both men. After the draw Hearn gave Benn and Eubank the option to go with King if they wanted to. Benn, still pissed off at the result did just that, but Eubank stayed with Hearn's Matchroom. In his autobiography Eubank blessed the draw as 'a tremendous result for me…the last thing I wanted in my career was to be tied to Don King'.

Eubank was free to fight whoever he wanted, so in 1994–95 he signed a £10 million deal with Sky to fight eight bouts in the space of a year. This deal put to bed any talk of a second rematch with Benn or any immediate big time fight in America with either Michael Nunn or James Toney.

The eight-fight schedule was demanding even if most of the opponents were not, and Eubank even became Sugar Ray Robinson in disguise by fighting two bouts in the space of a week. Most would be 'bum of the month' contests, but an initially intriguing aspect of the Sky deal was that if Eubank won all eight bouts then a showdown with James Toney could follow. While the fight was in the pipeline of possibility, Eubank said of the IBF champ, 'He is the most unreasonable, the most pig-headed man', a statement confirming the contrast in personalities that such a contest would have provided; Toney the foul-mouthed gangster versus Eubank the monocle-wearing gentleman. 'Simply the Best' may have questioned Toney's manners, but not his ability, and added, 'He has the most fire in his stomach, more even than Nigel Benn. Can I beat him? Where there's a will there's a way. If I take the fight, I will not be saying "ouch, that hurt", or be looking at the referee for help. They will have to carry me out'.

Rival promoter Frank Warren did more than question the direction they took after the second Benn fight and said, 'Chris Eubank was picking his own opponents. Some of those opponents, or fights, were bum fights. Might have done his bank balance a bit of a favour, but it didn't do him any favours as far as credibility was concerned'. Even during the financial negotiations for the Eubank-Benn rematch the 'Dark Destroyer' mocked his rival face to face as terms were being argued over. 'I'll go and do what you do…look in the top 10, or the top 30, in fact bring him up from the top 30 and put him in the top 10!'

Benn may have given the unproven Eubank a shot for the title in 1990, but directly afterwards the winner and new WBO champion was not so generous in granting a rematch and stated, 'If I should decide to give you the opportunity to fight me again you should think yourself privileged. But for now I think I'll make you wait in the queue for a while'.

Nunn was at the end of the queue, as was Mike McCallum and anyone remotely frightening. Eubank's instructions on opponents were that the biggest risk he would take was a 60/40 chance in his favour, though hardly were the odds as close as that. If personality, mannerism, and fighting style separated Benn and Eubank then so did their approach to taking on a challenge. Eubank was simply unwilling to take a chance, while Benn would gain a reputation for being prepared to thrive on fear. Despite not beating Eubank in both their fights, Benn ended up with a more respected legacy because of being prepared to take on formidable Americans. While Eubank would not accept a risk beyond 60/40 in his favour, the 'Dark Destroyer' put his belt on the line against Gerald McClellan with chances being somewhere in the region of 20/80 against.

Barry Hearn's son and protégée Eddie Hearn described some of Eubank's opponents as 'quite frankly embarrassing' in an *Evening Standard* interview in 2013. The young boxing promoter said that such fights are not the direction he wants to take his top Matchroom stars and that the 'landscape has changed for fans and broadcasters. Fans want to sit down and watch a match not knowing the result before the fight starts'.

Barry Hearn, however, has always defended and stood by the scheduling that he and his champion took and admitted:

> I did give him easy fights and Eubank wasn't at his best in easy fights, Eubank needed the challenge. We as the paying public... don't have the right to watch a man kill himself every week. You have to have the odd war to sustain the interest. But then some days you go to work, it's an ordinary day at work. And some days it's a special day at work. The special days however, come with special payment...

While at a boxing event in the York Hall I was able to personally ask Barry Hearn if he felt that Eubank-Nunn was a fight that should have happened. 'No way', responded Hearn. The Matchroom boss' reasoning was more honest than I was expecting:

> He'd have got killed. Eubank was a great fighter but there's a step up where you don't go if you don't have to. Some fights are right for you and some fights are not...Don't forget, Eubank was only ever in it for the money'. Hearn added, 'Take Carl Froch v Andre Ward. Froch is a great fighter—don't get me wrong. But when taking on someone like Ward, that was a level too high.

The very approachable Hearn agreed to my request for an interview and invited me for a tea at the Waldorf Hotel in Aldwych to talk about his and Eubank's conservative methods of operating. After a quick chat about football and Hearn keenly agreeing with my description of Alan Sugar in *Theatre of Silence,*[2] we got on to the subject of whether Eubank should have gone across the pond to fight in America. Regarding Nunn, Hearn repeated his reservations about such a tough opponent. 'I didn't like the fight, nor did Chris. Nunn was a southpaw and Eubank hated southpaws. Especially a tall southpaw because they're the worst. So Nunn was never a prospective opponent. Like Herol Graham, no one wanted to fight him. Nunn was 6 foot 3, great long arms and a front foot so far forward you couldn't get close to him. He was top of the "not wanted list" as Mickey Duff used to say'.

Eubank's first five professional fights were in Atlantic City, but he never returned to fight in the country of his teenage years. Considering that Eubank was such a charismatic personality, an attribute which could have made him a saleable name Stateside, I wondered if there were the slightest of regrets about not taking a chance, but Hearn insisted, 'There were a lot more easier fighters to import, rather than to export yourself…There's an awful lot of good fighters in America in comparison to the names who we chose to fight. Eubank was run like a proper corporate business. In other word—risk-reward'.

Eubank was a very successful business and the CEO Hearn added, 'It worked out very well. We both made money out of it. I kept mine, he didn't keep his, that was the sad thing about it'.

Hearn was not convinced that an American adventure would have been lucrative; despite James Toney saying that the 'only way to make real money' was through fighting him. Hearn stressed that 'Eubank was virtually unknown in America so there was no HBO scenario where they were courting him. It would have taken some time to have gotten his message across'.

The one time Eubank's fame and celebrity got tested in America was when he was present at Madison Square Garden for Lewis-Holyfield. He was working as a pundit for British radio and claims to have received a great reception: 'When I walked into the arena, the clapping filled that cavernous hall…In my opinion, Jack Nicolson got the biggest round of applause, then Keith Richards, then me'.

One thing for certain was that Chris Eubank's fighting style had become more cautious even by his own conservative standards. Before the second Michael Watson fight in 1991, ten out of his last 12 wins were via stoppages. Since the trauma of nearly killing a man, that stat would be reversed, and ten of Eubank's next 12 wins would be via decisions. Hearn felt that Eubank's conservativeness would not have been a seller in the US and said, 'I'm not sure the American audience would have loved Eubank's style. They would have liked the charisma of the man if they got to know him. But as a fighter, he wasn't the most exciting to watch…Mayweather, for example, is clinically brilliant but I personally wouldn't buy a ticket to go and watch him'.

In his autobiography, Eubank openly admits to a preference of being a big fish in a small pond, rather than to going to America, which he describes as 'a vast pond with some very dangerous large fish in there'. He also had no intention of allowing the large fish in his small pond, as James Toney was more than happy to come to England to 'whoop some British ass'. Toney enjoyed being jeered by the fans, which in turn made him perform better, and he expressed a desire to fight either Eubank or Benn in England. The main reason being that there was a guarantee that he'd be booed!

'Toney was a tough guy', said Hearn. 'I met him a couple of times. I remember he had a gun on him once. For Eubank though it was just a business and quite rightly so. He was there to maximise at minimal risk and Toney wasn't minimum risk. Toney was a counterpuncher, but he could bang as well. Crazy guy though! Everyone says he's now punchy and slurs but he always talked like that'.

Regarding Toney's hatred of British fighters Hearn pointed out, 'Yeah, but he hates everybody!'

My conversation with Barry Hearn was in October 2013, which was 20 years to the month since James Toney insulted and called out Benn and Eubank in front of millions of ITV viewers. Even at the age of 45, 'Lights Out' was still keen to 'whoop some British ass', and Hearn's Matchroom promotion had him booked to lead a USA team against a GB team at the York Hall. Before the event Toney said that he loved UK boxing fans and expressed a regret that it had taken so long for him to debut here. 'It should have happened twenty years ago; Benn and Eubank were around. But it is what it is; they avoided me. I wanted those fights, to show what I always knew, that I was the best middleweight and super middleweight in the world…I can't wait to let everyone in England know I'm the best fighter they've ever had over there'.

Twenty years earlier when Toney was a young genuine talent, he, like Nunn, was far too dangerous to be included on a list of potential Eubank opponents and Hearn recalled, 'We had rules. No southpaws. No undefeated fighters. No one under 25. No one without a stoppage loss. It was like a shopping list'. One person to be quickly ticked off the list in 1991 was an American who was becoming more feared than anyone. Hearn admitted:

> We vacated the middleweight title in order to avoid Gerald McClellan who was the mandatory challenger. I said to Eubank, 'I don't want you in there with McClellan. I think he's a fucking monster'. I'd seen McClellan a few times and thought—don't like the look of this character at all. Powerful fucker. Horrible, nasty bastard. We then used that as an excuse to move up to super middleweight and challenge Watson.

The promoter would also advise Nigel Benn to stay clear of the 'G' Man, to which Benn grunted a few words, which implied that he wasn't worried.

Hearn looks back to the time as a complete success for the corporation of Eubank Ltd, but there was one business venture he does think should have happened—a kind of war to settle the score. He told me, 'I've promoted around 500 shows over the years…The only fight that I regret in my career that I didn't see was Benn-Eubank III. Financially, with the pay-per-view market just beginning to evolve, it's frightening to think how many buys we would have got for that'. Hearn added that the fight would have surpassed the one million UK buys that Ricky Hatton once commanded and said, 'The ITV figure for Benn-Eubank II was over 18 million viewers. Plus the 13 million who watched the repeat on the following Monday, so that's over 30 million viewers'.

Other than finance, Hearn was also intrigued by the outcome of a third match. 'I like trilogy fights anyway to put the result beyond dispute. And I don't know who would have won. If anything Benn was probably in the ascendancy'. Eubank had asked what a draw meant for his career to which Hearn told him, 'It means we get to do it again'.

'I like draws!', replied the WBO champion.

Sky had hoped that Eubank's first match with them would be another fight with Benn, but the 'Dark Destroyer' instead signed with Don King and Frank Warren.

Eubank would go on to tackle quantity over quality, to which Hearn joked that 'the match making was tougher' than the actual fights. It may have been a busy schedule but Hearn knew that Eubank was a consistent trainer who never fell out of shape even without a fight scheduled. 'When we sat down with Sky and did the deal with Kelvin McKenzie, he said to me "it's a lot of money. They'll be proper fights, won't they?"

Hearn insisted that they would, to which McKenzie replied, "But you won't get him beat, will you?"'

Therefore, the biggest pressure was to keep Eubank undefeated: a record that became his selling point. One such easy opponent was supposed to be Steve Collins, who had just moved up from middleweight. His CV was unspectacular enough to have ticked all the boxes on the 'shopping list', but to the surprise of many, the 'Celtic Warrior' not only took away Eubank's WBO title, but would also beat him in the rematch.

It was a pleasure to talk to Barry Hearn, but his standpoint does contradict the narrative of the chapter, which is that these are fights that should have happened. I still can't help but to be intrigued about the idea of a showman like Eubank taking on fewer fights, but against top opponents. Losing to the best would probably have done his legacy more credit than to have mostly beaten a checklist of beatable bums. Fans of the football team who win the Premier League title then want to see them take on the best in the Champions League. It's the obvious next step of progression; but then again boxing isn't like other sports: when Manchester City takes a beating from Bayern Munich they don't risk brain injury. Is Chris Eubank v James Toney or Michael Nunn a fight that should have happened? In terms of the natural order of things, then yes, without a doubt. In sport the champions should meet and give clarity to the division. In terms of an individual's right to choose his own path in dangerous sport, it makes the term 'should' one that is hard to conclusively justify.

In his autobiography Eubank insists, 'Dodging a fighter is a cardinal sin in boxing and is something I can never be accused of, unlike one such character who came on to the scene at the end of my era.[3] Roy Jones, James Toney and Michael Nunn for example I did not dodge'.

Eubank's interpretation of a 'dodge' is all down to the ratings and whether or not the WBO rated a fighter as number-one contender. If an opponent offered to Eubank was not rated number one, he could turn the fight down and claim it was not a dodge. To some, that interpretation is highly questionable, primarily because the best super middleweights in the world could never have been rated as WBO number-one contender because of this rule: if you are champion of a body like WBO, you cannot be rated number-one contender for anyone else. So in the early to mid 1990s IBF champ James Toney and WBA champ Michael Nunn could never have been rated as WBO number-one contender. For the same reason as WBO title holder Chris Eubank could not have been rated number-one contender for the IBF, WBA and WBC titles. That one ruling gave carte blanche for champs to dodge other champs. Imagine having four Super Bowls?

After Eubank retired he was offered comeback fights against some big names, which did include the 'abrasive' James Toney, but he couldn't be tempted. 'Why come back? I retired just before my 32nd birthday, which in boxing terms meant I was an old man. If the phone rang tomorrow and I was offered £1 billion, then no, I wouldn't do it. My dignity and respect are more valuable'.

'No fighters in England, they're all bums!' After hearing that statement, the patriot in me wanted the attacking Nigel Benn to go to America and declare war on the masterful counterpuncher James Toney. Personality-wise, however, Benn's moody temper was not the total opposite to Toney's short fuse. Unlike the sensitive Eubank, Benn had the take no shit personality to match fire with fire. Benn may have lost, but he wouldn't have done so on a whim, and if one man had the attitude to stand toe to toe with Toney it was Big Bad Benn, who once said, 'If you hit me, I will get back up. I'm not one of these Brits whose gonna lay down and die. I'm going out on my shield, I'm proud to be British'.

A rivalry between Toney and Benn could have been a microcosm of the edgier elements of two different countries. The London street fighter against the American gangster; Toney and Benn were the bona fide bad boys of the societies they came from. Benn had the swagger and attitude of a man who had fought more wars out of the ring than inside. Toney, a former crack dealer, came from the ghettos of America and was known to carry a gun, even to press conferences. The violence of American society outweighed anything on our shores. British street gang culture back then may have had bad intentions and plenty of attitude, but its American counterpart was ruthless to a more fatal and graphic extreme. Benn had mouth, but he never went so far as to tell his most hated rival that he wanted Mother Eubank to suck his dick.

Don King had tried and failed to lure James Toney by telling him that his manager, a white female called Jackie Kallem, was a Jew who would only look after her own interests, and to give a brother a chance. With Toney, the race tactic did not work. His respect for the blonde Kallem was strong enough for him to wear a Star of David on his fighting shorts as a gesture of friendship. Benn having signed with Don King in 1993 was a stumbling block to a matchup with Toney, who made his feelings on his choice of promoter very clear in his victory speech after beating Mike McCallum in 1992: 'I'll talk to Bob Arum because he's my man. Don King kiss my ass!'

The only King that James Toney wanted to deal with served cheeseburgers on the high street, and in the post-McCallum interview the IBF champion bounced up and down in excitement while piping up 'Yo, Burger King, baby…Burger King! '

Benn would have been the underdog against James Toney, but 'Lights Out's' struggle with weight and the fatigue that came with it may have provided the factor which would give a warrior like Benn a fighting chance. Going by past evidence, weight issues had nearly cost Toney a defeat against an unrated fighter in 1992. Dave Tiberi from Delaware had outfought Toney and ended up on the wrong end of a scandalous decision.

In later years Toney admitted that Tiberi won the fight and blamed exhaustion, which came from meeting the 160 lb (72 kg) middleweight requirement. Before the bell sounded Toney looked in prime, million pound condition, but he would put in a lacklustre two bob performance. As the bell ended the contest, an ecstatic Tiberi was picked up and paraded like he was the new middleweight champion. Toney looked to the canvas, exhausted, despondent and defeated. Toney would win by split decision and was too embarrassed and tired to even raise a smile as boos of disgust rang out from the crowd. Tiberi would quit boxing as a direct result of the decision. The super middleweight class did not end Toney's weight issues. In 1994 he was dethroned of his super middleweight IBF title by a points loss to Roy Jones Jr. in his first ever defeat. Jones badly outclassed a below-form 'Lights Out', who blamed his loss on tiredness due to trying to make the weight. Toney held his manager, Jackie Kallem, responsible and the day after the loss went looking for her with a gun, which naturally ended their friendship. Just like Don, Burger King can also have a detrimental impact on a fighter's wellbeing and Toney's days as a super middleweight were coming to an end. The cheeseburgers took their toll and Toney would come to resemble a black version of the Marshmallow Man from *Ghostbusters*. 'Lights Out' moved up weight, where he never excelled to the same great standards as he did in the middleweight divisions. It was at this point that Eubank decided to call out the man he never previously expressed any desire to face. Eubank had lost his WBO title to Steve Collins and said, 'James Toney come down from light heavyweight, you've insulted my mother once too often…'

If some fighters favoured staying clear of Don King, Benn saw the benefits and noted, 'I think, why deal with the small rats? Why not deal with the biggest rat? So I'd rather deal with him. I didn't care how much he was taking, I was just worried about what I [got]…He paid me good money, so whether he made £20 million good luck to him. But you pay me what I want and I was happy with that'.

With the Eubank-Nunn deal now out of the question, King offered Nunn to Benn, who the 'Dark Destroyer' described as, 'The most slippery southpaw I've ever met'. Benn refused the Nunn fight, claiming that he didn't see why he should take a smaller slice of the purse: 'I'm the world champion and they want me to take less [than Nunn]? I told them just what I was thinking—bollocks to that!'

It wasn't the first time that Benn had sidestepped an offer to fight Nunn. Early on in his career, before his loss to Michael Watson, Benn was offered $3 million to go to America and fight Nunn but said, 'We rejected it out of hand. Nunn was my age and had just knocked out World Boxing Association champion Sumbu Kalambay in 88 seconds in Las Vegas. He was undefeated in 33 fights, 23 of them inside the distance. Ambrose [Mendy] told the press that they could stick his offer. I would continue to fight for the British and European titles before thinking about the World Championship. . .'

After Benn ducked Nunn for a second time in the mid 1990s, Don King then warned, 'If you don't [fight Nunn] we're gonna bring in the mini Mike Tyson'. To which Benn replied, 'Okay bring him on'. In an interview in 2012 Benn recalled, 'Usually a fighter will say, okay [I'll fight the easier guy]. Not me. I used to fight the National Front, I was in the army. If I go out, I'll go out on my shield. I fight anybody'.

The rest is history. Nigel Benn-Gerald McClellan goes down as one of the most talked about, tragic, notorious and monumental fights in history. James Toney's accusation that Benn lacked guts took a hammer blow as the British boy somehow rose from a first-round knock down to beat an opponent who trainer Emanuel Steward claimed had the biggest mean streak of anyone he had worked with.

It was one of the greatest and bravest fights in the modern era, but marred by a horrible outcome which left the American with chronic brain damage and a loss of sight and hearing. Had the 'G Man' not been so horribly injured, one can only imagine the epic showdowns that he would have gone on to compete in.[4]

Toney, however, withheld credit to Benn and told Donald McRea that McClellan won via a first round KO but was denied by a slow count. In later years, however, something incredible happened which challenged everything human beings thought we knew: James Toney talked about Benn and Eubank without insulting them, or even Eubank's mother. If that wasn't stunning enough, history was made when 'Lights Out' actually hinted of praise for the British boys. He told the writer Ben Dirs:

> There was never any hatred, all that was just hype to get a fight between us. I wasn't very complementary but I just wanted in on the action. The truth is I don't think the WBO is a joke. I wanted every title out there, every title looks good in my belt case. So I never thought of either Benn-Eubank fight as something inferior. Believe me, I was watching that night of 18 November 1990—is that right?—because I wanted every middle and super

middleweight belt that could come my way. I was hoping the winner of that first fight would come over to the United States or I could go over there. But it never came off that way. But I give Nigel Benn all the credit in the world because he came over here and fought some of our good guys and blew them out. I liked his style—he came at you, he didn't dance, he didn't run from no friendly fire. And that's also why I wanted to fight him, because I knew when we got in the ring he wasn't going anywhere and I wasn't going anywhere, but I had a better chin. Chris Eubank was a pretty good boxer but more on the scary side of things. He was a very strange guy, and I'm not the only one who thought that. But Chris wasn't brave enough to come to America. The closest I came to fighting him was when I was hooked up to that satellite feed.

1. Part one is a fight that nearly didn't happen. On the morning of the bout, Benn woke up to the shock that he was 6 lbs (2.7 kg) over the weight limit and only had three hours before the weigh in. Incredibly he lost the weight in a manic last-ditch morning training session that included steam room shadow boxing while wearing a winter puffer jacket.
2. 'An over-publicised bearded troll'.
3. Eubank did not go on to elaborate who that elusive boxer was, which leaves us guessing! My guess is Naseem Hamed.
4. A fight that did happen is Gerald McClellan-Thomas Hearns. It was an exhibition bout hosted at the famous Kronk gym in Detroit in 1990, and footage can be found on Internet sites like YouTube. Footage can also be found of an exhibition bout in the Kronk between Gerald McClellan and James Toney.

ROUND 4

SCHMELING IS DENIED A DATE WITH CINDERELLA

Yes I had dinner with Adolf Hitler, but that doesn't make me a Nazi. The same way I had dinner with Roosevelt but that doesn't make me a democrat!'
Max Schmeling in conversation with boxing historian and writer Bert Sugar

'The [1930s] Depression-starved fan identified with him. He'd been on welfare. He had made something of himself, come off welfare and was a champion.'
Bert Sugar on James J. Braddock

In a debate over Christmas 2012 with my great uncle, Reg Calcagni, a passionate boxing fan in his 90s, we were on the subject of fights that should *never* have happened. I mentioned Rocky Marciano-Joe Louis in

1951, considering that Marciano was in his prime and Louis was old, tired and washed up. After the fight, Rocky went to the loser's dressing room to tell Louis that it was a fight that he didn't want, but that he had no choice. Watching the footage of Louis falling through the ropes is spectacular, but also sad considering the 'Brown Bomber' was such a great champion years beforehand. Uncle Reg responded with, 'Eh, don't give me that. Remember, what goes around comes around'.

'What do you mean by that?'

'Listen, boy, when he fought Schmeling the first time Schmeling was an old man. Then it was another two years before he fought him again'.

Uncle Reg then got on his soap box about how Schmeling should have been given the chance to fight for the world championship directly after his first fight with Louis in 1936. As you delve into the heavyweight division in the period 1936–37, then you see that, yes, a clear fight that arguably should have happened was Max Schmeling against the world heavyweight champion James Braddock, the 'Cinderella Man'.

Max Schmeling was born in Klein Luckow, Germany in 1905 and is a boxer who will forever be associated with Nazi Germany. When discussing whether or not Schmeling was actually a Nazi, the debate ends when you learn that he saved the lives of two Jewish children during *Kristallnacht*, the notorious night of Nazi persecution in Berlin. On a holocaust remembrance website that I stumbled upon, there is a page dedicated to Schmeling in which he is proclaimed as a hero due to his protection of the two children, and also because he refused to sack his manager Joe Jacobs who was a Jewish American. In contrast to being a Nazi, Schmeling had the courage to refuse to join the Nazi Party and Goebbels was said to be angry that he still associated with German Jews. Schmeling himself never revealed to the world the fact that he saved the lives of the two Jewish brothers (sons of a friend) by hiding them in a hotel room and giving orders to staff for nobody to disturb him while he pretended to be ill. It was not until 1989 when one of the brothers, a hotel owner called Henri Lewin, invited Schmeling to Las Vegas to honour him and tell the story.

In the 1920s the sport of boxing was thriving in Germany and there were around 40,000 registered amateurs. Schmeling's professional career spanned 1924 to 1948 and he retired with a record of 56 wins, four draws and ten losses. Known as 'The Black Uhlan of the Rhine' (German's don't do short nicknames), Schmeling obtained the unique honour of being the only man to win the world heavyweight title lying on his back. In 1930 he was awarded the vacant title when Jack Sharkey floored him with an illegal left-hand low blow in the fourth round, which sent Schmeling rolling around the floor in pain. The crowd at the Yankee Stadium thought it was a legitimate body shot from the Boston Gob and were cheering a knockdown, only for the referee to disqualify Sharkey. The German was lifted off his feet by two of his corner men, carried away like a wounded soldier and certainly not looking like a man who had just won the championship of the world; slow motion film replays confirmed that the punch was below the belt. As the newest and oldest member of the Berlin Boys' Choir, Schmeling had become the first man to win the title from a disqualification and also the first ever German world heavyweight champion..

Two years later at Madison Square Garden, Jack Sharkey won the title back from Schmeling in a split decision that has been hotly disputed over the years. There were many who believed that Schmeling should have been awarded the bout and was robbed of victory. One of those people (aside from Uncle Reg!) who felt that the German won was the great Gene Tunney who had retired and vacated the title that was up for grabs in the first Schmeling-Sharkey contest.

After beating local legend Mickey Walker at Madison Square Garden later on in 1932, Schmeling was given a shot at the new world champion Max Baer at the Yankee Stadium in 1933. This was an event promoted by former champ Jack Dempsey and although Schmeling was stopped by the referee in the tenth round, the fight had the honour of being declared Match of the Year by *The Ring*.

But it wasn't a world title contest that gave Schmeling the golden moment of his career. In 1936, at the Yankee Stadium, the German took on Joe Louis, who had won all of his 27 fights and was making a name for himself as the emerging superstar in the sport. He had already convincingly beaten some top-rank fighters and the young 'Brown Bomber' from Detroit was the clear favourite to beat 31-year-old Schmeling. In one of heavyweight boxing's biggest upsets Schmeling not only beat Louis, but did so convincingly. Before the fight, Schmeling had watched videotapes and noticed that Louis dropped his left hand after throwing a jab. Schmeling's game plan was to counterpunch after every Louis jab. The plan worked a treat and the young superstar was dominated by the experienced German and eventually knocked out in the 12th round.

If all had gone to plan, then waiting for the victorious Joe Louis in the next fight would be the reigning champion James J. Braddock who a year earlier had beaten Max Baer in a huge upset to win the title. Braddock, portrayed by Russell Crowe in the 2005 film *Cinderella Man*, was an embodiment of desire and the overcoming of social hardship. Born in Manhattan's Hell's Kitchen, Braddock's biographer Michael C. Delisa notes that, 'Rarely was a slum so aptly named'.

Previous to the Max Baer fight, Braddock was highly respected but not viewed as championship material. His professional career didn't even get off to a winning start as his first ever match was declared a draw. Even so, it wasn't until his 26th fight that he suffered his first defeat. But then numerous broken hand injuries dogged his career and he registered countless losses, many of which were against journeymen. During the Great Depression in 1933, the ongoing hand injuries forced Braddock into retirement, but he was able to find labour work at the docks to support his impoverished family.

In June 1934 at Madison Square Garden, Max Baer fought for the world championship against the Italian giant Primo Carnera. If Schmeling was unfortunate to have Hitler as a supposed admirer, Carnera couldn't really boast about his fans either, as they included Benito Mussolini.[1] Six-foot-six Primo Carnera had beaten Jack Sharkey for the title in 1933 in a match that many at the time claimed was a fix. The Italian was huge but untalented, and controlled by the mafia who are thought to have fixed most of his fights; very few of Carnera's wins were thought to be on the level. Outside the ring the 'Ambling Alp' was a gentle giant who was left penniless after his boxing career and it's thought that he only ever received 10 percent of his purses. Max Baer versus Primo Carnera was a blueprint in how to cut down a giant. 'Madcap' Maxie's destruction of the big man was frightening, brutal and described by Bert Sugar as 'the most one-sided fight ever'. In today's more merciful culture the fight would have been stopped long before Carnera hit the canvas for the 11th time. On a couple of occasions Carnera was so dazed that he turned his back to Baer, who continued to pummel him with a sadistic smile on his face. Nicknamed 'Madcap Maxie' with good reason, Bert Sugar lists Baer as the most colourful character in the sport's history, even ahead of Muhammad Ali. 'Honestly his antics and statements were the things of 1930s headlines. Before his title fight with Primo Carnera, Baer nonchalantly picked hairs off Carnera's chest chanting "She loves me…she loves me not"'.

By the 11th round Primo Carnera himself actually appealed to the referee to stop the fight, to which the official obliged and Max Baer was declared the new champion of the world.

On the undercard for this fight at the Garden was Braddock. He had been retired for a year but made a comeback for $250 and beat Corn Griffin who was considered a bright prospect. Griffin needed some respected names on his CV and this fight was supposed to help propel his career, not re-launch Braddock's, who had been offered the match two days prior and had no time to train. The win did not immediately bring a turn of fortune for Braddock and in order to pay bills he had to register for welfare, just like so many others of the Great Depression generation.

He soon got back in the ring, and surprising wins against the highly rated John Henry Lewis and Art Lasky then suddenly put Braddock in line for a title shot against Max Baer. It was thought that Lasky would be the one to fight for the title, and once again Braddock was supposed to be the stepping-stone for up-and-coming talent. Braddock used the earnings from the Lasky fight to pay back the money he had received from state welfare, which he was under no obligation to do. It became a gesture that immortalised him as a people's champion and a generous person.

Because of the decisive nature in which Baer had cut down Primo Carnera, the perceived chances of Braddock winning were understandably viewed as very slim and his odds were at 10/1. The pre-match build up was good spirited and Baer expressed a desire that after the fight the two men would remain friends. Baer also boasted that he was in great shape and that he'd been training hard, which is a claim that many have doubted; in contrast, the champ was said to be enjoying life too much and hardly spending any time in the gym, unlike Braddock who trained intensely.

Braddock did not intend to out-brawl his heavier opponent and the Irishman's game plan, which was to beat Baer by jabbing and moving, worked perfectly. This was a tactic he noted and copied from Tommy Loughran, who beat Baer with that style in 1931(Loughran had also registered a win over Braddock in a light heavyweight title contest in 1929).

There's a wonderful moment in the Baer-Braddock fight when 'Madcap' took a right shot to the face, stepped backwards with a punch-drunk expression as if he'd been pole axed, then came forward again with his trademark insane grin to let us know he was playing possum. That moment was never portrayed in the film *Cinderella Man*, perhaps because the filmmakers thought that people wouldn't believe that such a thing would really have happened in a world title fight.[2]

After 15 rounds the judges awarded the decision to Braddock and the match still stands as one of the sport's biggest upsets. Baer's post-fight response was fairly pragmatic and typically colourful. 'Braddock can use the title. He has three kids. I don't know how many I have'.

The priority now for the ageing Braddock was to get as big a purse as he possibly could in his next fight to see him into a comfortable retirement. His manager Joe Gould had the same priority and told the press, 'We're in the saddle now and we can say whom we'll fight. We want the guy who will draw the biggest gate'. Braddock himself was realistic about his chances of a long championship run and admitted, 'The only thing a guy can do is cash in while he's hot. Everybody is going to be licked some day'.

At this point in time Max Schmeling was a hot, sellable name who would draw good money. But the man he beat up, Joe Louis, was still the bigger attraction and remained the one who Gould felt could pull in the most revenue. The German's shock win against the 'Brown Bomber' placed him as number-one contender for the title and Max Schmeling-Jim Braddock was announced and booked in for summer 1937. Braddock, who was under contract from Madison Square Garden, did sign for the bout and large billboards went up advertising the fight, which would take place on 3 June.

But things were about to change very quickly. Just two months after losing to Schmeling, Louis made a decisive comeback and knocked out the former champ Jack Sharkey in front of a huge crowd at the Yankee Stadium—a demolition job on the 'Boston Gob'. After the fight, Louis said he wanted a rematch with Schmeling. The one-sided nature of Louis-Sharkey was enough to convince Joe Gould that Joe Louis was still the right man to pursue. Despite losing to Schmeling, the 'Brown Bomber' remained the man in the division who could draw the most money. The very next day Gould pulled Braddock out of the Schmeling fight and claimed that the champion had injured his hand. To quote Dan Margolick, author of the Joe Louis-Max Schmeling-themed book *Beyond Glory*, 'Everyone assumed

Braddock was trying to get out of the fight, angling for a more lucrative match with Louis, and hadn't known he was injured until Joe Gould told him so'. The fight was postponed until August 1937 and Schmeling cynically noted, 'I hope the 21 doctors will be able to keep him alive until next summer'.

Soon afterwards, Gould began to look for ways to get out of the Madison Square Garden contract, scrap the Schmeling fight and sign a deal for Braddock to fight Louis in Chicago with a local promoter. The politics of the sport was about to run wild and the Madison Square Garden big wigs declared 'war' on the Chicago promotion and insisted that any Braddock fight outside of New York was illegal and would break binding agreements. They called themselves 'old fashioned' in that they believed in seeing out contracts. 'We're holding our fort. We know our legal rights and will stop any Louis-Braddock fight until Schmeling has had his chance', insisted the Garden's boss Jim Johnston.

Joe Gould didn't have a venue preference for Louis-Braddock and was prepared to go with the highest bidder, which was looking likely to be Atlantic City in New Jersey. Schmeling was being erased from the title picture and asked, 'What is the heavyweight championship? Is it a joke? Is it stuff like wrestling?' Braddock, however, felt no remorse at denying the German a title shot and said, 'I'm not going to sacrifice my family just to please some fighter who never in his ring career has done anything to please anybody but himself'. The champion was backed by writer Bill Farnsworth of the newspaper the *Evening Journal,* who wrote, 'Why should Jim, who was on welfare relief for years, who hasn't made a real dollar since winning the title, who has a bunch of youngsters he wants to educate, who has a wife he wants to build a home for, take $75,000 to fight Schmeling instead of $700,000 for facing Louis?'

In February 1937, Braddock signed to fight Joe Louis in June of that year in Chicago, the same month in which he was contracted to fight Schmeling. The deal, worth half a million for Braddock, included a masterstroke piece of negotiating from Joe Gould: Joe Louis was managed by Mike Jacobs, the most powerful boxing promoter of the time. In return for them breaking the Garden's contract, Gould somehow managed to convince Jacobs to sign a legally binding agreement that entitled him and Braddock to 10 percent of all profits on Jacob's heavyweight title bouts for the next ten years. The argument from Gould must have been along the lines of: 'You need to give us this incentive because by going with Louis we're burning all bridges with the Garden'.

This deal was kept secret; otherwise Schmeling would have been even angrier than he already was at how the situation had developed. Even though the politics and legal disputes were still ongoing, Schmeling returned to Germany a despondent man. His chance to win back the title, which he felt cheated out of against Sharkey, was slipping away.

To broker Louis-Braddock, Joe Gould's team had found flaws and potential get-out clauses in the Garden's contract with Braddock, but a new problem was about to arise. State legislators in Chicago put forward a bizarre bill that would make it illegal for the Braddock-Louis promotion to charge more than $10 for any ticket, including ringside. This now put the fight in major jeopardy, as the top-price tickets would potentially be significantly below the expected amount. One has to wonder how that proposed law came about, as it would not make sense for state officials in

Chicago to propose legislation that would jeopardise a major world sporting event taking place in their city. Maybe the Garden had secretly been in touch with some influential Chicago lawmakers? Speculation, perhaps, but there aren't any other obvious reasons why some in Chicago would want to bring in such legislation. The law was never passed, however, fearing it would be, Gould was ready to change his mind over a match with Schmeling if his asking price of a $400,000 purse for Braddock was met. That ray of hope for Schmeling did not last long. Once the proposed $10 ticket law was scrapped, Braddock-Louis was back on despite a continuation of legal battles. In May 1937, a judge ruled in favour of Braddock's right to fight Joe Louis.

Braddock could have potentially taken on both men, Schmeling first, then Louis. But if he were to lose the belt against Schmeling then a follow-up match with Louis would have lost its kudos with no title on the line. It would not have grossed anywhere near as much money or held the same amount of interest. Braddock's winning streak would have been over, along with the Cinderella story. From Braddock and Gould's point of view, Max Schmeling represented far too great a risk and was best avoided.

For side-stepping a title match with Schmeling, Braddock was fined $1,000 and banned from competing in New York, a measure in which the ducked German protested, 'Is that a punishment for a world champion who chickens out? The whole decision is a joke. The championship, it is a joke. And your commission is a bigger joke. I cannot help it that I beat your Joe Louis. Louis will be your champion June 23, and I knocked Louis out. Can you figure that?'

Even though the fight had long since been cancelled, on 3 June 1937 Max Schmeling still turned up to a rainy Long Island City for a mock weigh-in. The press, umbrellas in hand, followed him to report on this bizarre event, and some rumours circulated among boxing fans that the fight was going ahead. Schmeling simply wanted to make a statement and afterwards the angry German screwed up a newspaper picture of Braddock and growled to reporters 'This is your champion. Bah, he is a coward!' before booting the crumpled-up picture in disgust. A few days beforehand the German propaganda minister Joseph Goebbels had proposed the idea of the Reich declaring Schmeling the real world champion, but no such announcement was made.

Braddock-Schmeling didn't happen for the main reason that the champion felt his time in the sport was limited and he wanted to earn as much money as possible from just one match. But there is also the factor that a German champion in that period of time was viewed with great trepidation. Boxing historian Mike Silver speaks of the fear some Americans had of losing the title to fascist Europe. 'Schmeling was from Germany. And the fear was that if Schmeling were to defeat Braddock for the heavyweight championship, the Nazis would keep the title in Germany, where they would use it as a propaganda tool'.

Schmeling had, of course, already held the heavyweight title, but that was before the Nazis took power in 1932. As a German in the 1930s, Schmeling would have had to fight under the Nazi swastika because that symbol had replaced the black, yellow and red tricolour as the official German flag between the years 1933 and 1945.[3] After the fight with Braddock was postponed/cancelled, options were explored by shady political figures in Germany to stage the fight in the Olympic Stadium in Berlin, in negotiations, which, supposedly, had the support of Hitler. Had that event gone ahead, and had Braddock won, it would have been immortalised alongside the triumphs of Jesse Owen in the 1936 Berlin Olympics. On the flip side, had Schmeling won the world title in Berlin, the Nazi regime would have no doubt hijacked the glory for themselves and had a field day with the propaganda. There were worries that they would do whatever they could to hold onto the title and not give shots to any credible American opponents, most notably Joe Louis. Max Schmeling's preference was to fight in America and he openly stated to the *New York Post* that he had no desire to fight Braddock in Germany because it would not generate the same amount of money as it would on US soil. He stated, 'Here is where I made my money. Here is where I will make more money when I win the championship'.

Max Schmeling's prospects of drawing big money were hindered, though, as he become a major target for Anti-Nazi League protesters. The protest movement saw Schmeling as a Hitler stooge and had threatened the sport with a boycott if 'Nazi Max' were to be given a title shot against Braddock. Many American Jews hated Max Schmeling, which was hardly surprising, as this was a man who had been photographed smiling with Adolf Hitler during an era when German Jews had been ghettoised and stripped of rights. To the casual observer, Max Schmeling was a Nazi who was fighting for the glory of his home country's regime. The Anti-Nazi League played on the fact that Schmeling had gone on an exhibition tour of the southern states of America after his defeat of Joe Louis. In their eyes it was a cynical attempt by Schmeling to maximise the fact that he had beaten the world's most famous black man to a bunch of appreciative Deep South racists. Schmeling's reasoning regarding his motivation for the tour was that winter had set in and it was a lot warmer in the south. From his point of view that sounds like a reasonable explanation, especially when you consider that in 1930s America there was also no shortage of racists in the northern states. In terms of black equality, America and Germany were by no means sitting at different ends of the table. At this point in time, no black man had ever been granted the right to fight for the world heavyweight championship on American soil. The racist manner in which Joe Louis was portrayed by the German Nazi media was no less offensive than the way Jack Johnson was regularly attacked during his fighting years by the American media. In relation to Jewish prejudice, however, there was a clear difference. In 1930s Germany, Jews were viciously persecuted, while in America they were free and in many cases thriving; nowhere more so than boxing, both in and out of the ring. The worry that a Braddock-Schmeling fight would be targeted by the threat of a boycott could have had a big influence in Joe Gould's thinking and future planning. Gould was reported to have said, 'Not only is three out of every four fight fans at title fights Jews, they sat in the most expensive seats'. Author David Margolick, however, claims this didn't bother Madison Square Garden, whose view was, 'For every Jew who spurned the contest an extra Irishman or German American would go'.

It didn't help matters that the doomed Braddock-Schmeling bout was at one point moved to a day in September which fell on Yom Kippur, the holiest day in the Jewish calendar. Joe Gould was lobbied by his mother and so the fight was moved to 24 September, before, of course, being aborted completely.

The leader of the Anti-Nazi League Samuel Untermyer himself did not support boxing boycotts for fear of turning the public against his group, and there were some in America who took offence to the boycott threats of Max Schmeling fights. A letter to the *Herald Tribune* from a reader warned, 'God help the Jews in Germany if the proposed Schmeling-Braddock boycott forces cancellation of the bout…The suffering the German Jews have already endured will be nothing compared with the attacks, both financial and physical, to which they will be subjected if Schmeling is cheated of his hard-earned shot at the title. I suggest that the boycott committee arrange to evacuate all Jews now in Germany if it insists on going ahead with the boycott'.

Schmeling tried to turn the concept of boycott into a tool with which to enhance his status and reputation. He told the boycott movement that he felt complemented by their stance and 'if they thought Braddock could beat me in two or three rounds there wouldn't be a boycott movement'.

After all the politics and lawsuits, James Braddock versus Joe Louis for the heavyweight title eventually took place in Chicago on 22 June 1937. Max Schmeling refused to be in attendance. The defending champion Braddock knocked down Louis in the fourth round, but the 'Bomber' got back on his feet and dominated the fight. Gould wanted to pull Braddock out of the contest for his own safety, but the 'Pride of Jersey' insisted on going down fighting; which is what happened in round eight when Louis floored the beaten Braddock, who lay down on the canvas in a motionless, crumpled heap. Joe Louis described the fallen ex-champ as the bravest man he ever faced in the ring.

Had James Braddock beaten Joe Louis then he most probably would have gone on to defend against Max Schmeling. Instead, he had one last fight against the top contender Tommy Farr and won a close points decision against the highly rated Welshman.[4] He ended his career with a record of 46 wins, 23 losses, five draws and 11 no decisions.

The good news for Schmeling was that he finally got his chance for a title shot in June 1938. However, the bad news was that it was against a

'Brown Bomber' intent on avenging his defeat from two years earlier. This was a career definer for Louis who brutally knocked the German out in round one in a super-fight dubbed the 'Battle of the Century', an event which went far beyond sport and became one of the most famous bouts in boxing history. The pressure on the 'Detroit Bomber' to win this fight was immense as it was seen as freedom versus fascism. President Roosevelt had told the champion, 'We need these fists for democracy'. That was the feeling at the time, anyway. Years down the line, the tagline of freedom vs. fascism seems a harsh burden on Schmeling, who was a victim of world political circumstance. In a 1975 interview, Schmeling expressed no regrets for his defeat in the Louis rematch and said, 'Looking back, I'm almost happy I lost that fight. Just imagine if I would have come back to Germany with a victory. I had nothing to do with the Nazis, but they would have given me a medal. After the war I might have been considered a war criminal'. Joe Louis would be the last non-German that Schmeling would fight in the ring. In 1939, the foreigners he would go on to face would be in the Second World War, in which he served as a paratrooper for the German Air force. In 1947, 'The Black Uhlan of the Rhine' resumed his boxing career. He won a few and lost a couple, but these fights were for domestic honours and his days as a top world title champion and contender were in the past. He retired for good after a loss in Berlin against Richard Vogt in 1948.

Whether or not Braddock-Schmeling is a fight that should have happened is all down to one's own interpretation. From Schmeling's point of view he had good reason to feel hard done by. From Braddock's angle, sidestepping the dangerous German was a move that more than took him out of poverty for the rest of his life.

In terms of sporting fairness, Braddock-Schmeling for the world title was an opportunity that the German had merited, but was denied. But who could possibly fault James J. Braddock for taking no chances and holding out for as big a payday as he could, especially in a sport that lacked the structure to enforce scheduling fairness. If being denied a championship fight against Braddock contributed to Schmeling being hard-up for cash and down on his luck in later life, then it would have been more of a travesty. On the bright side, Schmeling's post-boxing career was productive and fruitful and he led a comfortable life as an executive for German Coca Cola. He built up a tremendous friendship with Joe Louis and financially supported him when the 'Brown Bomber' fell on hard times. Given that Schmeling at one point in his life was made to fight in a World War in which tens of millions of people died, with some worse luck, he may not have lived to the ripe old age of 90. Just like James J. Braddock, Schmeling is one of boxing's genuine good guys who upset the odds when everyone expected him to lose. In their own different ways, both these great fighters were Cinderella men.

1. Another fight that perhaps should have happened in the 1930s was between these two European heavyweights (Schmeling-Carnera, not Hitler-Mussolini).

2. The filmmakers also used a bit of creative licence in their portrayal of the Baer-Carnera fight. They showed Carnera as being knocked out and then picked up off the canvas. In real life Carnera was retired while standing up, despite being knocked down 11 times throughout the fight.

3. If you look at fight records, a listed German boxer fighting between the years 1933 and 1945 will probably have a swastika next to their name as the national symbol.

4. Tommy Farr vs. Max Schmeling was a fight that nearly happened as a rebellious counter-act to Louis-Braddock. German promoters suggested a Farr-Schmeling bout in Europe, which they would have marketed as the 'Real World championship'. The Germans described Farr as an 'Englishman', even though he was Welsh, and Schmeling was happy for this fight to go ahead in London as opposed to Berlin. The prospect of Farr-Schmeling was hijacked by the management of the actual world champion, Joe Louis. They offered Tommy Farr more money to fight Louis and so the Welshman flew to the other side of the Atlantic. As a result, Tommy Farr became as popular in Berlin as James Braddock was.

INTERLUDE

THE HAWK FALLS OFF THE MONEY TREE

'I didn't see it, but I've been told by the guys that were there, that Aaron was so good in that weight class—Ray Leonard moved up to get away from Aaron Pryor.'

Butch Lewis, boxing promoter

In September 1981, at Caesar's Palace, Sugar Ray Leonard beat Thomas Hearns in one of the all time great welterweight title matches. Having disposed of the formidable Hearns in stunning fashion, the most charismatic star of the 1980s had confirmed his status as Ali's successor and the prime superstar of boxing. At the post-fight press conference the victorious Leonard held stage while wearing an audacious white yachting suit and captain's hat. 'I beat Thomas Hearns…I wanna fight…I beat Thomas Hearns, I wanna fight'.

Those were not the words of the 'Hitman' conquering Leonard, but those of Aaron Pryor who was reminding the press at Caesar's Palace that he too had beaten the 'Hitman' in an amateur bout in 1976.

Sugar's limelight on the press conference podium had just been ambushed by Pryor, whose look resembled a real-life version of Apollo Creed from the film *Rocky*.

'I just been told that you want to challenge me, and that I knocked you down and that you knocked me down', said a hesitant Leonard regarding sparring sessions, to which Pryor in later years recalled, 'We've had workouts as amateur but I've actually knocked the guy down as a pro and amateur. Well whaddaya know…he knows me!'

Much to the visible displeasure of Leonard, whose style was being cramped, Pryor decided that it was a shared press conference and told the world, 'I just beat the number-one contender in my weight division [lightweight]. I got nothing to prove there, so why don't I come up?'

'This is my show', replied the nautically-clad 'Money Tree' as he brushed aside the wannabe challenger, turned to the press and asked, 'Any more questions please?'

Regarding Pryor's challenge Leonard predicted: 'Aaron Pryor says he wants to get in the ring with me. He says he wants to retire—and he will for health reasons!'

'I wanna fight Leonard because I feel like I'm king of the junior welterweights for what I've already done', insisted Pryor, though he had once turned down an offer of $500,000 to fight Leonard because he felt the disparity of Leonard's $4 million fee was too imbalanced. In 1982, the 'Hawk' had a record of 30 unbeaten professional fights as a lightweight and had even been compared to the great Henry Armstrong because of his irresistible speed and energy. $750,000 was enough of a temptation for Pryor to accept a deal to fight Leonard for the welterweight title in what was set to be one of the super-fights of the decade. All Sugar had to do was beat Roger Stafford in Buffalo and the match was on. Pryor was going to be in attendance in order to be a nuisance and drum up hype for the future showdown. On his way to upstate New York he received the news that Leonard had suffered a detached retina in training and all immediate plans were to be postponed. Pryor is said to have stopped the car and cried his eyes out on the side of the road. Sugar Ray then announced his retirement, and would not make a return until 1984. Pryor would not join the likes of Hearns, Leonard, Duran and Hagler in the golden era of the Four Kings. It could have been Five Kings but the 'Hawk' remained a welterweight while the other four legends moved to middleweight. His biggest battle was an addiction to drugs, which did little to move him up the scales. In 1986, Pryor's demons were destroying his career and his weight had plummeted to 110 lbs (50 kg).

The 'Hawk' retired in 1990 with a record of 40 wins and 1 defeat, and he would finally turn his back on his drug habit in 1993. Talking to the Boxing Channel at the Hall of Fame, the 1996 inductee said:

> I was close to making that fight, until I sparred with him a few times and I don't think they liked what happened in the sparring sessions. But me and Ray Leonard, we're great friends…I wanted to fight him and he turned me down but he's still my friend. His brother Dale once came over to me and said, 'Pryor you're my brother we thought you would have won', and so I said, 'go and ask your brother that!' I didn't say I was going to beat Ray Leonard, I said I wanted to fight him. I think it would have been a great fight.

ROUND 5

DON'T LET ME CALL YOU CHICKEN, BOWE!

'Them two big clowns [Lennox Lewis-Tony Tucker]. Holyfield would beat both those bums hands down. Take away his one big weapon, his right hand, Lewis is pitiful. I better fight that guy before somebody else gets him.'

Riddick Bowe

'I stopped Riddick in the 1988 Olympics. He can't forget that. I think after this fight [Lewis-Tucker] the American people will demand he fights me. Until he does, they won't give him any credibility.'

Lennox Lewis

'Lewis and Bowe is one of the all time super-fights never to happen. Sometimes there just isn't enough will from the people who matter the most in making these things go ahead. Each camp could accuse

the other of ducking and could probably form a case, be it fair or not. Egos get in the way, and not necessarily the egos of the two fighters.'
Steve Bunce

The structure and scheduling of amateur boxing is the same as most sports, apart from, of course, professional boxing. As many of you reading this are aware, Lennox Lewis-Riddick Bowe is a fight that did happen. The history books will record that these two men got in to the ring and boxed in a sanctioned bout, and did so because of the stipulations of round by round competition, not politics. Both men had to fight each other—no questions asked, no manager bullshit, no purse disputes and no accusations of ducking.

The fight happened at a time when the names Riddick Bowe and Lennox Lewis were not familiar to the casual boxing fan, let alone household names. However, the stakes for this match were incredibly high, as on the line was the super heavyweight gold medal in the 1988 Olympic Games in Seoul.

Both boxers were relatively slimmer than what we became familiar with at the height of their professional careers, particularly Bowe who was sporting a shiny Afro mullet that could have got him an audition with Five Star. Aged 21 at the time, Bowe weighed in at 216 lbs (98 kg) and by the time he became world champion in 1992 he had filled out to 246 lbs (111.5 kg). Lewis, who had lost a quarter-final to Tyrell Biggs in the 1984 Olympic Games at the age of 19, weighed in at 220 lbs (100 kg) for the 1988 gold medal match. By the final fight of his career in 2003 Lewis was carrying an extra 36 lbs (16 kgs).

The beginning of the first round of the 1988 gold medal match was an even exchange of jabs, until, with 1.28 minutes to go, Bowe rocked Lewis with an upper cut. Lewis, representing his adopted home nation of Canada, weathered the storm but overall Bowe had the better of the first round, aside from the final few seconds when Lewis caught him with a strong right hand. The American commentator praised the aggression of Bowe and accused Lewis of being lethargic. No such accusations could be directed at Lewis in the following round and within seconds he forced Bowe to a standing eight count. 'Lewis has come out inspired', conceded the American commentator. With 2.28 to go in the round, Lewis hit Bowe with another great right hand and forced another standing eight count. During the count the referee then changed his mind and surprisingly stopped the fight. It was all over and Lennox Lewis was crowned the new Olympic champion. Bowe didn't look happy about the decision, although his protests were not particularly animated. Well, certainly not compared to the hissy fit that we'd seen in another fight during Seoul in 1988. In the bantamweight division, South Korean homeboy Byun Jong had lost a decision against Bulgaria's Alexander Hristov, due to Jong being deducted two points for consistent use of a low head.

This decision sparked a violent attack on the New Zealand referee Keith Walker, as fists and other weapons were thrown in anger by members of Jong's corner. One hour after the riot, Jong's protest continued in an in-ring sit-down sulk, this happening despite the fact that two more fights on the card were scheduled. The judges decided to call a stop to the event and the lights of the arena were turned off with Jong still sulking in the ring. Keith Walker had to be flown out of the country for his own safety and the New Zealand Embassy was inundated with complaints from angry South Koreans. So, all things considered Bowe took the decision very gracefully, especially as the stoppage did seem very harsh on him. Yes he was getting beat, but not to the point where he was out of it, and he looked in reasonable enough shape to be able to continue. From the referee's point of view, Lewis had gained the advantage in the contest and was probably going to win, therefore it was best to spare Bowe any potential injury. In the post-match interview Bowe admitted to have been 'shaken up', but that he felt the bout was stopped prematurely. In later years Lewis expressed regret at the fight not going on for longer and said, 'His eyes were glazed and he was gone. I wish I'd knocked him out because he kept complaining he was robbed'. Lewis also claimed that Bowe's US teammates didn't like Big Daddy and wanted him to beat their teammate up.

At the end of the contest in 1988, both men came together in a friendly embrace, which was totally in tune with the Olympic spirit. They bowed their heads in unison to the crowd in a wonderful show of respect. That moment would be so far removed from the bitterness that would go on to dominate their future relationship.

Both men turned professional in 1989, and within a few years they were world title contenders, with Lewis already the European champion and claiming British nationality (his country of birth and childhood). In 1992 they were part of a four-man WBC mini-tournament to decide the best heavyweight in the world, along with the much-fancied Donovan 'Razor' Ruddock and Evander Holyfield. Lewis had built up a record of 21-0 and Bowe was on 32-0. By this point Evander Holyfield was also undefeated, which made Donovan Ruddock the odd one out; however, Razor's losses to Tyson in 1991 had been spirited and he had won well in his last two matches against Greg Page and Phil Jackson.

The structure of this WBC competition looked like a step in a sensible direction as it was round-by-round elimination scheduling. Lewis was to face Ruddock in the first semi-final and Bowe was to take on Holyfield in the second. The winner of each match would then meet in the decider. However, there was one major flaw: it was all a load of bollocks. The tournament was nothing more than a gentlemen's agreement and there was no hint of a binding contract. Therefore, after the semi-finals, one of the winners was under no legal obligation to fight anyone. If one semi-final winner's next fight were to be against Barney the Dinosaur or Mickey Mouse then they could choose that route.

In the first of the 'three' fights in this mini-tournament, Lewis, many people's underdog, flattened the favoured Donavan Ruddock in two rounds at Earls Court in front of a pumped-up British crowd. Ruddock was Lewis' first world-class scalp and the two-round KO win on Halloween night was unexpected and decisive. In the post-match interview Lewis cried out, 'I'm going after Holyfield', and predicted a win for the 'Real Deal' because 'he's a workaholic'. So, next up, the WBA, WBC and IBF champion Holyfield fought Bowe in his fourth defence of the titles. After beating Buster Douglas for the belts in 1990, Holyfield had successfully defended against Larry Holmes and Mike Weaver, as well as an enthralling showdown with a gutsy George Foreman at Atlantic City. His semi-final fight with Bowe at the Mirage Hotel in Las Vegas was a classic, in which round ten was hailed by *The Ring* as the best round of the year. In the 11th, Holyfield fell to the canvas and after 12 rounds Bowe won a unanimous decision to become a three-belt world champion. During the post-fight interview, Lewis, who was ringside doing TV commentary, called out 'Bring it on…or are we gonna call you chicken, Bowe?

'Who's next?', was the question HBO asked Bowe's manager Rock Newman, who replied, 'We're going to choose who we will fight next. We will go to the negotiation table with Lennox Lewis. I want to give Lennox a guaranteed shot at Big Daddy'.

Bowe then left the ring and confronted Lewis in the HBO commentary box, which confirmed to the world the ill feeling between the two men. 'I'm not afraid of you Lennox. We gonna get it on. I owe you one. You lied on me. You're not the man I thought you were'.

Lewis looked calm, nodded and in a mixed English and Canadian accent replied, 'Yo, bring it on man'.

The on-air verbal dispute ended up with both men insisting that the other one would be knocked out, until Rock Newman in his normal abrasive manner got involved in the confrontation by telling Bowe, 'You're the champion. You're the man'.

After Bowe walked away from the incident, Lewis addressed the viewer and proclaimed, 'I beat him before, I'll beat him again. I look into Riddick Bowe's eyes and he fears me. I see absolute fear…I think he's gonna sidestep me. Hopefully he doesn't. Don't let me call him chicken, Bowe, bring it on Bowe!'

Lewis claimed after the fight that he would have liked to have hit Bowe there and then. However, considering that Bowe had just gone through twelve intensely tough and courageous rounds, Lewis conceded that such a move would have made him look bad.

Boxing fans watching this confrontation would have automatically assumed that both men would soon be meeting in the ring. It was clearly the natural order of things. World title belts would have been on the line.

Both men were considered the best two heavyweights on the planet. Both were undefeated. Both despised one another and represented rival boxing nations. The predictions for the winner would have been a 50-50 call. Everything about Lewis-Bowe would be box office gold; it's very hard to see what extra promotional tools were needed to sell this match. The Bowe-Holyfield post-fight press conference was no less friendly between Lewis and 'Big Daddy'. Lennox praised the new champion for the win, but Riddick, still upset that Lewis had tipped Holyfield for the win, replied with sarcasm and claimed that both his sisters could 'whoop you', before calling Lewis a 'faggot'.

The outcome of the second title eliminator was the last thing Lewis and his manager Frank Maloney wanted, as they had immediate reservations about Bowe's commitment to the final match. With Evander Holyfield they didn't have those reservations and there was no concern that he would duck Lewis. Before his man was even crowned champion, Rock Newman was already looking elsewhere than Lewis for the next title fight. There are even claims that Newman tried to arrange a Bowe title defence during the 20-minute halftime break at the 1993 Super Bowl. 'That shows you how serious the fight would have been', brushed off Maloney regarding the time limit of such a fight.

The name George Foreman was mentioned as an opponent for Bowe, and Newman's objective was to keep 'Big Daddy' champ for as long as possible. Bowe never did face Foreman, whom he described as 'old, slow and immobile, but he still packs a punch, though I don't think I'll have any trouble with him'.

In the early 1990s, Bowe was one of the highest grossing sportsmen in the world and commercial endorsements were making him a very wealthy man. A fight with Lewis would have been a huge earner for him, but he could still sidestep this fight and live a luxurious lifestyle. If Bowe was running scared, as Lewis claimed, he covered it up with dismissive assessments of Lewis' ability with remarks such as, 'For a guy who's been a pro for a while now, he still looks like an amateur in the ring. Take away his left jab and he doesn't know what to do'.

Considering that Lewis wore down and defeated so many opponents with his effective jab, some may say that such an accusation is a bit like saying 'Joe Hart is a good goalkeeper, but cut off one of his arms and he'll struggle'. Bowe claimed on Sky Sport's *Ringside* in 2013 that he had the perfect strategy to put a stop to the Lewis jab, and demonstrated how he would have caught the jab with his right hand and counterpunched. 'My thing was to get past the jab and hit him on the inside. By me getting on the inside he would be overwhelmed and I would tear him apart systematically and he knew that…That's why the fight never happened', said an out of breath Bowe as he gave a demonstration in a UK boxing gym.

Throughout 1993, Lewis-Bowe remained an unsigned super-fight and the blame was being put firmly in the corner of the New Yorker from Brooklyn and his manager Newman, who were going down easier routes. Evander Holyfield aside, during Bowe's prime and title reigns, he never faced one world-class opponent, and instead fought fringe contenders like Michael Dokes, Jesse Ferguson, Herbie Hide, Larry Donald, Buster Mathis and Jorge Luis Gonzalez. Between them, those fighters never beat one marquee opponent in their entire careers.[1] Bowe's reputation may not have been enhanced by fighting lower-calibre opponents, but it did allow him to stay champion and also win a new belt, as Herbie Hide was WBO champ when he faced Bowe.

In 1993, the WBC ordered that Bowe be stripped of his title belt for ducking the number-one contender Lennox Lewis, resulting in Big Daddy going down from three belts to two. Therefore, at the St James' Court Hotel in London, in front of the world's media, Riddick Bowe, on the advice of Rock Newman, dropped the WBC belt in the bin to be fished out by Lewis. It's worth pointing out that the belt was actually a replica, which had been sold to them by Evander Holyfield, so neither the WBC nor Lewis would have been remotely interested in picking it out (Bowe reportedly picked it back out and took it home). After the dumping of the fake WBC belt, Rock Newman boasted, 'They didn't strip us, we stripped them'. Newman's designs on empowerment backfired. The episode ended up looking bad for him and his fighter, not least because Frank Maloney had assembled a group of people dressed as chickens to gather outside the hotel. In 2013, Bowe expressed regret at the dumping of the WBC title belt and told *Boxing News* that it was something he should not have done and that he was ill advised.

Lewis was formally awarded the WBC belt in a small boxing hall in England, becoming the first British heavyweight champion for nearly 100 years and the days of Bob Fitzsimmons. WBC President Jose Sulaiman was told by Newman, 'You forced Riddick out because I would not do business with Don King'. Sulaiman responded to the dumping of the title by hitting out , 'The belt thrown into the trash bin has been worn with dignity and pride by Muhammad Ali, Larry Holmes and Mike Tyson…We expected that Bowe would try to duck the winner of Lewis and Ruddock. Bowe has reneged on his agreement to fight Lewis. He is running scared'. Lewis' first defence of the WBC title was against the Don King-controlled Tony Tucker, which leads to speculation of a conflict of interest in the WBC's decision to strip Bowe of the belt, considering that Jose Sulaiman was viewed by many as a stooge for Don King. Not that Lewis and Maloney were keen on a fight with a Don King-controlled fighter in America and they unsuccessfully lobbied for the Tucker fight to be held in the UK. The match went to Las Vegas and after 12 rounds Lewis won on the scorecards despite his fears that in a US-based Don King promotion 'Anything could happen'.

Beating Tucker did Lewis no major credibility favours. To be the man he had to beat Bowe who claimed to be the man, who beat the man, who beat the man, who beat the man. In other words, he beat Evander Holyfield, who beat 'Buster' Douglas, who beat Mike Tyson. Whether Bowe was 'running scared' or not, money as usual was the deciding factor in this super-fight not going ahead. $32 million was the combined amount this fight was reported to be worth for both camps, and Newman had no intention of splitting that fortune down the middle. He reportedly offered Lewis a mere $3 million, which was flatly turned down by Frank Maloney who accused Newman of 'taking liberties'. A smaller offer of $2 million was then made to Lewis to fight on the undercard of a Bowe main event. In return was a promise that Lewis would be next in line for a shot at Bowe. Once again this was turned down by the Lewis camp on the grounds that promises from Bowe's camp didn't hold much substance. Maloney said, 'They've broken their word to us once after the Ruddock fight…why should we trust them again?'

More disputes about shares of the purse continued. From Lewis' point of view, he'd already beaten Bowe in the Olympics, so if anyone was entitled to an even share of the purse, it was him, and yet he was expected to take less. Frank Maloney claims that Newman offered them a stipulation in which the winner would end up getting the bulk of the purse. According to Maloney, Lewis accepted the challenge only for Newman go quiet on the offer, which put that idea to bed. When asked why he never fought Lewis, Bowe has always put the blame on the Brit and will claim that he would have won the fight easily. The only problem is that his accusations don't get followed up with much evidence. 'He didn't want to fight me', is what Bowe will say, but substantial examples of ducking don't tend to follow. But it's not conclusively to say that Bowe did not at any time want to fight Lewis. In October 1993 a below-par Lewis defended his belts against Frank Bruno in Cardiff and got out-boxed for the first six rounds before winning by knockout in the seventh round. After watching the fight on TV, an encouraged Bowe is reported to have called out to Rock Newman, 'we got to get him quick'. Tommy Morrison's name was being lined up as a Lewis opponent and Bowe was worried that Morrison would expose him before he could get the chance. (Lewis-Morrison was delayed until 1995 and 'The Duke' was stopped by Lewis in round six.)

In December 1993, Evander Holyfield won back the WBA and IBF belts from Bowe in their first rematch, so talk then emerged of a Lewis-Holyfield title unification in 1994. Lewis never had reservations about 'Real Deal's' guts and willingness to fight him and had said, 'I wanted Holyfield to win [against Bowe in the first fight] because I knew that if he didn't Bowe would be reluctant to box me, and that's the way it turned out, exactly'. So, in April 1994, all Holyfield needed to do was dispose of the respected but little-fancied southpaw Michael Moorer and then the big title unification with Lewis was on. Holyfield made his intentions clear on the direction he would take after he saw off Moorer. 'I would like to fight Lennox Lewis, to unify the titles. I hope it will happen, because I have a lot of respect for him'.

But, in a huge upset, Moorer won a close-points decision and became the new WBA and IBF heavyweight champion. So the fight that should then happen would naturally have been Lewis-Moorer. However, the new champion's post-fight response put pay to any hopes of that happening. 'I don't have to fight Lewis. I don't have to fight anybody…I'll do what I like, it's my right now'. Chicken Bowe was off the menu, but only to be replaced by Duck Moorer, leading Lewis to say 'If Moorer doesn't want to unify the title, he will just die of shame'.

In hindsight, Michael Moorer's decision not to fight Lewis backfired massively and shame was about to be served. His first title defence was against 45-year-old George Foreman in May 1994, which at the time seemed like a walk in the park considering Moorer's skill and Foreman's age. Moorer, by the tenth round, was way ahead on points and seemingly strolling, until Foreman floored the southpaw with a famous old right hand to win the title. Had Moorer taken on Lewis and lost there would have been no shame attached, as many considered the 'Lion' to be the best heavyweight on the scene. By losing to the 'Punching Preacher', Moorer had the indignity of being the man who made way for the oldest heavyweight champion in boxing history.

So from that point on, the natural match-up was Lennox Lewis-George Foreman for the latter's IBF and WBA titles. Tony Tucker was rated as WBA number-one contender but was sidestepped by Foreman, which resulted in him being stripped of the title. Foreman still held the IBF belt, but was protected and went on to defeat Axel Schulz on a split decision.

The ageing legend was then stripped of the IBF title in 1995 for refusing a rematch with Schulz, who most people thought should have been given the decision by the judges in the first match. A clear duck by Foreman, but at least he wasn't bull-headed enough to have dropped his belt in the rubbish bin in front of the world's media in protest at the IBF's decision.[2]

In 1994 something else happened, which for Lewis was detrimental in terms of allowing him the fights that he desired: Don King took centre stage by getting his hands on a heavyweight title which had eluded him since the first Mike Tyson era. King, who Lewis always refused to sign with, had been lurking in the lower weight classes and was no longer calling the major shots in the heavyweight division. And it was Lewis' complacency and focus on fighting Bowe that allowed King back in. Things turned back to the Don's favour when Lewis surprisingly lost to the un-fancied Oliver McCall in London, in what was his first ever professional defeat. Losing the fight was bad enough, but the catastrophe for the Lewis camp was that it gave back title control to the most cunning shark in the pond. Straight after McCall's win there were talks of an immediate rematch, to which King responded, 'His [Lewis] chances of a rematch are slim and not at all, and slim just left town'. Lewis underestimated McCall and wasn't in prime condition mainly because talks had resumed between his and Bowe's camps. The fight that went missing was back on the agenda. Things looked positive and terms were said to have been agreed. Now that Riddick was without a world title, his management were more open to the idea of fighting the WBC champ Lewis. Of a combined $20 million purse, Lewis was to take the bigger slice and get a $12 million payday. All he had to do was to see off McCall and then it was a showdown with Bowe in a super-fight the following year in 1995. The fact that Lewis even had to face McCall was a distraction that he didn't want and he said, 'If it was up to me, I'd rather skip this fight and get ready for the big one…McCall is just a stepping stone, an indifference in my plans. But he will help me get ready for Riddick Bowe'. That stepping stone knocked out the WBC champion in the second round to the shock of millions of Brits watching on terrestrial television in the final days of mass-boxing viewing in the UK; the glorious homecoming of a British champion had turned into a nightmare. Watching the match back home in America, Bowe would have had mixed feelings. Yes, there was the satisfaction of seeing Lewis get spattered, but the return of the King did him no favours. On that Saturday night in London, Don King's smile had never been wider and Lewis blamed himself for allowing 'my mind to stray to Bowe, and not to keep it totally focused on McCall…I was excited because I wanted to ram Bowe's insults right back down his throat'.

With Lennox dethroned as the champ, the title fight with Bowe, scheduled for 1995, once again went to the scrap heap.

The way in which the title scene was unfolding was not good for Lennox Lewis. The aging WBA and IBF champion Foreman was being protected, Bowe went on to beat Hyde for the WBO belt and with King now controlling the WBC title belt, Lewis would spend the following few years in the wilderness. By losing to McCall, the most feared lion in the jungle had lost control of the only title he was realistically able to fight for.

One final attempt was made for the match between Lewis and Bowe in an event that carried an overall budget of $175 million. Time Warner's president, Seth Abraham, who did not get along with Rock Newman, had plans for a heavyweight super tournament in 1996 which would involve both men, along with George Foreman, Tommy Morrison, Ray Mercer, Michael Moorer and Evander Holyfield. No Don King fighters were put forward, so that excluded Mike Tyson and Oliver McCall. But those two aside, Abraham's list was the cream of 1990s heavyweight talent. Abraham was hoping that this eight-man tournament would go some way to establishing who the main heavyweight was at a time when championship belts were being passed around like cold viruses in winter.

Of course, the problem with Abraham's concept for a scheduled elimination tournament was that it was far too structured and organised to have a place in professional boxing. There were too many managers and promoters to keep happy and predictably the idea of the super tournament faded away. Riddick Bowe's management were not getting along well with HBO, whom Lewis had just signed a contract with, and from this point onwards the general idea of Bowe-Lewis fizzled out for good. The most natural matchup of 1990s heavyweight boxing went straight to the top of the scrapheap of great fights that never were.

Both Lewis and Bowe retired from their professional careers having never faced an opponent they didn't beat. Lewis only lost to two opponents. Along with Oliver McCall, Hasim Rahman is the only man to register a professional win over Lewis and like McCall he got avenged in a rematch. Rahman was brutally knocked out by a Lewis left/right combination in the fourth round in November 2001, seven months after shocking the world with a fifth round KO of Lewis in South Africa.

Oliver McCall famously had an emotional breakdown during his rematch with Lewis in 1997 and was stopped in round five for not being in a mentally fit state to continue. The farce did no favours for Lewis' credibility but the win earned him the vacant WBC title and he was once again crowned a world champion.

Tyrell Biggs, the man who beat Lewis in the 1984 Olympics, was also avenged by Lewis in a professional bout seven years later. Biggs's career never lived up to the promise he showed as an amateur and Lewis knocked him out in the third round. The TV commentator's immediate response was that Lewis had finished off Biggs five rounds earlier than Bowe had done. Those were the innocent days of 1991 when one assumed that the two men would naturally fight each other and so comparisons were being drawn.

Bowe's professional record is highly impressive. He lost only one fight, which was the rematch with Holyfield, who he beat twice in a trilogy. With Bowe, however, it's the names that don't make the list which are the ones that stand out the most. Aside from Lennox Lewis, the fighter that leaves a gaping 'what if' in Bowe's career was a showdown with another native of Brownsville New York. Normally a star like Riddick Bowe would be his neighbourhood's ultimate boxing claim to fame, but when Mike Tyson comes from the same district, it means you come in second.

While Tyson was in prison between 1992 and 1995, there were talks of a future showdown, and, once he was released, Rock Newman and Don King held amicable discussions for Tyson-Bowe. The talks were described by Newman as 'pleasant conversations'; however not friendly enough to come to an agreement.

When asked in 2012 about not fighting Tyson, Bowe insisted, 'It would have been a blockbuster. But I think as the fight progressed, with me being relaxed, my left hand would have taken over and Mike would have been in a lot of trouble. I've got respect for Mike but I truly believe that I've got the better left hand'.

During Tyson's time in prison he received a visit from Bowe, who promised a title shot to the thankful ex-champion. After Tyson's release from prison Bowe pleaded, 'I really want Tyson. I want there to be no doubt who is the greatest heavyweight out there today, and the best way to do that is to give Tyson the whooping of a lifetime'.

The year 1996 was when this dream match could have happened, but both men took different roots. Tyson went for the title and unified the WBA and WBC titles by beating Frank Bruno and Bruce Seldon.[3]

Meanwhile, Bowe went on to fight Poland's Andrew Golota in two battles that the big Pole would have won had he kept his disciple and not delivered low blows that got him disqualified in both bouts. In each contest, Bowe was out-fought and out-punched by Golota and had lost his cutting edge. In the first contest, Bowe's supporters in Madison Square Garden threw far more punches than he did in the most notorious and uncontrollable boxing riot in modern history. A year later in 1997 and Lewis had no such problems with Golota, who he knocked out in the first round in Atlantic City. Golota's face after falling on the canvas was one of total shock and awe at the mauling he was receiving. Bowe's star was fading while Lewis was on the way to cleaning up the heavyweight division.

Bowe effectively retired in 1996 after the second Golota contest, although between 2004 and 2008 he fought three times against non-box office names and maintained his record of losing only once in his career

A huge question mark will always hang over him as to whether that record would read more than just one loss had he faced Lewis. And this is the problem, because a great fighter with a record like Riddick Bowe's should be viewed with nothing but admiration and respect. When Bowe gets interviewed he tends to get asked about the fight that should have happened more so than the ones that did. When a reporter has the chance to question Bowe, the lost fight with Lewis will be a higher priority question as opposed to asking Bowe to recall his title defences against the likes of Jesse Ferguson and Michael Dokes. When many people think of Bowe they see the man who ducked, not the man who won 43 out of 45 fights (the record includes a no-contest when Bowe punched Buster Mathis who was already down on a knee). Bowe's great legacy is tarnished by being viewed as the man who dropped his world championship belt in the bin so that he could sidestep the most worthy opponent of his era. Instead of Bowe the Great, many people think of him as Bowe the Avoider. Instead of 'Big Daddy Supreme' it's 'Chicken Bowe'. Taken from Mills Lane's biography, the legendary referee sums up Big Daddy by saying, 'I considered Bowe to be the best of the heavyweights'.

'Bowe had it all—size, strength, an impressive chin and a devastating punching ability…Although I liked the guy, in my mind he was a failure because he didn't go as far as he could'.

Even if Lewis wasn't to blame for the fight not happening, it still leaves holes in what would be an unblemished record. In the book *The Ultimate Book of Boxing Lists* Gareth Davis writes, 'The only gray clouds over his [Lewis] career are the fact that he faced Mike Tyson well after the American's prime and that he never met Bowe in his professional career'. When rating the best heavyweights of the 1990s, *Boxing News* holds back Lewis from the number-one spot on the grounds that he never obtained a professional win over Bowe, as opposed to their number-one pick Evander Holyfield.

Throughout much the 1990s, Lewis had been lambasted by the US media, who did not rate him as a great champion. Many US writers and pundits shot him down for fighting non-marquee names while never acknowledging the obstacles put in front of the 'Lion', which prevented him from proving the doubters wrong. Lewis was denied fights and then castigated for not beating the same people who ducked him. He partly silenced those critics with decisive wins at the end of his career against Holyfield in 1999 and Tyson in 2002. But the doubters will argue that he beat them after they had both passed their primes. His final match, against Vitali Klitschko in 2003, wasn't seen at the time as a career definer, but years later is viewed as a huge scalp due to Vitali going on to become a dominant world champion. Before and after that fight Lewis spoke of fighting Wladimir Klitschko after he disposed of his older brother and joked, 'One for breakfast one for lunch!'

Wladimir would now be a very worthy name in Lewis' legacy, however, after the Vitali win the 'Lion' called time on his career at the age of 37, and retired with a record of 44 wins 2 losses and a draw.[4]

As late as 2008 and five years into retirement, Lewis caught word that Bowe had been hinting of a possible future showdown. Lewis responded, 'He waits until I am in retirement to call out my name…I will come out of retirement to beat up that guy. I'll beat him up for free!' 2008 would have been around 15 years after the fight should have happened. So ,with no guarantee of a great payday they may have had to do it for free.

In an interview from 2012 Riddick Bowe formally challenged Lewis to 'Come out of retirement, let's fight. Let's give the people want they want. Let's give them the fight that never had. You don't like me, I don't like you…Come shut my mouth, come knock me out'. The overall interview did Bowe little credit as he mainly concentrated on overtly homophobic taunts towards Lewis. He even implied that the two fell out because Lewis tried to sexually come on to him. He told Lewis, 'I've got a wife at home and kids, I'm straight'. The story is not convincing and just when you thought that the Bowe-Lewis affair dragged the sport through the mud in 1990s, 'Big Daddy' may not be finished just yet. In the same year, 2012, he was asked about what would have happened if he and Lewis had fought. The interviewer was Bowe's biographer and implied that before Lewis hired Emanuel Steward as his trainer, most people believe that Bowe would have won. 'A lot of people are absolutely right', replied the former champ. 'I think within the first four or five rounds I would have knocked Lennox Lewis out. That's before he got Emanuel Steward. After Emanuel, I would have won the fight a little later but eventually I would have got him'.

In this interview, Bowe looked and sounded worryingly punch drunk, which was why in June 2013 people were aghast to see him step into the ring of combat once more. In Thailand he fought a mixed martial arts contest against a 30-year-old Russian and he got kicked to the floor in a horrible second-round defeat. To see such a great former boxer humiliated in that way was depressing and even for fans who would have been rooting for Lewis, this was a painful and sad farce to witness. Unlike Bowe-Lewis in the 1990s, this was something that nobody wanted to see.

Minutes after I'd finished this chapter in summer 2014, I noticed on social media a message that Riddick Bowe had tweeted to Lennox Lewis, 'I officially chalenge (sic) coward @lennoxlewis to a fight ill beat his ass so his mama feel it. I fight him anyplace 4 free to shut his big mouth'.To which

Lewis responded, 'and I officially challenge Bowe to a spelling bee!'

Lewis then uploaded two pictures on his twitter account: one of him standing next to Bowe on the Olympic medal podium in 1988. The second picture was of Bowe dropping the WBC belt into the trash. Above the photos, Lewis simply tweeted, 'Nuff said'.

1. Larry Donald beat Holyfield in 2004 when 'Real Deal' was nearer his free bus pass than his prime.

2. In 2002, Foreman spoke of coming out of retirement again in order to fight Vitali Klitschko, on the condition that the Ukrainian was able to beat Lennox Lewis for the unified titles in 2003. Asked if he was joking, Foreman responded, 'No, not joking at all…I'm tired of waiting around. I get examined every year. Doctors looking for something. They're not going to find anything…I'm tired of that. I've got things to do with my life…Sure people say you can wake up with your wife and watch the Dow Jones report on CNN. I'm tired of that! I'm not worried about a new car, I wanna fight'. Foreman was a Lennox Lewis fan and rated him as one of the best heavyweights of all time. Immediately after Lewis beat Klitschko, HBO asked Big George if he would be willing to come out of retirement to face Lewis. With a comical expression he faced the camera and replied 'No…no'.

3. Mike Tyson was supposed to fight Lennox Lewis in 1996 instead of Bruce Seldon. Lewis was blocked by legal disputes and then paid off $4 million to step aside for Seldon-Tyson, which was a one-sided farce that lasted all of one and a half minutes. Many have suggested foul play and accused Seldon of going down to punches that barely connected.

4. Before Lewis retired, not only were there talks of him facing Wladimir Klitschko, but Roy Jones Jr. was another main name being touted around. Jones, by 2002, was now fighting at heavyweight but was still considerably smaller than Lewis. When asked about fighting Roy Jones, Lewis responded, 'Yeah that fight could happen…[but] now he wants to fight Evander Holyfield. Makes no sense. Evander Holyfield's slow; he's an old man. If Jones wants to be a true heavyweight he might as well come to Lennox Lewis. They call him the superman. Well I've got some kryptonite for him. This is my weight class. If he wants to test I'll take the 'S' off his chest!'

ROUND 6

DODGING THE 'BOMBER': HEROL 'BOMBER'

'One fighter I was relieved never to see at number-one contender rank was the skilful Herol Graham. That fight would never have happened unless he was number-one contender, in which case I couldn't dodge. McCallum and Nunn were quality fighters but not like Herol Graham. You couldn't hit him—he was so elusive, they say in the business, "You couldn't hit him with a handful of stones".'

Chris Eubank

'They avoided me like the plague because I am the plague! My hands were all over the place, they hated my movement—Excuse me, wait a minute, he's supposed to be here, he's supposed to be there, no he's not, he's here, where is he now…they couldn't cope with that…I wanted to prove I was the best but not everybody wanted to box me.'

Herol 'Bomber' Graham

I first met Herol Graham at an amateur event at the Emirates Stadium in 2012. The 'exclusive' diamond club rooms was where the boxing action was taking place and were occupied with a more traditional class of Arsenal fan, most of whom don't normally set foot in the Emirates Stadium let alone the belly of the corporate beast (I don't remember seeing any diamonds by the way). Outside the stadium I approached Herol and explained the nature of this book and that I'd like to chat to him. Within a few seconds of knowing a complete stranger, he gave me his phone number and told me to call him.

Herol Graham, born in 1959 in Nottingham, was Britain's standout middleweight star in the early to mid 1980s and is commonly referred to as the best British fighter never to win a world title. Some people even refer to Graham as the best British fighter, period. His pro career began in 1978 and he soon gained a reputation for quick hand and leg speed and having the ability to elude punches for fun. As a demonstration of how hard he was to hit, he'd hold contests in pubs where he would tie his hands behind his back and lay down challenges for people to hit him. Nobody ever won.

But it's not to say that no one ever got close to him in the professional ring. Despite an enthralling and impressive career, the first image many will conjure up of Herol Graham will be when he was famously knocked out by Julian Jackson in a world title fight in 1990, the 'Bomber' lying on the canvas totally sparked out. Herol had out-boxed and battered Jackson for the first three rounds and the referee told Jackson at the start of the fourth that he only had one round to save the fight due to a badly damaged eye. Heavy hitter Jackson, known as the 'Hawk', went hell for leather but couldn't get through to Graham who was his usual elusive self. 'He can take Graham with one shot, be under no illusion about that', remarked the worried commentator whose support for Herol was undisguised.

Herol dominated the fourth round then dropped his game plan and went in for the kill, only to be caught with a devastating Jackson right hook that knocked him out cold. A decisive one-punch knockout if ever there was one.

'Oh no, that's what we were worried about. He won't get up from that. Oh, would you believe it'. Despair in the commentary box and despair for Herol as he lay motionless for minutes, his dream of winning the WBC title now a nightmare. In later years the British Master of Ceremonies Bob Williams discussed the fight with Julian Jackson who had become a devout Christian. Jackson recalled the knockout and claimed that he closed his eyes and the punch came from the power of God. Bob Williams replied, 'If you ask Herol's opinion he'll tell you that punch was more likely to have come from the devil!'

For people who followed Graham's career during the early 1980s they may remember a man whom champions wanted to stay clear of, and this was what I wanted to discuss with him. I arranged to meet Herol for a coffee in North London. On entering the café the 'Bomber' noticed a framed picture on the wall that made him smile. 'Look at the first thing I see when I come in here!' Displayed was a picture of Muhammad Ali standing over a beaten Sony Liston in their infamous (and some say fixed) second fight. Like so many boxers, 'The Greatest' was Herol's favourite when he was growing up and he wanted to emulate him as a middleweight, the division which, in his eyes, outshines the heavyweight scene. 'The lighter weights will control things. They've got the speed and the power. Good movers, good boxers. If you're a middleweight you can hit as hard as a heavyweight sometimes. No one can take a punch if you hit in the right place, I don't care who you are. The heavyweight division is lacklustre. The Muhammad Alis are gone'.

Graham's an instantly engaging person and wears a smile, but it doesn't by any means tell the whole story of what he's feeling inside and he's suffered from bouts of chronic depression since his second retirement in 1998. It can't be easy to go from being great at something that people love to then being out of the limelight and not knowing what to do with your life. The feeling of emptiness came to a tipping point in 2007 when Herol slit his wrists in a suicide attempt that led to him being sectioned.

Through the loving help of his partner Karen (who was with us at the café), he has come through that horrific and traumatic time and seems to be doing well. Depression is a struggle that he still faces from time to time, but I wanted to discuss battles that he should have been given the chance to face in the ring. What's noticeable about the 'Bomber's' career is the list of people he didn't face of the same era, much more so than the names he did fight. The biggest stars in the middleweight division from both Britain and America managed to stay clear of a man who some of them may have viewed as a southpaw perhaps too tricky for comfort.

The staggering, and perhaps scandalous, statistic of Graham's career is that he had a record of 43 wins out of 44 before he got a world title shot at the age of 30. When he finally did against Mike McCallum in 1989 he narrowly lost on a split decision. Many of Herol's fans would argue that, although the 'Bomber' was still a class act in 1989, it was too late. The early to mid 1980s were his absolute prime and was when he would have won a world title. The big-name overseas fighters who Herol never got the chance to face include Marvin Hagler, Ray Leonard, Roberto Duran, Thomas Hearns, Iran Barkley, John Mugabe and Wilfred Benitez, who all got a shot at a world title well before reaching the 30-bout mark. In contrast, by 1987 Graham was undefeated on 38 fights and yet was a nowhere man.

I asked Herol to look back at his career and say which fighter he wished he could have been tested against. He thought about it for a couple of seconds before replying, 'Hagler…I'm not saying I would have beat him but I would have liked it because he was the top man. Whether I won or lost, he would have been the benchmark to compare myself with the best'.

Hagler-Graham could have been scheduled for any time in the early to mid 1980s, but it wasn't until 1986 when the WBA rated the 'Bomber' as number-one contender to Hagler's world title. By then the American had notched up over 60 fights and was looking for a huge payday to set him up for a comfortable retirement. Therefore he sidestepped Graham and fought Sugar Ray Leonard in one of the greatest fights of all time, in any division, of any era. No one can damn Hagler for taking a multi-million dollar fight with the 'Money Tree' for his last ever match, even if it meant being stripped of the title for not fighting the number-one-rated contender. The boxing world wanted to see Hagler-Leonard and it's undeniable that a match with Herol Graham would not have been anywhere near as high grossing. The argument for Hagler-Graham is that the two men should have clashed a few years earlier when 'Marvellous Marvin' fought opponents less talented and exiting than Graham. Hagler did take on decent British middleweight stars Alan Minter and Tony Sibson in that time, yet Graham was in the shadows despite arguably being the UK's most exciting prospect in that weight division. The 'Bomber's' unconventional style did him no scheduling favours and Herol implied to me that Hagler didn't like the fact that he was a southpaw and so sidestepped him for that reason. Herol's trainer in the 1980s Brendon Ingle insists that the 'Bomber' would have beaten Hagler if given the chance, a claim naturally not denied by Herol. 'Brendon's right. We had a plan to beat him on movement. Plans don't always come to fruition but I'd have had a chance for sure. Hagler's a heavy puncher, so if I fought him I would have to be elusive. In and out, get behind him and jab, get tipping and tapping'.

Although Hagler tops the list for missed opportunities, it's also a close call with Sugar Ray Leonard, who Graham always admired. 'He had the razzmatazz. Our styles would have made for something special. He was the man everybody wanted to beat. We were both thinkers and movers so I think that could have been a classic', Graham added. 'With Ray, nothing conclusive was ever put on the table, but there was talk. He was the champion, the best one there. We put the word out, but nothing came back. I'd love to have fought him'.

The third American king in that classic era of middleweight boxing was Thomas Hearns, but Herol never had a shot at him either. 'Hearns also would have been good, but he didn't want to fight me. They put the fight in front of him but he didn't want it. It was always difficult with Hearns because we all expected him to go up in weight so you never quite knew where you stood. Bob Arum and Mickey Duff were involved in what talks did happen, but nothing came about. The way I was, I had something that they didn't want. Not that they didn't move either, I mean Hearns was fast! But it was my contest movement that really put them off'.

When Graham speaks of Hearns, Hagler and Leonard he does so respectfully, but when I mentioned the great Roberto Duran as someone he could have fought, he shook his head in contempt and referred to him as being 'ignorant'. He then said, 'Roberto Duran would never ever box me'. Graham went on to recall how he was Duran's sparring partner before an upcoming title fight:

> I was hitting and moving, and he stopped in the middle of the ring and said 'Who you think you are? Stand still…why you move?' I told him I was moving because I didn't want to get hit! He couldn't touch me for three rounds and that's when he started moaning. I told him that he was supposed to hit me and if he can't then I'm winning. I was hitting and moving and he hated it.

Throughout his career, being too good as a sparring partner would do Graham no scheduling favours in a sport without a structure. Suppose in football Liverpool played Manchester City in a pre-season friendly and got outplayed and out-classed. Upset at being so humiliated, Liverpool decide that at no point will they agree to play Manchester City again and are free to make that choice.

If Graham attributes one thing to being in the shadows and missing out on the fights that mattered, then it was geography and being based in the north of England:

> If I came down to London at an earlier time I think it would have been different. In the north, things are slower. Mickey Duff was in

London and was the main person, and then Frank Warren. If you wanted the world championship and were based in Britain you had to go through them. Boxing's all about contacts and fitting in with the right people. It's more politics than sport. I knew what was going on. We call it a syndicate. If you weren't in the right group you were nowhere. As far as the Americans go, you had to be in with Bob Arum. He was the matchmaker for all the top middleweight names there. I was out that circle.

Now Herol's retired he does live in London, about which he concedes, 'I did it the wrong way round!'

When Graham finally got a shot at a world title in 1989 against the awesome Jamaican Mike 'Body Snatcher' McCallum, he lost on a split decision which was a result that he still questions. 'He was a good champion, but I thought I beat him. If I count the points up and the punches I think I should have got the decision. And I won it by moving jab, moving jab. But it wasn't convincing enough for the judges to say "The new world champion is…"'

McCallum-Graham may have happened, but perhaps that too should have come sooner. While Herol was in his prime in 1984, the 'Body Snatcher' won the vacant WBA middleweight title against the average Irish fighter Sean Mannion. The Irishman had a half credible record, but had also registered five defeats against journeymen. Meanwhile Herol was undefeated and causing havoc for every opponent put in his way. For the following two years after winning the WBA title, McCallum beat four journeymen before successfully defending against Julian Jackson in 1986.

Graham recalls, 'If I'd have fought McCallum years earlier, me being hyper and young, probably moving even more, I probably would have beat him'.

Talk of Mike McCallum's career and being sidestepped usually goes the other way round. The Jamaican from the Kronk was the bona fide danger man who people avoided like Jabba the Hut's own brand of perfume. One of the few names who did stand up to face him was Michael Watson, who said, 'McCallum was the best middleweight in 1990 and had been for a few years. The biggest names from that period, Marvin Hagler, Sugar Ray Leonard, Thomas Hearns and Roberto Duran all shared one thing in common, none of them shared a ring with the "Body Snatcher"'.

After Graham's narrow loss to McCallum, it was the nightmare world title fight in 1990 against Julian Jackson which will probably always be imbedded in the psyche of the 'Bomber'. I asked Herol if he would have taken a rematch with Jackson and he didn't hesitate with his answer:

> Yeah, why not? I'd have had nothing to lose. I could have out-boxed him again. If he knocked me down again, then it had already happened before, therefore, so be it. I could have handled that. But he had a problem with his eye, and he wouldn't have wanted a rematch anyway. In the first match I should have just kept off him, but I messed around with Jackson. I wanted to finish him off. I leaned over him, which I wouldn't do normally, and boom, he got me on the chin.

Regarding Graham's attempts to lure Hagler into a fight, the author

Ben Dirs notes, 'Talk of challenging the undisputed world middleweight champion was wildly optimistic when even Graham's domestic rivals didn't want to know him'.

Aside from not fighting the top overseas names, the other surprising aspect of Herol's career is the lack of matchmaking between him and the other top UK middleweights such as Tony Sibson from the East Midlands.

'Sibson beat me in the Schoolboy's. But we never fought as pros even though we were in the same weight division. Me and Sibson would have been a good one'.

There was heat between Graham and the man known as 'Sibbo', who snarled, 'I'll play the piano on his ribs'.

The two men were separated as sparring partners after a contrast of styles, when, as usual, Herol's dancing and movement were not appreciated. In 1986, Sibson won a decision against a Ghanaian fighter called Abdul Sanda for the Commonwealth middleweight title. After the fight, TV interviewer Gary Newborn asked him about fighting Herol. Sibson said that Graham had disrespected him and that he was ready to get him in the ring. In that era of Sibson's career he was fighting predominantly in Alexandra Palace in Muswell Hill (where Herol now lives). Instead of fighting Graham, Sibbo fought Luis Jose Rivera, Dennis Andries, Brian Anderson and Frank Tate and then retired in 1988 with a record of 55-7-1. Of the seven career loses the most notable one was in 1983 when Sibson was given a shot against Marvin Hagler in Massachusetts. Outclassed, he was stopped in the sixth round. Of his 55 wins, Sibson's most notable victory was against Alan Minter in 1981 at Wembley Arena. Minter's reign as world middleweight champion was during the young 'Bomber's' prime and Graham mentioned to me that 'Boom Boom' Minter was another boxer who didn't appreciate his elusiveness as a training partner. The two sparred in preparation for Minter's WBA and WBC middleweight title defence against Marvin Hagler at Wembley Arena in 1980. 'He [Minter] told me "I can't hit you," so I was sacked as a sparring partner again! The way I see sparring is, if you can't hit me in training how are you going to hit the other person?' Alan Minter retired in 1981 with a record of 39 wins and nine losses. In his fight with Hagler at QPR's Loftus Road, 'Marvellous' knocked Minter out in round three—sparking a riot. Before Hagler could be announced as the winner and new champion, he had already fled the ring as Minter's fans launched a tirade of missiles in a shameful episode in British boxing history. The fight was infamously marred by racism from sections of Minter's following and 'Boom Boom' himself didn't help matters in the build up by saying, 'That black man is not going to take my title away'. On that note, maybe it's a blessing in disguise that Graham and Minter did not meet, considering the potential racial connotations during less tolerant times.

Another middleweight from the same era considered to be one of the best British fighters never to have won a world title was Coventry's Errol Christie. With Christie, not being a world champion was less a case of him being dodged and more a case of a fighter not living up to his potential. He had a tremendous ABA record and showed lots of promise in the beginning of his professional career, gaining a fearsome reputation as a good mover and knockout specialist. Christie had earned enough credibility to spend time in the famous Kronk gym in Detroit, and Emanuel Steward let him wear the yellow Kronk branding on his boxing shorts. In hindsight it seems strange that Herol-Errol didn't happen, as they were two top British middleweights from the same era. However, on the subject of a fight with Christie, Herol seemed to dismiss the suggestion by shaking his head and muttering, 'No chance…No way, Jose. But I had it with his younger brother Michael Christie in the amateurs and beat him. In the ABAs, me and Errol missed each other because he was light middle and I was middle'.

I didn't press Herol too hard on the subject of Christie, but my impression was that Herol felt it would have been a mismatch in his favour. A comparative link between Christie and Graham is East London brawler Mark Kaylor. In 1985, Kaylor beat Christie at Wembley Arena in a classic British showdown that was marred by overt racism towards Christie from NF-linked supporters of Kaylor.[1] A year later in 1986, Graham defeated Kaylor with a stoppage in the eighth round.

Herol not being matched up with big-name British fighters in the early to mid 1980s is one part of a common theme. The other part is not being in the mix against the next generation of emerging British superstars of the super middleweight division. The likes of Chris Eubank and Nigel Benn had become household names due to huge charisma and talent that was showcased on terrestrial television. Even if the average person didn't know much about boxing, there was a good chance that they'd know who Eubank and Benn were. As opposed to Herol, who, despite his superior boxing credentials, wasn't a recognisable figure in mainstream culture to anywhere near the same degree.

During an amateur boxing event in Finchley in 2012, I got chatting to former boxer and TV pundit Jim McDonnell, who rated Herol enough to say, 'During the 1980s and 1990s you had our fabulous four, Michael Watson, Chris Eubank, Nigel Benn and Steve Collins. In my opinion Herol was better than all of them'.

Herol Graham never got the chance to take on one of those great fighters and said, 'We wanted the opportunity, but an opportunity never arose. By that time there was a lot of money involved and their promoters and managers didn't want me'.

So how could they all have slipped away from the fighter who many considered the most talented middleweight in England? There were talks, rumours and hints but nothing conclusive ever got put on the table. Herol attributes these missed chances to the same reason he never got to fight the top Americans: 'Had I been based in London I think that things would have been different, but again, even with the Brits, me being up north was the same problem'.

Perhaps the most intriguing lost matchup is Nigel Benn-Graham in the bona fide bull versus the matador. People loved the rivalry between Eubank and Benn because of the contrast of styles and Benn-Graham would have represented the same chalk and cheese scenario. Graham, the happy go lucky nice guy who once said, 'I hate the sight of blood', against the former squaddie who said, 'I'm a fighter not a boxer. I just love standing there toe to toe and having a good whack!'

Herol liked the idea of the fight and told me, 'Benn would have been a good match because it would have been a classic boxer against a fighter. But my style was all wrong for him'

It's an accusation that Benn doesn't deny. When talking about why the two never faced each other the 'Dark Destroyer' admitted, 'He was the kind of fighter I avoided. I couldn't have hit him. He's a style of boxer who I didn't want to fight. I like opponents that would come to me full on…I like a war…that's my type of fight. He was a great fighter though'.

That statement is a clear contradiction to how Benn had described Graham years earlier when he said, 'Herol Graham was, in my view, the perfect example of a second-rate fighter. He was just wasting his time hanging around for a title fight. I said he was not in the top drawer and that's why he wouldn't fight me'.

When Benn was asked about his great rival Chris Eubank not fighting Graham, the 'Dark Destroyer' added, 'Eubank was a counterpuncher and he liked people coming to him and he wasn't gonna get that with Herol'.

Chris Eubank makes it very clear in his autobiography that he wanted no part of Graham. As long as the 'Bomber' wasn't rated number-one contender by WBO then Eubank would never have accepted a title fight with him. He already had firsthand experience of Graham's ability, as the two sparred together when Graham was preparing for Mike McCallum in 1989. 'Simply the Best' was in the process of making a name for himself, but Herol by this point had not caught word of the name Christopher Livingstone Eubank. 'To be honest I never knew who the hell he was, so when we sparred, straight away he caught me on the chin and knocked me down. Knocked me down— not out. I thought, this guy's a bit handy, so I raised myself. He never touched me again, he hardly got near me'.

During these sparring sessions, Eubank was frank with his elusive partner and said, 'Herol, there's one thing that I want to tell you. I will never, ever box you, ever!' Talking to Sky Sports after retirement Eubank conceded, 'I hit him once in two week—and it was a great shot – but I got punched to pieces every day…Why would you fight a man you can't hit? Herol's an amazing fighter'.

A young Prince Naseem Hamed was at the sparring sessions and remarked that it was so embarrassing for Eubank that people looked away.

Herol would attend Chris Eubank's fights to try and drum up interest in a showdown, but on these occasions, Eubank would be the one turning away when Herol tried to say hello. The 'Bomber' claimed that Eubank refused to even look in his general direction.

Graham retired in 1992, one year after Michael Watson's career ended in horrible circumstances after losing to Eubank at White Hart Lane. Throughout the late 1980s Watson and Graham could have faced one another in what would have been a purist's dream domestic matchup. In 1988, Watson was deeply frustrated, in that he had just beaten Nigel Benn, and yet he was made to take a backseat while all the media attention and title prospects remained with the 'Dark Destroyer'. The winner remained Mr Nobody while the media wanted to talk to Benn about how he would make a comeback, as opposed to building up Watson. His lack of media recognition mirrored Graham's and the two could have perhaps done each other a favour by meeting in a British super-fight. According to Herol's account to the writer Ben Dirs:

> Michael Watson was a better fighter than both Benn and Eubank but he didn't want to fight me either. He could have had the fight anytime, anyplace, anywhere. I was the one squealing, saying, 'Let's fight, and if you beat me you've shown you can beat a good flashy guy—a matador'. But he wouldn't go for it because I was too big an obstacle. The only way any of them could get rid of

me was by stepping over me. Which they did, the three of them together. I didn't mind in one sense, in that I was better than them anyway.

Herol also missed out of on fights with Steve Collins and Joe Calzaghe who were on the super middleweight scene when the 'Bomber' made a surprising comeback in 1996, which he refers to as his 'second peak'.

In 1997, he caused two big upsets by beating both Chris Johnson and Vinnie Paz in fights in which he was supposed to be the washed-up underdog. He was the stepping-stone who ended up stepping on his younger prey. Those two impressive victories set him up for a final shot at a world title as he was pitted against IBF champion Charles Brewer in 1998. The 39-year-old 'Bomber' put 'Hatchet' Brewer down on the canvas twice in the early rounds and it looked like he was finally going to achieve his world title dream. But unfortunately for Nottingham's finest, Brewer recovered and won by a TKO in the tenth round. That defeat called time on Graham's career.

When talking to Herol I didn't sense any anger or bitterness, although there is regret about being considered a world-class fighter with no world title to show for it. Not to mention missing out on the money that he could have made by being a defending champion. At the amateur boxing event in Finchley where I was talking to Jim McDonnell, he too told me that he regretted never winning a world title. I drew the comparison with Herol, who was also in attendance, and came to the conclusion that respect is in many ways far more important than winning titles. When people talk of someone like Herol Graham they do so with incredible admiration of the talent he had. In contrast, there have been numerous world champions over the years that carry nowhere near the same degree of kudos.

1. For Christie, it was all downhill after the Kaylor loss, which in many ways was
    his last chance to get his career back on track. He had already suffered some
    bad losses to opponents considered below his pedigree. After fighting Kaylor,
    he went on to lose on a whim to more low-calibre opponents. When he lost in
    two rounds to Michael Watson in 1990 it signalled an end of what is considered
    a disappointing professional career given such early promise. Christie blames
    undiagnosed condensed muscles in his lower legs as to why he lost his speed
    and movement. This problem was finally diagnosed by an off-duty army officer
    who took Christie back to the barracks to get free treatment and heal the prob-
    lem. Unfortunately, it was far too late in his career to make a difference.

ROUND 7

SAM LANGFORD: TOO BLACK, TOO DODGED

'Sam Langford was one of the great greats of all time…he could call a round [predict the time of a knockout] better than Ali. One time, he came out for the start of a round and touches gloves, and his opponent says, "Why you touching gloves, this isn't the last round?" and Langford replied, "For you it is!"'

Bert Sugar

In 1907, a writer by the name of W. O McGeehan composed a nine-verse poem called 'Who will fight Sam Langford?' The poem featured the names of many fighters of the time who each responded to the question by saying, 'Not I', followed by an unconvincing excuse for not being available. This is the last verse of McGeehan's poem:

'Who will fight Sam Langford?'

'Not us.' The low brows cried

And they turned around to hide

'Nix: The colour line is wide,

And we're going to stay inside.

We'll not fight Sam Langford'.

By the standards of any era, the stocky but short Langford was tiny for a heavyweight. His measurements were 5 foot 7 inches in height and he typically weighed between 180 lbs and 190 lbs (81.5–86 kg) once he made the step up to heavyweight. But being small doesn't mean you don't get ducked and, luckily for the dodgers, Langford's terror on the heavyweight scene came at a time when the colour of a man's skin was a socially acceptable reason to shun someone.

In the opening chapter of this book, I said that Sugar Ray Robinson would not be heavily featured, because with a fight tally of over 200 he'd had more than had enough fights. Not to mention the fact that he is universally recognised as the best pound for pound world champion of all time, with few question marks over his legacy.

Sam Langford's professional career spanned between 1902 and 1925. He had in the region of 300 fights, the vast majority being wins, and yet there is a chapter in this book devoted to him. The argument with Langford is not that he should have had more fights than 300. The argument is that he should have had at least one world title bout which would have given him the chance of a great and universally celebrated legacy. If I was saying this on a radio interview I'd repeat that last fact because it's absolutely mind boggling. What the hell, I will do anyway…300 fights and not one world title shot! In the reference book where I have Langford's total record of fights, the list of opponents is so long that it stretches from page 415 to page 429. When one looks into the career history of Sam Langford, a farcical pattern stands out, which is that he fought the same opponents multiple times. In the early decades of the 20th Century, the heavyweight title scene was repressed by racial apartheid against black fighters like Langford and their choices for opponents were limited. Therefore, Langford fought Harry Wills 16 times, Sam McVea 15 times, Joe Jeanette 14 times and Big Bill Tate a comparatively few ten times.

Sam was born in Nova Scotia in 1886 and like most black families in that part of Canada the Langford's were descendents of slaves. In the late 18th century the British had promised freedom to black slaves who fought with them against the Americans in the War of Independence. Nova Scotia (New Scotland) was where many of the freed slaves were resettled. Raised in a farm by an abusive and violent father, by the age of 13 Sam moved south of the border to the city of Boston where, during his boxing career, he would acquire the nickname 'Boston Tar Baby'.[1] His debut match was in April 1902 when he beat an opponent called Jack McVicker, though Langford would not fight again that year. In 1905 he fought 28 contests, one of which was against Joe Gans who goes down in history as only the second black man to be a boxing world champion. Gans was the world lightweight champion and Langford beat him, however, 'Tar Baby' was not awarded the world title because he had entered the fight 2 lbs (1 kg) above the agreed weight. Joe Gans refused to fight Langford in a rematch and would remain lightweight champion for another five years.[2] The failure to meet the weight was an important crossroad for Langford who then decided to be a small man on the heavyweight scene rather than try and shed the pounds. The problem with that decision was that he would be entering a division where being too good could be a major flaw for non-whites.

The first black man to ever win a world title was the Canadian George Dixon in 1891 when he beat Cal McCarthy for the featherweight belt. The perseverance and success of fighters like Joe Gans and George Dixon proved that it was hard but possible for black boxers to get a shot at the title in lower weight classes. The heavyweight title scene was viewed differently. It represented the ultimate fighting honour and in society at the time it was deemed that honour had to be held by a white man. During the early years of the 20th Century, legalised slavery in America had only been abolished for a handful of decades. The idea that descendants of the slaves could reign as the ultimate fighting male was seen by many whites as unthinkable.

Langford's career spanned a time when vicious, open and overt racism was completely normal and socially acceptable. The open prejudice in boxing simply reflected the time. Black men were feared, hated and ridiculed, none more so than by the boxing media. In 1895 one editor of a New York daily expressed his fear of black fighters by saying, 'We are in the midst of a growing menace. The black man is rapidly forging into the ranks of athletics, especially in the field of fisticuff. We are in the midst of a black rise against white supremacy'.

One very easy way for white boxers to maintain superiority was to not let anyone black compete for the world title. The term 'drawing the colour line' was coined for a white fighter who would duck an opponent purely on race grounds. Such a thing was acceptable and lost no credibility for a white champion. Former world heavyweight champion John L. Sullivan thought nothing remotely improper by insisting, 'I will not fight a Negro. I never have and never will'. In 1891, Sullivan sidestepped the Australian black heavyweight Peter Jackson who instead went on to fight a 61-round draw with 'Gentleman' Jim Corbett. A year later, Corbett would beat Sullivan for the world title, but now he was heavyweight champion, Peter Jackson would not be getting a rematch.

Newspaper journalists felt completely justified in writing anti-black articles, which we, in this era, would find astonishingly unacceptable. On the issue of interracial matchups the boxing writer Bohun Lynch said that black people had an advantage because they had thicker skulls and were less sensitive about being punched in the face. In an article that would make even Eugene Terre'Blanche cringe Lynch added, 'Niggers are usually like children in temperament, with the children's bad points as well as their good ones. The black man's head is easily turned, and when his personal and physical success over a white man is manifest he generally behaves like the worst kind of spoiled child'.

Essentially, what Lynch was saying was that he didn't want a black man to gloat at beating a white opponent. He added: 'In extreme cases, his overwhelming sense of triumph knows no bounds at all, and he turns from a primitive man into a fiend. His insolence is appalling. When the black man is in this condition ignorant white men lose their heads, their betters are coldly disgusted'.

Not a man who will ever be celebrated for services to anthropology Lynch concluded, 'As a rule, it is far better that Negros, if fight they must, should fight amongst themselves. No crowd is ever big-hearted enough, or "sporting enough" to regard an encounter between white and black with purely a sporting interest'.

In America it wasn't just boxing where people were legally excluded on the grounds of race. Baseball also drew the colour line with a ban on black players that started in 1887 and lasted until 1947. In contrast, during the same period of time FIFA ran soccer tournaments where countries of different colours and races played against one another in an equal attempt for world superiority. America was proclaimed as the land of the free, yet if you were a black baseball player in the first half of the twentieth century you were only free to play in the Negro World Series.

Sam Langford was only free to fight for the World Coloured Championship, a now notorious body spanning all weights, which compensated black fighters for the fact that they never got title shots anywhere else. The first ever World Coloured heavyweight champion was Charles Smith in the year 1876. In 1903, a fighter by the name of Jack Johnson would be crowned as the new World Coloured champion and would soon become one of the standout names in sporting history, let alone boxing. Jack Johnson's career started slowly, as he only won four out of his first 13 professional fights. But after winning the WCC in 1903 he established himself as the most credible challenger to the world heavyweight title. Johnson knew he was good enough to win the belt, but fighting the colour line would be harder than any battle in the ring. While Johnson went on a winning streak he was ducked by the world champion Jim Jefferies, who drew the colour line. Jefferies had fought and beat black fighters, including Peter Jackson, but now a world champion he insisted, 'I will never fight a Negro'. In 1905, Jefferies retired an undefeated champion and claimed, 'There's nobody to fight me', using the term 'logical challengers'.

Jack Johnson's biographer Geoffrey C. Ward notes, 'by which he meant white challengers'.

By 1906, Tommy Burns from Canada was the new world champion. The chances of Johnson getting a title shot on American soil were remote, so it was good news for him to learn that Burns was touring on foreign land and Burns had said that he was prepared to fight challengers of all races. The intention for Burns was to fight people of any colour in their homelands and prove he was a truly global world champion. He certainly didn't intend to encourage someone like Johnson to pursue him on his travels, which is what the 'Galveston Giant' did.

Johnson followed Tommy Burns to England, then to France then back to England again, all to no avail. A London promoter wanted to stage the fight, but the deal fell through because Burns was asking for too much money. Tommy got on a boat to tour Australia. Meanwhile, Jack Johnson was booked in to fight Sam Langford in London, but he too got on a boat destined for down under and continued his pursuit of the champion. Before leaving for Australia, Johnson signed an agreement that whether he won or lost against Tommy Burns for the world title, he would go back to London to face Sam Langford. Once on Australian soil, a member of Johnson's team asked if little Sam Langford would be able beat Tommy Burns, to which Johnson is reported to have said, 'It wouldn't be much of a match. Langford would finish him off in no time'.

Eventually, Tommy Burns was offered a sum of money too good to refuse and fought Johnson in Sydney, Australia in 1908. Johnson-Burns ended up a one-sided slaughter and the white Canadian hadn't done himself any favours beforehand by referring to Johnson as 'Mr Coon'. Burns was battered for 13 rounds, before the fight was stopped by a police officer who feared crowd trouble. Johnson described the fight as the easiest of his career and claimed he could have knocked Burns out any time he wanted to.

In later years, former world champion John L. Sullivan would heavily criticise Burns for agreeing to fight a black man for the heavyweight title and blasted, 'Shame on the man who upsets good American precedents because there are dollars, dollars, dollars in it'.

The initial outcome of this fight looked like good news for black fighters such as Langford. His biographer Clay Moyle noted, 'It looked like Sam Langford would be fighting for the title in a few months'.

Johnson then dismissed the contract he signed stating he had to fight Langford in London and argued that the money wasn't good enough. He then went on to claim that he never signed the contract and that his signature was forged.

Sam Langford being dodged by white fighters was something that he was used to. Since the start of his career in 1903 he had established himself as a formidable force that fighters in the middleweight and heavyweight divisions should stay clear of. In 1908 a reporter warned, 'Now is the time for [Stanley] Ketchel[3] and, yes, even Tommy Burns to draw the colour line tight and put up reinforced concrete fences around it. The lily-white champions had better keep themselves lily white for some time to come. There is a dark man looming up their horoscopes and they had better duck him'.

And ducked he was, but now the man who would become most famous for dodging Langford would be Jack Johnson, who refused to defend his world title against the 'Boston Terror'. Langford-Johnson, however, does go down in history as a fight that did happen. They officially fought once and it was for the World Coloured Heavyweight Championship in April 1906, in Langford's adopted home state of Massachusetts. The 28-year-old Johnson outweighed the 21-year-old Langford by 40 lbs (18 kg) and was awarded the decision after 15 rounds. Some records state that Johnson won the fight easily, as did Johnson's testimony, which stated:

> I did all the forcing. One great feature of this fight was Langford's ability to take punishment. It was a wonder he could stand what with the beating I gave him. I didn't try very hard for I did not have to as was very evident to the spectators. I left the ring without a mark while Langford's face looked like it had been through a war.

Then came the contradictions. Firstly, Langford's people spread the word that Johnson had been knocked down in the second round, which was a claim not verified by anyone else. In his excellent biography of Langford, Clay Moyle sources a match report from a Boston newspaper, which claims that the first two rounds went by without much action, before Johnson picked things up from the third round and dominated the fight. Some sources claim that Langford dropped Johnson in the fifth round.

Langford would go on to admit that Johnson beat him decisively. Then to add a bit more of a cloud over what really happened, Johnson would later claim in his autobiography:

I found him [Langford] one of the toughest adversaries I ever met in the ring. I weighed 190 and Langford only 138. In the second round the little Negro hit me in the jaw with a terrible right hand and I fell as if up-ended by a cannon ball. In all my pugilistic career, not before and not afterwards have I received a blow that struck me with such force. It was all I could do just to get back on my feet just as the referee was about to count to 'ten!' I made it, but I assure you that I felt the effects of that punch for the rest of the fight. (I recovered but I would have to take my hat off to him if I hadn't had so much science at my command.) In the 15th round I was declared the winner on points.

One thing is, without any confusion, Jack Johnson refused to fight Langford again and is reported to have told his pursuer, 'Sam, nobody wants to watch two black men fight for the heavyweight championship. I'm the only black who's won it and gonna stay the only black who's won it'. Unofficially, it seems that they did have a rematch of sorts. Two days after their fight in April 1906, the two men appeared at a charity event at a theatre in Boston for an exhibition bout. Langford had a point to prove, and what transpired was a manic rumble which should have been filmed and released to rival other slapstick comedies of the time. According to Langford's account in the newspaper *Halifax Herald,* he said:

There wasn't any ring on the stage of the theatre. It was just a stage, no ropes, nothing. We battled from one side to the other, back to the curtains, forward to the floodlights, fighting like two tigers. I was out to knock Johnson cold, if I could, and he was trying to finish me. We punched, wrestled, mauled, hauled and did everything but knock down the building. Before the first round was over we had upset the water buckets and our chairs, knocked over the referee and timekeeper, broken about ten electric bulbs in the floodlights and twice, in the cyclonic stuff we were doing, almost fell into the orchestra pit. Somewhere in the middle of the second round I drove one home into Johnson's face. I jumped at him to land a follow-up. He backed up and as he did I just threw myself at him. He grabbed me [back], the two of us bumped into the scenery and a second later the scenery tumbled down on us. Some of it landed straight on our heads. The canvas pit and the scenery lay on our shoulders, with our heads sticking out. We shoved it down over our bodies, jumped away and it landed on the floor, and went on fighting…The house was in uproar…So we went ahead slugging, wrestling, mauling, butting until somebody called time. And that ended what started as an exhibition and turned into the wildest nine minutes of fighting I ever was mixed up in during 23 years of war.

In 1909, and in pursuit of the first ever black heavyweight champion, Langford said:

Jack beat me in that Chelsea fight. There's no disputing that. I didn't have the experience then, and above all else, I hadn't really learned the trick of beating men bigger than myself. I'll make Jack Johnson fight harder than he did with Burns, if he beats me in 20 rounds, which we are scheduled to go. I realise Johnson is taller and heavier, but he isn't any faster, and I know I have a harder wallop than he has.

Jack Johnson's view that nobody wanted to see two black men fight for the title was not shared in the UK or France. In 1909, Sam Langford returned to London and beat local boy James 'Iron' Hague. The 'Tar Baby' was so impressive that English fight fans demanded that Johnson have the guts to defend the title against the little Canadian. Some even went so far as to declare Sam Langford the real world heavyweight champion and the International Boxing Union in Paris would do the same for Langford in 1915. The beaten 'Iron' Hague's assessment of Sam Langford was, 'That nigger can fight. I'm not surprised that Jack Johnson didn't want to fight him. I've had enough of him'. Despite his use of language, which today would be unacceptable, 'Iron' Hague was not a bigot. He denounced the concept of the colour line and said, 'Unless all men are allowed to freely compete then how can you ever find the true champion?'

Instead of Langford, the scenario the American public were crying out to see was a white hope beat the champion, but there was nobody out there capable. Such was the desperation for a great white hope that middleweight legend Stanley Ketchel felt compelled to have a go in October 1909. Ketchel knocked Johnson to the floor with an overhand right in round 12. The crowd rose to their feet in anticipation of another knockdown. It came within a couple of seconds—Johnson got up and knocked Ketchel out for the count.

At this period of time the best and most equal match that could have happened in the heavyweight division was Johnson-Langford for the title, but promoters were far more obsessed with finding white hopes than give a chance to the most worthy contender. This suited Johnson because a match with Sam Langford represented a war that he didn't need to have. There were easier white challengers out there who had the 'complexion to get the connection', as Muhammad Ali would go on to say.

Langford had the complexion to get sidelined, as did other worthy challengers including Joe Jeanette who had registered a win, a draw and another no-contest against Johnson in a run of matches in 1905. Jeanette said of his former rival, 'Jack forgot about his old friends after he became champion and drew the colour line against his own people'.

The desperation for a white champion forced the former world heavyweight champion Jim Jefferies out of retirement to fight Johnson for a combined purse of $120,000, which was a huge blow for a frustrated Langford. The 'Boston Tar Baby' felt that he was entitled to a shot and wanted to go to Johnson's training camp and dare the champion to force him to leave. 'If I want to go to that niggah's (sic) camp and he orders away from that place, ah'll smash him in the jaw', threatened Langford, who was talked out of doing so by his manager Joe Woodman.

The aftermath of the Johnson-Jefferies title match would be an even bigger hammer blow for Langford and other black heavyweights of the day. Johnson comprehensively beat Jefferies in a one-sided match, to the humiliation of many whites . Former champ John L. Sullivan praised Johnson's performance as the most one-sided title fight ever. 'Johnson played fairly at all times and fought fairly', said Sullivan. However, race riots followed in which hundreds of people were injured and 19 people killed. The promoter of the fight Tex Rickard would always remember the violence and mayhem that the fight caused.

Jack Johnson's breakthrough as the first ever black heavyweight champion was now a paradox in fortune for other black heavyweights. On the one hand Johnson had struck a blow for black people and ended the white-only reign of the belt, to be followed by defeating all white challengers put in his way. Unfortunately, the hysteria and bitterness it caused meant that promoters like Tex Rickard would not want anything to do with interracial title matches. Along with good old-fashioned ducking, social disorder would be a crucial factor in preventing other black hopes from fighting for the title.

Jack Johnson would reign as world heavyweight champion between the years 1908 and 1915, where he successfully defended the title ten times. That same period of time was Sam Langford's prime and there were occasions when he thought he might just get a shot. To do so meant travelling the globe in a way similar to Jack Johnson's pursuit of Tommy Burns. Langford had already tried and failed to get Johnson to fight him in the States. In 1910, he confronted Johnson in the ring in Boston to the delight of his hometown supporters. Both men were suited and had been watching a fight between Jimmy Walsh and Young Britt. Johnson was a guest of honour and was addressing the crowd when Langford showed up and formally challenged the heavyweight champion. Langford said he'd fight him anywhere before Johnson accused him of not posting a money guarantee of $20,000, which would make him accept the fight. Langford denied that the money had not been sent and the two shook hands and agreed to meet the next day to discuss terms. Langford told the crowd at Boston, 'Gentlemen, I am ready to post $20,000 within three days, or tomorrow morning, and I'll fight Johnson before any club, or I'll go down to the cellar with him and have it out'. The meeting the next morning did not go well. Arguments regarding deposits, how much should be paid and who should pay first, were not agreed upon and it finished in stalemate.

In 1911, Langford travelled back to England to defeat Bill Lang for a fee of £10,000, which would turn out to be the biggest payday of his career. The local magazine *Boxing World and Athletic Chronicle* was so desperate for someone to beat Jack Johnson that it suggested that Langford should be considered an honouree white man until somebody better with the right, or you could say 'white', credentials come along. In another British magazine, *Boxing*, Langford was featured in an article titled 'Why won't Jack Johnson meet me?' In this piece, the little Canadian complained, 'He has given quite a lot of reasons. First of all he said that we wouldn't draw any gate worthy of his attention, but that was bull as every genuine fan knew'.

In the same piece, Langford expressed a desire to fight Johnson at a round schedule of over 20. He figured that a longer fight would favour him and claimed that he finished their first fight the stronger of the two. He added, 'He will have course have to fight someone before long, and he knows it, but I somehow fancy that he is praying some big white fellow will come along who will be fancied by the fans. Someone without any great amount of experience, because it keeps looking more and more as though I shall be the proposition he shall have to tackle'.

Langford returned to America near enough the same time that Johnson travelled to England to witness the coronation of King George V. Johnson told Britain that he was man enough to fight a bear. Someone asked, 'Will you fight Sam Langford?', to which the champion replied 'He ain't no bear, he's a wildcat'.

A year later, in 1912, attempts were made by the promoter Hugh McIntosh for a Langford-Johnson title match in Australia. Langford sailed down under at the end of 1911 with one man firmly in mind: 'I've got an old score to settle with this coloured gentleman. We met in Chelsea five years ago in a fifteen round bout. I weighed 140 pounds then, while Johnson weighed 190. He was as much of an unknown as I was'.

By now both men were boxing stars on each side of the globe and Langford vowed:

> I am goin' to Australia to make him fight me or show him up as a rank coward. If Johnson can get Hugh McIntosh to agree to give him $30,000 he'll probably agree to meet me, which means I'll come back here [to the US] with the championship of the world. But I'll not be satisfied that Johnson really wants to take a chance until I see him in the ring pullin' on the gloves.

Johnson swerved the prospect of fighting Langford in Australia and instead fought 'Fireman' Jim Flynn in Las Vegas, who he beat via a ninth round TKO. 'Fireman' Flynn had fought and lost to Langford two years earlier and would go on to beat a young and up-and-coming Jack Dempsey in 1917. When asked who his toughest opponent was Flynn replied, 'I fought most of the heavyweights, including Dempsey and Johnson, but Sam could stretch a guy colder than any of them'.

Langford fought out of Australia Between 1912 and 1913 and built up a feud with Sam McVea, beating him on five out of six occasions.

Born in Texas, McVea was inducted into the Boxing Hall of Fame in 1999, and was another black heavyweight who would have been a title contender had his skin been a lighter colour. By the end of his time in Australia, McVea said he'd had enough of fighting Langford, but would end up meeting him another seven times over the coming years. McVea would die of pneumonia in 1921 while still an active fighter. Despite having nearly 100 fights to his name, McVea died penniless and his fellow Texan Jack Johnson saw fit to put the money up for his burial and gravestone.

During Langford's run of matches with McVea down under, there were reports that his promoter McIntosh had signed up Jack Johnson to set sail to Oz to fight both Langford and McVea for a fee of $50,000. While Sam was thousands of miles away from home, Johnson had bragged, 'I will meet the rest of these white, black and blue hopes at the rate of one a week. This means Sam Langford too, but Sam must post a side bet. I'm feeling fine, and believe me, I could put Palzer, McCarty and Langford in a ring and whip the bunch without exerting myself'.

Johnson then announced his retirement, but by September 1912 newspapers were reporting that Johnson-Langford was due happen in Sydney on Boxing Day. Four years to the very day since Johnson made history by winning the title from Tommy Burns in the same city. Johnson confirmed that the reports were true. The next month the champion was arrested for taking a white woman from one state to another. He was charged under the Man Act, which was supposedly designed to tackle prostitution and drug and alcohol use. The woman in question was Lucille Cameron and she married Johnson two months later, which effectively destroyed the case for the prosecution. The episode, along with disputes over advance payments, put pay to Johnson being welcomed back in Australia. Langford's biographer Clay Moyle notes, 'Johnson wasn't very popular down under to begin with, and the recent news of his troubles with the law over a white woman had further decreased interest in bringing him to the country. Already aggravated by his dealings with Johnson, McIntosh decided he would be inviting trouble if he brought Johnson to Australia, so he quickly put an end to negotiations'. After Johnson was arrested a month later for once again violating the Man Act, Clay Moyle concluded, 'Any possibility of a Johnson-Langford bout extinguished'.

The promoter Hugh McIntosh would go on to say:

> Langford, he is by far and away the best heavyweight in the world right now. I have tried time and time again to get Jack Johnson to meet Langford but Jack would never accept terms or sign for a meeting with the little black fellow. When I would get near the point of a match with Langford he would stall off with some excuse. Finally, I made things so hot for Johnson that he admitted to me that Langford was too tough a game to tackle, and he passed the little fellow up.

From Johnson's point of view, he had to stay champion for as long as possible, because once dethroned he wasn't going to get another title shot. Being the world champion was the only way a black fighter could command big fight fees, and the threat of Langford was too big a risk to take. For 17 straight months between 1912 and 1913, a match with the now experienced Langford would have been well suited, but Johnson was too busy fighting the law to defend his title. Not surprisingly, the law won. In June 1913 he was found guilty of violating the Man Act and sentenced to a year and one day in prison. With an all white jury Johnson never stood a chance, especially as the judge was Kenesaw Mountain Landis, the same man who would become the first commissioner of baseball and introduce the colour line that lasted until 1947.

The champ who had been granted bail didn't stick about to taste prison food and quickly fled to Canada and then on to France. Langford followed him across the pond in the fading hope that he could finally get a shot at the title. Sam was popular in France and there was also talk that he could fight the future light heavyweight champion star Georges Carpentier.[4] As Johnson now had money issues it gave Langford hope that this fight would finally happen because Johnson had been guaranteed a $30,000 purse. Langford's end of the deal was to get 25 percent of the attendance money.

So Johnson did fight in France in what would be the first ever time that two black men would compete for the world title. But instead of the 'Boston Terror', he faced 'Battling' Jim Johnson to a 10-round draw. Jim Johnson was no Jack Johnson and was a regular victim of Langford for the World Coloured Championship. With hardly a marquee career win to his name, the only reason he was able to take the champ to a draw was because Jack had suffered a fracture to the bone (caused possibly from a wrestling bout earlier in the week). The following year, in 1914, Jack Johnson stayed in Paris and defended the belt by beating Frank Moran on points. Langford, meanwhile,

beat Joe Jeanette, as the two most worthy title contenders competed for
the World Coloured Championship. Jeanette rated Langford and claimed
'Sam would have been champion anytime Johnson had given him a second
opportunity. Man! How that baby could hit…Jack was afraid of Langford,
though. He beat Sam when Sam was only a middleweight, but he wouldn't
have anything to do with him when Sam got bigger and better'.

Still a wanted man by the law back home, Jack Johnson then flew out to the
Argentine capital Buenos Aires for one last successful title defence in which he
beat Jack Murray. His next match, against the Kansas farm giant Jess Willard in
Havana Cuba, would result in defeat for the out-of-prime Johnson and the loss
of the heavyweight crown. If Langford's prospects for a world title fight were
bad before, they were catastrophic now, especially considering that Willard
wouldn't fight Langford before he even became the world champion.

Even if Willard was willing, white America once again had a champion
and there was no way Langford was going to be allowed to ruin things.
In the coming years Sam continued to fight on for the World Coloured
Championship in multiple contests against Harry Wills, Sam McVea, Joe
Jeanette and 'Big' Bill Tate.

In 1919, the 'Manassa Mauler' Jack Dempsey would go on to brutally
cut down Jack Johnson's conquer Jess Willard in just three rounds to win
the heavyweight championship. Willard was pummelled by the small
heavyweight Dempsey who was barely bigger than Langford, but like Sam
was a brutally hard puncher.

Before Jack Dempsey became world heavyweight champion he had
fought black opponents, but now he had the belt his promoter Tex Rickard
did not want to promote matches that could lead to riots and jeopardise

his career; which, needless to say, also put an ageing but still active Sam out of the picture. Dempsey had avoided Langford once before in the year 1916 when the soon to be superstar was an unknown. The Manassa Mauler admitted in later years that he felt he could not have beaten Langford at that time in his career and said, 'The hell I feared no man. There was one man, he was even smaller than I was, I wouldn't fight him because I knew he would flatten me. I was afraid of Sam Langford'.

By the time Jack Dempsey was a boxing superstar Langford was blind in one eye and in the twilight of his career. But there is still a suggestion that he posed too big a threat and historian Bert Sugar claims, 'In 1923, Langford pleaded with Tex Rickard for a title shot.

Rickard told him, 'Sam we were looking for somebody easier'.

Sugar added, 'Langford was blind in one eye and forty years old. That's how great Sam Langford was, and yet nobody's heard of him. It's such a shame'.

With Johnson and Langford now old and well past their best, the younger heavyweight Harry Wills took on the role of being too black and too dodged. Sam Langford fought Wills more than any other opponent and 'The Black Panther' was a constant thorn in the ageing Tar Baby's side, winning 14 of their 16 bouts. Despite being in decline, Langford was still described by Wills as the toughest man he ever fought. The final fight between these two men was in 1922, which was a time when Wills was being touted as an opponent to take on Jack Dempsey for the world title. *The Ring* magazine were putting out editorials in favour of Wills being given a chance, which then began to sway the American public in favour of Wills-Dempsey. Sam Langford also believed his old foe deserved a shot and said:

Jack Dempsey ought to give Harry Wills a chance at the title. By not doing so I believe he shows he is somewhat afraid of Wills. It proves it to me by all the fooling around he's done with Harry. First, he goes West and signs with Floyd Fitzsimmons to box Wills and then he comes back East and signs up with Rickard for a bout with Tunney. I guess he doesn't care much for Harry's game, else he would give the man who has been chosen as the logical contender for his title a chance with him.

Tex Rickard feared such a match for the same reason he had denied Langford one. He was terrified of the prospect of race riots and even claimed that politicians were against any such match happening. As the pressure grew for a Wills-Dempsey showdown, Rickard told everyone that the fight would happen. According to Dempsey's biographer Randy Roberts, this was a typical Rickard ploy: he would keep everyone quiet by telling them that a fight would happen, only to then do nothing and let the idea slowly fizzle out. He would sign contracts but they would be no more than goodwill gestures, which were not legally binding. By the early 1920s, Harry Wills was in his early thirties, but still carried enough fear to be sidestepped by those who held the key to a world title shot. Dempsey was said to be open to fighting Wills and by 1926 they had signed a contract to do so. Dempsey, however, never got paid his $100k guarantee, therefore went off to face Gene Tunney. The fight was held in Philadelphia instead of New York where Wills had a legally binding contract. In hindsight, Dempsey may have wished the Wills contract was universally binding, as Tunney would famously beat him to become the new world heavyweight champion.

Between the title reigns of Jack Johnson and Joe Louis (1915 to 1937) there were no black heavyweight champions. Larry Gains was a Canadian heavyweight who fought out of the UK and would have been considered a strong title contender were it not for the colour curtain. Like Langford, Wills, Jeanette and McVea, Gains never got a shot despite registering 115 wins. He was the last ever holder of the World Coloured Heavyweight Championship, which he won in 1935. Then Joe Louis beat James Braddock for the world title in 1937 and consequently the World Coloured Championship was dissolved in the heavyweight division. Louis-Braddock was the first time a black challenger had ever fought for the world heavyweight title on American soil and Louis would reign undefeated for 25 straight matches. In his autobiography Malcolm X recalls what Louis' win over Braddock meant to black Americans: 'And all the Negroes in Lansing, like Negroes everywhere, went wildly happy with the greatest celebration of race pride our generation had ever known. Every Negro boy old enough to walk wanted to be the next "Brown Bomber"'.

In 1951 Jersey Joe Walcott beat Ezzard Charles for the heavyweight title. Not only was this match significant because Walcott became the oldest champion in history, but it was also the first time the heavyweight title had changed hands from one black fighter to another.

In 1983, the average white South African Gerrie Coetzee won the WBA title by beating a cocaine-ridden Michael Dokes. This made Coetzee the first white heavyweight champion since Ingemar Johansson in 1960. Coetzee lost the WBA title a year later to black American Greg Page at a time when most people viewed the WBC holder Larry Holmes as the only legitimate heavyweight world champion. Holmes himself was offered big money to defend his championship in apartheid South Africa during the 1980s.The money was very tempting, but Holmes turned the offers down on principle. Had he accepted, he would have been accused of endorsing a country whose openly racial laws were no less extreme than the ones that kept down Jack Johnson, Sam Langford, Harry Wills, Sam McVea, Joe Jeanette and Larry Gains among others.

Here is a contender for the most scandalous statistic in boxing history: Sam Langford, Harry Wills, Larry Gains, Sam McVea and Joe Jeanette, between them won over 600 professional boxing matches. All that endeavour, all that blood, all that sacrifice and yet not one of those wins led to one heavyweight world title match.

Langford believed his career earnings were somewhere in the region of half a million, yet he retired penniless and explained, 'Yes I earned about $500,000 but [after expenses] all I got from it was about $9,000 a year, and I was in a profession where a man had to be a fairly liberal spender to get along and where he was nearly always the boy who had to grab the dinner checks and pay them'.

After retirement, the 299 fights had taken a horrible toll on Langford's wellbeing and he lost the sight in his good eye. Thankfully, efforts were made to partially restore his vision and a contented Langford beamed, 'It's great to be able to see again. When you can get out and look at the birds and the young girls going by'. Langford then disappeared out of the public gaze until he was tracked down by a sports writer in the middle part of the century. He was found to be living in a cellar in a small room in Harlem Manhattan. The writer's article on Sam's plight generated publicity and through fundraisers he was able to live on a guaranteed benefit of $49 a month. If ever a man should have been financially secure for his services to boxing it was Sam Langford. If ever a man were to feel justified in being bitter for the way things turned out, it was Sam Langford. In contrast, the 'Boston Terror' was content and humble in his old age and reserved no spite for his lack of recognition. 'Well I've got my guitar. I've got my memories. I'm okay'.

1.   One explanation for this unusual nickname is that some female boxing fans referred to him as 'our baby', and one reporter noted that tar was black and so was Langford.
2.   Gans and Langford shared mutual respect for each other. After their fight, Gans taught the less experienced Langford some tricks of the trade in a training session to help him in his career. Langford rated Gans as one of his toughest opponents.
3.   Middleweight legend Stanley Ketchel met the challenge and faced Langford in 1910. Their match was declared a no decision after 6 rounds, which had been signed and agreed beforehand. In real terms Langford was declared the winner by most of the press and some suggested he was holding back on the aggressive Ketchel so as not to jeopardise a longer-round title fight in the future. The re-match never happened. Later that year, Ketchel was murdered by the boyfriend of a woman who he supposedly tried to bed. Langford described Ketchel as the toughest opponent he ever faced.
4.   In 1922, Carpentier would have drawn the colour line against a black fighter called Battling Siki, had he not underestimated him. Siki, from Senegal, West Africa, was un-fancied and expected to be easily knocked out by the French-man. The fight was filmed for cinema and had an exhibition tone to it, until Carpentier was knocked out in the sixth round. The French crowd booed Carpentier for dirty tactics and were outraged when the judges tried to disqualify Siki. Their decision was overturned by the French boxing authorities who feared a riot from the local crowd that put fair play before colour and nationality. There have been suggestions that Siki was expected to take a fall and changed his mind halfway through the fight. Siki is the first ever black light heavyweight world champion and held the title for a year before being dethroned in Dublin by Mike McTigue. Siki was murdered in the streets of New York in 1925 at the age of 28. Before his death he claimed that he changed his mind from losing to Carpentier during the fight because the Frenchman was hitting him for real and thought he could win without a fix.

ROUND 8

WHEN LARRY DIDN'T MEET GEORGE

'I don't want no dried-up burger!'

Larry Holmes gives his opinion on the George Foreman grill

'Big' George Foreman and Larry 'Easton Assassin' Holmes were once scheduled to fight each other at the 67,000-capacity Houston Astrodome. The event was to be billed as a birthday bash and would cost the pay-per-view fan $39.95 for the privilege to watch it. However, the promoter Roger Levitt failed to meet the promised payment to George Foreman, whose purse was a reported $10 million. Larry Holmes' end of the deal was $4 million. Foreman kept his $1 million deposit and Holmes got to keep his $400,000. The fact that this fight was called off was probably a blessing in disguise, for one good reason—it was scheduled for 23 January 1999. The proposed birthday bash would have been billed as a celebration for Foreman turning 50. As for Holmes, he was a spring chicken at just 49 years of age. Had this fight at the Houston Astrodome gone ahead it could have been put in the category of 'fights that should have happened sooner', or perhaps even in the following chapter 'fights that should never have happened'. In 1999, both Holmes and Foreman were not just a few years past their primes, but two decades, and the ring announcer could have introduced both men as at combined age of 99, which would have been a record breaker. Not to mention the combined weight, considering that neither man looked like they had missed many meals in recent years. Before the fight was cancelled Foreman denied that age was a problem and told the media, 'I'm happy to be afraid of being hit right after my 50th birthday. Lots of people are afraid of losing their jobs at age 50'. He then joked, 'Usually, the doctors check a fighter's heart, but with Larry and me, they're just going to see if we have a pulse'. Holmes also dismissed the question of age and said, 'I don't care if we're 900 years old. You got two old guys almost the same age that are going to fight'.

Before signing for the matchup with Foreman, Larry Holmes had told *Boxing Insider:*

> I want to get that guy named George Foreman into the ring. . .If he comes, he comes. If he don't, he don't...George is a little afraid of me. He said he didn't want to fight. He says he's got all this money selling those grills. But I don't think that's true. The thing he wants to get excited about is getting into the ring. He definitely doesn't want to go around the world saying that he ducked Larry Holmes. Therefore, I think George would like to fight me...I think the public will want to see it, and I think they'll support it.

As it turned out, it was deemed that the public would not support Holmes-Foreman, which is why the promoter was unable to raise the $14 million combined purse.

Larry Holmes versus George Foreman, however, is a dream matchup that certainly resonates with boxing fans. It's not hard to find a debate on Internet boxing forums on what would have happened had the two men fought. But these forum debates have a common theme, which is: what would have happened if these two men fought during their primes in the 1970s, a time when both men were under the promotional umbrella of Don King?

There are two reasons why this dream matchup never happened in the era when it should have. Firstly, Larry Holmes' successful rise as a boxer came about under the radar. He was grossly underrated and not seen as championship material. Holmes' pro career started in 1973, and by the mid to late 1970s he was building up a very credible unbeaten record. Not that anybody was taking any notice of his credibility, especially not Don King who viewed Holmes as little more than Muhammad Ali's sparring partner and a future journeyman. In the promotion for the 1999 cancelled bout, Foreman said, 'Holmes was a second-rate fighter sparring for Ali when I had my original career'.

By the time Holmes caught people's attention in the late 1970s, unforeseen circumstances cut down any chance of a match with Big George. In 1977, Foreman retired at the age of just 28 with a record of 45 wins and two losses. His second loss (Ali, of course, being the first) was a surprise defeat to Jimmy Young, which resulted in the former champion having an emotional breakdown in his dressing room. Foreman fell in to a state of unconsciousness and was taken to a dark and desperate place in his mind where he had visions of dying. Foreman had been emotionally hit by what he describes as a 'Sledgehammer of sadness'. While still unconscious to the people in his dressing room, he claims that God spoke to him at that moment and became his saviour. God asked Foreman why he was so scared to die if he was a believer. The former champ was not a religious man and told God he could still box and earn money. God turned down the offer: 'I don't want your money I want you'.

Foreman awoke and went from a state of extreme fear and desperation to sheer joy. 'Hallelujah, I'm clean. Hallelujah, I've been born again'.

Whether Foreman really encountered divine inspiration or not, what is for sure is that the experience changed his whole direction in life. He quit boxing and focused on being a preacher. Religion had given him a degree of glory that he had never felt from boxing.

> I'd achieved all the greatness I'd aspired to. I was everything I'd ever wanted to be. The feeling that rocked me was the one I'd never experienced as the world champ. I finally had it all: fulfilment, peace, contentment…to knock a guy out, I needed to psych myself into a state of viciousness. But that George Foreman didn't exist anymore.

God, real or not, is to blame for the fact that Holmes and Foreman never met in a super-fight in the late 1970s. While Holmes became the main man in heavyweight boxing, Foreman was far away and busy spreading the good word.

Before Big George retired from boxing, 1976 was a feasible period in time when he could have fought the up-and-coming Holmes. According to the *Augusta Chronicle*, 'Holmes said he had the chance to fight Foreman in 1976, but couldn't take the bout because he had broken a thumb in beating Roy Williams that year.[1] Foreman instead fought Dino Denis and knocked him out'.

In 1976, Holmes-Foreman would not have been viewed as a clash of the titans because Holmes was not yet viewed as a contender. In the promotion for the doomed 1999 fight Foreman had no regrets that it didn't happen sooner and said, 'It's one of those things that should have happened a long time ago. But I'm happy it didn't because it wouldn't have meant anything'.

Fulfilment in boxing was Larry Holmes' prime focus and he needed George Foreman more than the other way round. Speaking to the Internet magazine *Ringtalk* regarding the cancelled bout, Holmes said, 'If there was ever a fight I wanted it's that one...it wasn't about the money...I wanted to show people that I could beat George Foreman, that he's not the guy people think he is. He's one of the greatest athletes out there but a phoney when it comes to being a fighter'.

The 'Easton Assassin' was always unfairly dogged with legacy issues and goes down in history as one of the most underappreciated heavyweight champions of all time; this despite defending the world title an incredible 20 times and not losing a fight until he was 36 years of age. It's been said that the biggest problem Larry Homes had as a champion was a lack of pedigree opponents and career-defining matches. For example, the trainer and broadcasting pundit Teddy Atlas said that Holmes was brilliantly consistent without ever having a great dance partner. Holmes won the

WBC heavyweight championship in 1978 in a classic battle against the much-favoured Ken Norton. The 15th round was one of the best in boxing championship history and Norton was certainly a brilliant 'dance partner'. Holmes was on the verge of a narrow points loss, but with seconds remaining he staggered Norton with a flurry of clean shots, which won him the title in a split decision. Holmes would describe the match, known as 'Bad Blood', as his toughest ever fight. However, it wasn't enough to win over a cynical boxing public who had been spoiled in recent years with the likes of Ali, Frazier and of course George Foreman. Holmes remained the unbeaten champion of the world for an incredible seven years. His first defeat didn't come until his 49th professional fight, which was a contested decision against Michael Spinks in 1985 and one match short of Rocky Marciano's unbeaten streak of 50.

Larry Holmes' hand speed was lightening quick and his left jab a thing of beauty. But in the 1970s that wasn't going to be enough to replace the golden boots of an ageing Muhammad Ali. When football manager David Moyes became manager of Manchester United in summer 2013, he was given the impossible task of following on from Alex Ferguson. It was described as the hardest job in sport. The torch that Holmes was expected to take from Ali was equally heavy and no emerging star could replace the most supreme personality in sporting and entertainment history.

George Foreman, on the other hand, never had legacy issues. His status and recognition were signed, sealed and delivered in just two matches. In 1973/74 he knocked down legends Joe Frazier and Ken Norton a total of eight times in a combined round count of just four. Both Frazier and Norton were knocked out by the second round. By cutting down two big trees in such a decisive manner, the 1968 Olympic gold medallist became the most feared boxer on the planet. Part of Foreman's legacy also includes a defeat and being the giant that was chopped down by Ali in the Rumble in the Jungle. He was one of two players in what was the most famous boxing match of all time. Therefore, the world has heard of George Foreman. He appears on mainstream chat shows and is a recognisable celebrity: an American icon. Boxing fans know of Larry Holmes, but you won't see him on the *David Letterman Show*. Even among many casual boxing fans, the name Larry Holmes does not come with the same awe as George Foreman. This is where the bitterness emanates when Holmes talks about his fellow legend. Before the doomed matchup that was planned for January 1999, Holmes had promised retirement but on this condition: 'Oh, I might make an exception for George Foreman. I've always thought I could beat that Texas fat boy. But otherwise [I'm finished]…'

It's fair to say that Holmes is not a member of the George Foreman Appreciation Society. Speaking at an appreciation event held in the 'Easton Assassin's' honour, the former world champion ranted, 'Bert Sugar says, "Larry Holmes you were one of the great guys, I rate you just behind George Foreman". What the heck was he thinking! Everybody knows that George Foreman can't fight. Everybody knew that he wouldn't fight me'. Holmes then gave his opinion on George Foreman's range of fat reducing grills, which have the slogan 'Knockout the fat':

> Don't listen to your husband when he says buy a George Foreman grill. I like my burgers juicy. I like my steak tender. I don't want no damn dried-up burger!. . .You know he's crazy. Anyone who names

their kids George, George, George, George, George and George…
he's got to be crazy. He don't like people. He likes himself. He only
likes you when you buy that George Foreman grill.

Holmes claims that the reason they never fought was down to Foreman,
who ducked, and remarked, 'It's not my fault that he was in the boxing game
and didn't want to fight me. Foreman's the biggest phoney ever'.

Steve Bunce said of Larry Holmes, 'If you don't have Larry Holmes
in your top five heavyweights of all time, then I think you need to get
some more DVDs out and read some more books'. On an EPSN televised
discussion on the greatest heavyweight fighters of all time, guest Bert Sugar
nominated George Foreman at number eight. The main criteria in Sugar's
reasoning was Foreman's achievement of winning back the heavyweight
crown against Michael Moorer 20 years after losing it to Ali in Zaire. Sugar
described what Foreman had done at the age of 45 as 'unprecedented'. Larry
Holmes was also a studio guest and also had something to say on the matter.
With a gleam in his eye Holmes said, 'I'm so happy to be here, to hear this
from Bert…How can he give George Foreman rated number eight? George
Foreman couldn't beat Jimmy Young. Couldn't beat Tommy Morrison. He
couldn't beat Shannon Biggs'. The host Brian Kenny then entered the debate
in defence of George Foreman. He reminded Holmes that George Foreman
essentially had two careers and that the losses to the likes of Morrison
and Biggs were when he was a lot older and way past his prime. Kenny
suggested that Holmes at least give Foreman credit for his destruction of Joe
Frazier in the 1970s. Holmes, however, wasn't in a generous mood:

I don't give credit for it because we don't have cash today…You can find anybody that don't move. George had problems with guys that moved, that's why he never fought Larry Holmes…Joe Frazier stood in front of George Foreman. Anybody who does that he takes out. But anybody who got a little boxing style like Jimmy Young did, he'd lose it, he can't take out.

Jimmy Young's win in 1977 was a major shock and Foreman claims that the reason he lost was because he was too focused on not knocking Young out early. Before the fight, Don King was concerned about the bout not lasting long enough to make good viewing. He expressed this fear to Foreman who in his autobiography claims, 'His [Young's] knees buckled. I thought he was going down. But instead of delivering the crowning blow, I wondered whether Don King would be satisfied with a seven round bout. In those seconds of indecision Young's wits returned and he ran for his life'. According to Larry Holmes, King had demanded the same from him for a fight in the 1970s. Holmes was on the undercard and claims that King had asked him to stretch his match out for as long as possible. However, nobody told this to the other guy who came out swinging. Therefore, the Easton Assassin felt obliged to deal with his opponent and finish things off early. King was furious and held back Holmes' purse for the crime of being too good.

Speculating on what might have happened between these two all-time greats regularly divides opinions on boxing forums. Many will agree with Holmes that his hit and move style would have beaten Foreman. Plenty of others counter by saying that Big George would have won through his punching power and would have done unto Holmes what he did to Norton and Frazier. Because of that element of doubt, it creates the biggest what-if of both men's careers, but it doesn't stand alone as the 1970s heavyweight classic that went missing. Holmes-Joe Frazier could have feasibly happened, and what if George Foreman had met Ernie Shavers in a war of the hardest hitters?

Holmes and Frazier fought many times in the ring but never in a sanctioned bout. Holmes used to spar with Frazier; one such time being in 1974 when 'Smokin' Joe' used him to prepare for the rematch with Muhammad Ali. Frazier's camp wanted Holmes because his hit and move style was similar to Ali's. In turn, Ali did not need his regular sparring partner because Holmes' smooth and elusive style was too different to Frazier's.

Smokin' Joe's career didn't officially end until 1981, but he was semi-retired after the Thrilla in Manila in 1975. A match with Holmes is a 'could have', rather than a definitive 'should have'. Between 1975 and 1981, Frazier only fought twice. These included a fifth-round KO defeat in a rematch with George Foreman. After drawing with the journeyman and former inmate Floyd 'Jumbo' Cummings, Frazier retired for good with a record of 32 wins, four losses and a draw. According to Larry Holmes in his autobiography, Frazier never held back in sparring:

> Joe trained like he fought, on full throttle, all burners blasting…
> Joe would walk in the gym and say, 'Let's go. We gonna go to war
> today'. And he wasn't fooling. Smokin' Joe sparred as if the whole
> world was watching. The man ripped that left hook like he wanted to
> bury it in you. He busted my ribs—actually fractured one of them.

Anyone with footage of the Frazier-Holmes sparring sessions would be a very popular person in boxing circles. Holmes-Marvis Frazier was a fight that did happen. 'Smokin's' son got a title shot against Holmes in 1983 in what turned out to be a mismatch. Marvis was knocked out in the first round, and went back to his stool in shame that he had let his legend of a father down. Joe Frazier ran up to the corner to tell his son how highly he thought of him and Marvis broke down in tears.

Hard-hitting Ernie Shavers' career spanned between 1969 and 1995, and he retired with a record of 74 wins, 14 losses and a draw. His standout bout was a disputed points loss to Muhammad Ali in 1977, in which many believed that he did enough to win. Not that Ali looked concerned just moments before the scorecards were read out, as he brought out a comb and groomed his hair. The crowd booed as all three judges favoured Ali for the win, and moments later Shavers told NBC's Larry Merchant, 'I thought I won, I'll fight him again'. There was no rematch. Ali had felt the power of the original 'Dark Destroyer' and literally thanked Allah for getting him through the experience. Larry Holmes describes Shavers as one of the most likeable guys outside of the ring, but inside the ropes his punches rained in from hell.[2] In describing Shavers' force Holmes joked, 'You'd punch him in his elbow and break your ankle'. In a Foreman-Shavers showdown, Big George would have been in the unusual position of fighting a man who many say could punch harder than he could. Speculation on boxing website forums focus on that one question: who banged harder, Foreman or Shavers? The answer has to lean towards Shavers, for no other reason than testimony from people who faced both men: Muhammad Ali, Ken Norton and Ron Lyle, who all claim that Shavers' strength had no equal. The actor Sylvester

Stallone is also someone who can testify for Shavers. In the 1980s the 'Destroyer' was invited to audition for a part in Rocky III as the character Clubber Lang. When role-playing in the ring, Stallone told Shavers to hit him properly and to stop going easy on him. Shavers obliged, and as a result Stallone soon went off to the men's room to throw up. In an interview with the *Guardian,* Shaver's attributes his strength to the fact that he did manual work before his life as a boxer, which built up his shoulder strength. On his technique he added, 'I always threw my punches at the guy's neck because, when he sees it coming, it's natural to duck and they drop their chin right on target. Bing'. When George Foreman was asked on the *David Letterman Show* about which boxers hit the hardest he responded,

'You only meet three genuine punchers in your career. Gerry Cooney, Ron Lyle and a kid I worked with by the name of Cleveland Williams. And they hit so hard that it vibrates your body'.

'What about Ernie Shavers?' asked Letterman.

'I never fought Ernie Shavers, thank goodness!'

Though the two men never met in the ring they would develop a friendship, and Shavers, (as well as Marvis Frazier) would follow Foreman's path as punching preacher by becoming a Christian minister.

The legacy of Larry Holmes cried out for a fight against a truly outstanding heavyweight in his prime. The irony is that by the time he got that opportunity, his prime had long passed. The year was 1988 and the man he would face would be none other than a 21-year-old Mike Tyson. In 1986, there had been talks to put on a Holmes-Tyson match after Tyson poleaxed Marvis Frazier. Iron Mike's manager Jim Jacobs said that he would go straight to the table with Larry Holmes, but the prospect temporarily fell though. By 1988 Larry Holmes was aged 38, which provided the contest with the second biggest age difference in heavyweight title history.[3] If Holmes were to win he would become the oldest man to ever win the world heavyweight title.

In the build up, Holmes slammed the media for his treatment over the years and said,

'Throughout my career they've [boxing fans] always been against me because of you guys. Don't bite your tongue. Say what you feel, write what you feel. If you think I'm going to lose say so, but when I win you write it'. He also had no fear of speaking his mind on his opponent and vowed, 'I'm going down in history not Mike Tyson. He'll go down in history as a S.O.B [son of a bitch]'.

The bout at Atlantic City was seen as a decent enough test for Tyson in his seventh title defence, but nobody really thought that the old boy Holmes could win. Preceding the opening bell, the former heavyweight champion was introduced to a mixture of boos and cheers, as was Tyson. In the opening three rounds, the young champion was the main aggressor but the old man stood firm even if he offered little in the way of attack. Muhammad Ali watched on in the front row, hiding behind a pair of sunglasses. In the fourth round, business was about to pick up. Holmes came out like a man on a mission to roll back the years, and for a brief period he reopened the school of How to Jab and Look Great Doing It. Holmes danced around and circled Tyson, hitting him with clean left jabs that got the crowd cheering. 'This is how young Larry Holmes would have fought Tyson', observed the HBO commentator. Some of the crowd were now on their feet, unlike Holmes whose feet were literally taken off the canvas by a devastating

Tyson right hook. Holmes beat the count, only to be knocked down twice more in the fourth round. The third knock down was brutal. The dazed Holmes went to counterpunch and caught his right arm on the ropes. That left a clear target for Tyson who knocked the former champ out cold for the first and only time in his career. Holmes was laid on the canvas and with dignity the former champ was raised from the canvas and helped back to the corner. Before the fight, Holmes had predicted that even if Tyson were to win, then further down the line he would destroy himself and end up in jail.

So where else could Holmes go from here? He was too old and out of shape to fight for the championship while Mike Tyson was on the scene and soon to unify the titles with a famous win over Michael Spinks. On the very same day in 1988 when Holmes lost to Mike Tyson, Mr George Foreman was celebrating his 40th birthday. It was also the 15th anniversary of Foreman's most famous win, the knockout of Joe Frazier in just two rounds in Kingston, Jamaica. Foreman a year earlier had come out of a ten-year retirement and was re-establishing himself on the heavyweight scene. Holmes recalls in his autobiography:

After a ten-year absence from boxing, a new and reconstituted George Foreman was out there in the hinterlands, knocking out a bunch of nobodies and getting well paid for it, even as he joked about the quality of opponents. 'You know', he said, 'there are some who claim I don't fight a guy unless he is on a respirator. That's a lie. He has to be at least eight days off the respirator'.

George Foreman looked different to the man that retired in 1977. A lot of the muscle had been replaced by fat and the menacing-looking moustache had gone. 'Man this stuff has shrunk', noted Forman as he tried and failed to get into his old boxing gear.

With Foreman back on the scene in the late 1980s there was talk of a showdown with Mike Tyson in a contest that would have beaten Holmes-Tyson in age disparity. 'Tyson's style is perfect for me. I can beat him, no problem', said Foreman. One can understand why Tyson would have been a motivation for Foreman, as beating him would have been the ultimate redemption for the Ali humiliation in 1974. On the *David Letterman Show* Foreman was asked about Tyson further down the line and claimed, 'That's what I wanted. I didn't come out of retirement to face Gerry Cooney…I came back to fight for the heavyweight championship of the world. I want this Mike Tyson. I will assure you that I will do it in the same fashion, in one or two rounds'.

'Is this fight actually going to happen?' said Letterman.

'It's going to happen. Don King came to visit my camp in Houston. He had a big contract. He offered me $5 million. Told me to sign on the dotted line. I'm more afraid of Don King and the dotted line than Mike Tyson!'

In his autobiography, Foreman claims, 'The more I continued to win, the more inevitable became the Tyson-Foreman showdown. Then in 1990 came the boxing shock of many years: Mike Tyson lost to journeyman James "Buster" Douglas in Tokyo. That disappointed me terribly'.

In a rare compliment, Larry Holmes claimed in his autobiography that a young George Foreman would have beaten Mike Tyson. 'After he hit Tyson, little Mickey would have been ready for social security'. Holmes also claimed that the bulk of great 1970s fighters would have done the same:

I'm going to give it to you straight. Smokin' Joe Frazier would have bombed Tyson out. So would have Bonavena, Lyle, Shavers, Norton and Quarry. Those were big strong punching suckers. Even Mac Foster and Ernie Terrall would have beat him. Ali would have ambushed him as Tyson charged forward…There are people who tell me I'm dead wrong about this. But I'm a student of boxing and while Tyson is a good fighter of today, he's not one of the great fighters of all time.

Of course we don't have a 100 percent definitive answer as to what would have happened in the Tyson-Foreman showdown that didn't happen; we can only guess that it would probably have been one-sided traffic in the young man's favour. It's unlikely that a 40-year-old Foreman would have been able to hold off the irresistible force of a raw and pissed-off 'Iron' Mike.

What would have been harder to predict was Holmes-Foreman during the same era, and it was highly feasible. If promoted as the fight that went missing from the golden era then it would have caught the imagination of the fans. Both fighters were unretired, active and still chasing greatness. This was the most realistic period of time when a Holmes-Foreman match could and should have happened. In the late 1970s, Foreman was retired and too busy preaching. In 1999, both men were too old and overweight for a potential farce in Houston, which was thankfully called off. So the fight that truly went missing between these two great legends would have been best scheduled for any time from 1987 to the early 1990s.

George Foreman ended his career for a second time with an overall record of 76 wins and five losses. After the Tyson loss in 1988, the old man Larry Holmes would go on to fight a whopping 24 more contests over the course of 16 years. Despite being a shadow of himself in his prime, only three of those fights ended in defeat and were against Evander Holyfield, Oliver McCall and Dane Brian Nielsen. Preceding the Holyfield fight in 1992, Holmes had caused an upset by beating Ray Mercer, which put him in line for one more title shot. However, one man still caused him a slight dilemma:

> My objective was to fight either Foreman or Holyfield, and now that I'd whipped Mercer it was pretty much my choice. I really wanted Foreman. I just thought he couldn't beat me now. Him on TV with that big phoney smile. He didn't fool me. What kind of man calls his children George or Georgette? Can't he take time to remember their names? I really wanted to kick his fat ass. But given that Holyfield was champion it was a no brainer.

Holmes' last ever contest was in 2002 against Eric Esch (aka Butterbean), a money-drawing white heavyweight known for a shaved head, an obese physic and Old Glory stars and stripe shorts. Butterbean is still active and known as a knockout specialist, providing the opponents are bums. Butterbean's biggest scalp would have been against the 'Easton Assassin', but the former champ won a ten-round decision, despite being over 50 years of age. He then retired with a record of 75 wins and six losses. His decision to finally quit was due to the realisation that any prospect of a fight with Foreman was over. Speaking in 2007, Holmes said:

I retired fighting because I wanted to fight a man called George Foreman. He didn't want nothing to do with me…If you're one of the great fighters you should fight one of the great fighters. So that fight will never happen now, because he's too old and I'm too old. And he missed a glowing opportunity to prove that he was one of the great ones.

More than any world champion, Holmes needed to beat someone great in order for the world to recognise his own greatness. Of course in 1980 he beat the most famous boxer of them all, the man known as the greatest of all time. But it did very little to enhance his reputation. It was a fight that should never have happened. .

1. In turn, Shavers describes Holmes as his best ever opponent. Holmes beat Shavers twice. In the second fight Shavers floored the champion in the seventh round. Holmes beat the count and went on to win the match.
2. Up to that point the biggest age difference in title history was when 21-year-old Floyd Patterson fought 42-year-old legend Archie Moore in 1956. Patterson knocked Moore out in round five.
3. Roy Williams is described by Holmes as a perfect example of a highly talented fighter that got held back and wasted by his management. Over the years he could have been pushed further, but was avoided and became demoralised and bitter. His most notable fight was one that only a select few people witnessed: in an angry and highly bitter sparring session he went hell for leather with Muhammad Ali in a dispute over money. According to Holmes, Williams matched Ali all the way, who then sacked him the next day after paying him the disputed fee.

INTERLUDE

THE WASTED ONE

'I was natural skill. I just wasn't disciplined enough. Imagine if I was sensible!'

Kirkland Laing

Kirkland Laing, born in 1954, was known as the 'Gifted One' and is up there, or perhaps down there, along with Errol Christie in the category of British fighters who did not live up to their true talent. But whereas Christie now lives a respectable, healthy and productive life as a fitness trainer, Laing ended up on the opposite side of the spectrum.

September 1982: Laing becomes the man who beat the man who was the only man to beat Sugar Ray Leonard. His points win over Roberto Duran was one of the major welterweight upsets of the decade. It should have set him up for mega-fights against the great American stars such as Thomas Hearns, Marvin Hagler and of course the 'Sugar Man' himself. An all-British super-fight against the 'Ragamuffin' Lloyd Honeyghan would have also captured the public imagination. The two men at one point had to stop sparring together because they were seen as natural rivals. As the decade wore on, Laing would have probably moved up in weight and gone on to challenge the great emerging British middleweight superstars such as Michael Watson, Nigel Benn, Herol Graham and Chris Eubank. 'That [win against Duran] should have been the start of something special', wrote Steve Bunce in the *Independent* on 4 September 2012, 30 years to the day since Laing's famous victory.

Instead, Kirkland's career was self-destructed by addiction and an over indulgence in drugs and partying. He was even caught smoking a joint in his place of work, the Royal Oak gym. He denied the accusation while a joint lay resting on his ear. 'I won a few fights and the next minute I'm partying', confessed Laing, whose career could not successfully coexist with his lifestyle. Meanwhile, the Laing-conquered Roberto Duran got disciplined, fought mega-fights and earned millions of dollars. Kirkland retired in 1994 with a record of 43 wins, 12 losses and one draw.

In 2003, Steve Bunce interviewed Laing on a park bench in Hackney. 'The Gifted One', by this stage in his life was, to put it harshly but truthfully, a tramp, with nothing but a few cans of beer to his name (bought by Steve Bunce). A passing stranger would not possibly imagine that behind the beard and old clothes was a man who used to be a contender. On the park bench, Bunce reminded Laing, 'You won the British title, then eventually the European'. Laing thought about it for a few seconds before replying, 'I did, didn't I?', while looking impressed at the realisation of his former talent. Poor Kirkland, and what a shame that he didn't have the discipline to warrant great fights that could have given the 'Gifted One' a hell of a reason to party. Not that he ever needed a reason.

ROUND 9

FIGHTS THAT SHOULD NEVER HAVE HAPPENED

'This fight [Holmes-Ali] was an abomination – was a crime.
All the people involved in this fight should have been arrested'
Muhammad Ali's former doctor Ferdie Pacheco

In football, if a member of the team can no longer perform at the required standard, a decision on future contracts and appearances will be made for the player, not the other way round. If you're way past your prime, the sensible thing to do is call it quits and to try and get a cushy pundit job on *Match of the Day*. Diego Maradona's name alone will not get him a professional game, only his talent will, and the majesty of that passed many years ago. In boxing, the legacy can sell more than the contemporary talent, so we see fights go ahead on the fantasy that someone can roll back the years and be great again. Once a fighter loses their cutting edge it never returns, but that reality rarely stops legends from trying. The comeback kid will tell us in the press conference that they are in the best shape of their career, but, along with a powerful punch, boastful chit-chat is also one of the last assets a boxer can lose.

The occasions when an old and tired-looking Muhammad Ali got battered around the ring highlighted this sad culture in the sport most starkly. In the opinion of many, any match that 'The Greatest' fought since the Thrilla in Manila against Joe Frazier should not have happened. The 1975 Thrilla was one of the bravest, gruelling, heroic and brutal matches in heavyweight history and described by Ali as 'The nearest thing to dying'. Afterwards, Ali's personal doctor Ferdie Pacheco told him to quit and recalls:

> That was the end of his career he should have never fought again. But he wanted to keep on going. And the [black] Muslims wanted him to keep on going. And Angelo Dundee wanted him to keep going. And the world wanted him to keep going. Except me. I'm the only one who said don't go again.

Instead of bowing out at the top, Ali would go on to fight ten more matches over the course of six years. Over the same period of time, Joe Frazier would fight only two more times before retiring. Ali still had accomplishments left in him, such as a win over Ernie Shavers, but he wasn't the great fighter who was seen for the last time in Manila in 1975. In 1977, while on a tour of northeast England, Ali told a crowd in Newcastle, 'I'm at the end of the road in boxing. In another year or less I'll retire…I enjoy boxing. I'll be sad the day I quit…[I'm] 35 years old now and I have to get out soon. I want to get out while I'm champion. I don't want to stay around like 99 percent of the fighters do, wind up on their back'.

He then went on to elaborate how being a boxing world champion gives him the chance to be heard and help change society for the better. He told of how he enjoyed the lifestyle and prestige that came with being the champ and his reluctance to quit the sport did seem to emanate from a fear of being a yesterday's man who people wouldn't listen to anymore.

Ali initially retired in September 1978, after impressively winning a rematch with Leon Spinks who had beaten him earlier that year. Then, two years later he was tempted to make a comeback. If any Ali contest since the Thrilla in Manila should be singled out as a fight that should not have happened, then it was this horrible showing against a world-class Larry Holmes in October 1980.

'Holmes is going to get knocked out. He doesn't stand a chance', proclaimed Muhammad while in training and in a mannerism similar to the build up to the Rumble in the Jungle. In 1964, he told the world that he would destroy Sonny Liston. No one believed him and he was proved right. In 1974, he told the world that he would whip George Foreman. Same scenario. In 1980, the 38-year-old Ali told the world that he would beat Larry Holmes. 'Mark my words. Take the films. If I get whooped, play it back because I'd be a fool'. Many people believed him. How could they not? In the back of people's minds there would have been a feeling that Ali was going to shock the world again, or at least go out in style. 'I always come through. I always figure out a way'.

The fight billed as 'The Last Hurrah' took place at Caesar's Palace, the same venue where Holmes had won the world title against Ken Norton two years earlier. Before the bell, Ali was waving his hands around in the air to whip the crowd up. 'Oh boy, this is going to be a brawl', gleamed the commentator in excitement of what he thought was going to transpire. What did transpire was a one-sided beat down of a boxing hero. From the opening round, an in-prime Larry Holmes outclassed his opponent who had nothing in the tank. Every round followed the same ugly pattern with Ali taking punishment and giving no offence in return. The one strength Ali had left was his resilience not to be knocked down to the canvas, but he was taking such a beating that his fans desired a knockout just so it could end. The commentator who was so excited before the opening bell was now sounding like a news reporter on the scene of a crisis: 'This must be stopped…Sad to witness this'.

Round after round, punches rained in on Ali who responded with nothing, and his tormenter Holmes was an emotional wreck. He was beating up his old sparring partner and a friend. Holmes made appeals to the referee for the fight to be stopped but they fell on deaf ears. Four years earlier he had been Ali's sparring partner and during those sessions Ali gave him a bruised face. Holmes was delighted for the memento and considered the bruise a badge of honour. The Last Hurrah was finally stopped by Angelo Dundee after round ten as Ali was finally deemed in no fit state to continue. Afterwards, Holmes cried tears of sadness over what had happened and went to visit the loser in his dressing room who in turn hugged the champion. But even a comprehensive whipping could not keep the great one from boastful hollering and as Holmes left the dressing room Ali piped up in defiance, 'Holmes…Holmes…I need to get Holmes!!'

In the coming years the 'Easton Assassin' had to live with the burden of being the man who beat up a washed-up Muhammad Ali. A woman walked up to Holmes in the street just to tell him how much she hated him for what he had done.

Unlike the Nevada State Athletic Commission, the hated Larry Holmes was not responsible for granting Ali a licence to box, despite a physical examination which showed worrying signs of slowness in his reactions. Film footage of Ali's training sessions survives and clearly portrays a man who didn't talk or move with the same irresistible energy as the world had become used to.

Nor did Holmes underpay Ali $1 million for the fight, unlike Don King was alleged to have done. Ali took legal action against the promoter and the matter was settled out of court with King paying a small fraction of the overall disputed amount.

Ali-Holmes should not have left any doubt that 'The Greatest' should retire. Unfortunately, two weeks before the fight, his preparation was not helped by poor medication. A doctor called Charles Williams was concerned about the fighter's weight and had stupidly prescribed him thyroid drugs, which were dehydrating and slowing Ali down. It gave an element of doubt to paper over the cracks that were clearly there anyway. The day after the fight, Ali was on the phone to the trainer Cus D'Amato and the Italian asked him to speak to an up-and-coming 14-year-old boxer by the name of Mike Tyson. Ali told the kid that he had been prescribed pills that slowed him down and that he would be back again to put things in order. The young kid told Ali that he would avenge the loss by beating Larry Holmes one day in the future.

A year after 'The Last Hurrah', Ali fought one more match. His opponent in 1981 was the 27-year-old Jamaican Trevor Berbick in a match that was lamely billed as the 'Drama in Bahama'. Ali entered the ring in Nassau looking sombre and overweight, even more so than the year before against Holmes. The TV commentator tried to be positive and claimed, 'This is just like the days of old'. In the opening rounds Ali threw punches and at times looked aggressive. But in a ten-round contest he was outfought by the younger man. In the later rounds Ali had nothing left to offer and once again it was horrible to see him take punishment that we now know with hindsight accelerated his illness. Berbick comfortably won the points decision and would also have to carry the burden of beating up a washed-up icon.[1]

A former opponent of Ali, Jerry Quarry was another top heavyweight star who fought for far longer than he should have done, leading to illness, in his case dementia in his 40s. Quarry was the 'great white hope' in the 1960s and 1970s, and somebody who in today's era of four governing bodies would have held a world championship. George Foreman described him as one of the best fighters never to win a world title and admitted to sidestepping the man known as the 'Bellflower Bomber'. Quarry was known for having a powerful punch and beat some top heavyweights such as Floyd Patterson, Mac Foster, Ron Lyle, Buster Mathis and Ernie Shavers. Unfortunately for him, when it came to a step up in class against Ali, Joe Frazier and Ken Norton, he came up short. By the early 1980s Quarry was washed up, broke and retired. An addiction to cocaine and alcohol also contributed to his physical and mental plight. So the fact that he had a comeback fight in 1992, at a time when he was already suffering from brain damage, was another sanctioning crime. Other boxing state commissions had refused Quarry a licence, but Colorado were willing and the 'Bellflower Bomber' was battered all the way through a six-round scheduled bout. He lost to a 31-year-old journeyman called Ron Cranmer who Quarry probably would have floored within a single round in his heyday. This fight would have only accelerated Quarry's illness and plight and he died of a stroke in 1999 at the age of 53. The stroke was probably a blessing, as his condition was so bad he needed permanent care and could hardly do anything for himself.

A contender past his prime in a sport like golf wouldn't be anything sinister, as we'd just have a middle-aged man competing at a lower standard to what we were used to. Fans might enjoy watching him and they could say that they'd seen a legend compete live. If anything, it would probably be good for that golfer's health to be out there on the green and having fun by being involved in the sport he loves. In boxing, the same scenario of trying to defy age and reality is painful in every sense. Of course, it's easy for those of us who have never experienced fame, glory and greatness to criticise others for finding it hard to give up. The degree of adulation and achievement that a top boxer must have experienced would be completely intoxicating. . .not to mention the money.

In his autobiography, entitled *Cyclone*, Barry McGuigan noted, 'There is something unique about boxing which puts you up on such an egotistical high that separates it from every other sport'. The only other 'sport' where we have a similar scenario is professional wrestling. There are plenty of occasions when a 60 year old will strut out to the ring in a pair of tights and try to bring back the glory years. Children will endure watching a washed-up wrestling legend and think to themselves, 'Why is this old man hobbling around the ring and why is this considered any good?' The film *The Wrestler* starring Mickey Rourke was an honest and accurate portrayal of a washed-up former legend not knowing when to quit and causing himself serious health issues. The boxing film *Rocky Balboa* also portrayed a middle-aged character who felt that he still had some fuel left in the tank. Stallone's character came out of retirement to fight the world heavyweight champion Mason 'The Line' Dixon, played by real-life boxing champion Antonio Tarver.[2] Just like in the original movie, Rocky went the distance, shocked the world and enhanced his reputation, which was a classic example of art not imitating real life. The idea represented people's desire to see a hero successfully defy age and be the champion they used to be. It had to be done in the movies, because in real life, the usual story is to see a washed-up former favourite showing us no signs of greatness and tarnishing a legacy.

Any match that Mike Tyson had after his loss to Lennox Lewis in 2002 certainly tarnished his legacy, if not his bank balance. In 2004, Tyson was knocked out by the 'Brixton Bomber' Danny Williams in Kentucky, and it was apparent that 'Iron' Mike was a shadow of the fighter he once was. A year later in his next and final fight, he would sink lower than that even, by losing to Ireland's Kevin McBride in Washington DC. Tyson's performance was so embarrassing that it made his loss to Danny Williams the previous year seem like a spirited defeat. Not only was Tyson beaten by a bum, he had become one. In the sixth round McBride leaned on Tyson, who, looking like a tired and worn-out wreck, slumped to the canvas and rested upright against the ropes, his legs spread out like a young child sitting on the floor. The crowd looked on in utter disbelief at the downfall they were witnessing. They didn't know whether to laugh, cry or boo. The referee generously called a push rather than a knock down and Tyson staggered up as the bell ended the round; but his manager told the referee 'no more' and Tyson's career ended with that call. Directly afterwards, Mike admitted to the world that he didn't love boxing anymore and that he was only doing it 'to pay a few bills'. Tyson's words were such a sad contrast to his early career when he was up and coming in 1985. After beating Sam Scarf he was asked if he enjoyed boxing and replied, 'You have to love the sport to be the best at it… it's good to be successful and [have] financial status, but if you only go in there for the money you're only going to reach a certain status and I'm in there for greatness and peace of mind. I love the sport and if I was in there just for financial reasons I wouldn't be doing as well as I am'.

When Tyson lost to Danny Williams in 2004 he looked like a depressed and broken man. However, on his admission after the McBride loss he looked contented at his acceptance of reality. He vowed not to disgrace the sport any longer by fighting and losing to such a 'calibre of opponent'. Despite offers, Tyson kept to his word.

Outside a small town in Derbyshire not many people would get excited over the prospect of Barcelona playing Burton Albion at The Nou Camp, as we could safely predict the outcome of such a contest. Boxing punters pay to watch a fight, not an assault. We want to see well-matched opponents and the right boxers get given opportunities based on merit. What we don't want to see is a one-sided farce. A wonderful contender in this category is George Mitchell versus the legendary Frenchman Georges Carpentier from the year 1914. Carpentier was a dominant figure in European boxing during that time and held the continent's heavyweight title from 1913 to 1923. He was also world light heavyweight champion between 1920 and 1922. In 1921, he fought against Jack Dempsey for the world heavyweight title, and so big was the fight that it created an attendance record for the time of 80,183. It was the first ever million-dollar gate. Dempsey beat the 'Pride of Paris' with a fourth-round knockout, but Carpentier had put up a credible battle up to that point. Despite losing to Dempsey, the 'Orchid Man' upheld his reputation as a world-class fighter. He was swish, handsome and talented. And he had a habit of knocking out British fighters.

So, who was George Mitchell? Well, he wasn't a journeyman because he wasn't even a professional boxer. Standing at 6'3" and weighing in at 196 lbs (89 kg), the 22 year old was an amateur with no record of prize fighting. He was, however, a proud Englishman, which in his mind put him in a good stead to take on anyone French. Mitchell-Carpentier came off the back of the Frenchman knocking out the British heavyweight champion 'Bombardier' Billy Wells in just 73 seconds. Boxing as we know it evolved in the UK, and yet a flash Frenchman was now knocking British boys out for fun. The Brits were not used to this kind of humiliation and to quote the April 1914 edition of the British magazine *Boxing News,* 'We have not been accustomed to repeated defeat, until these last few years, while the savour of victory has grown so familiar to the French palate that our friends can roll it over their tongues without any particularly undue excitement'. Losing to the French was unacceptable and George Mitchell from Bradford considered himself the man to put things back in order. Mitchell pledged to right the wrong of Billy Wells' lame showing and therefore challenged Carpentier to a sanctioned bout in Paris. The 'Orchid Man' accepted the fight for a £100 fee and vowed to do his best to knockout the amateur as quickly as he could. George Mitchell then agreed a £200 wager with Billy Wells that he would last longer than 73 seconds. Wells accepted the bet, although the fight organisers in Paris were optimistic and scheduled the bout at six rounds. The scenario today is a bit like an unknown amateur being upset with Andre Ward for beating Carl Froch and challenging him to a fight—and Ward accepting. Mitchell-Carpentier caught the imagination of the British press far more than their French counterparts, who for some strange reason did not take the contest seriously. *Boxing News* described the lopsidedness of the matchup as like a greyhound taking on a Bengal tiger.

'You're a plucky fellow', was Carpentier's message to Mitchell. According to a match report from the day, Mitchell came out swinging on the opening bell. Disaster. Fifteen seconds into the fight and Mitchell was down and given a count. Billy Wells' end of the bet was looking good, but 'The Mitch' beat the count and using all of his English resolve managed to fight on. He was knocked down two more times and got up before 73 seconds had past. After he was knocked down for a fourth time, Mitchell's corner threw the towel in. However, 95 seconds had now past, a whopping 22 seconds longer than Wells. Glory achieved and George Mitchell was able to restore British pride by being knocked out in a durable one minute and thirty five seconds. *Boxing News* commented, 'If the battered man did not show us that he could box, he gave proof of that good old British grit that borders on foolishness'. The journalist then elaborated, 'The only benefit to be gathered by this night's "sacrificial offering" is that it may deter other hot-headed amateurs from following Mr George Mitchell's example'.

A great moment of fame for the Yorkshireman, but Carpentier-Mitchell will not go down in history as a precursor to the Rumble in the Jungle. The story of the British hero George Mitchell ends on a sad note and as it turned out fighting for Britain became the death of him. In 1915 he was killed in the Great War. His brigade was practising bomb throwing and one went off in Mitchell's hand, making him one of 704,803 British soldiers to die in that conflict. Not the death that he would have wanted, but had he not perished from the exploding bomb his chances of surviving No-Man's Land were not great. To quote the boxing historian Miles Templeton, 'Mitchell's chances of surviving going over the top were probably less than his chances of beating Carpentier'.

Another classic contender for a fight that should not have happened, for the reason that one opponent was hideously overmatched, was Frank Bruno-Chuck Gardner from June 1987. Chuck Gardner from Minneapolis, was a boxer who made George Mitchell look like Joe Frazier. Weighing in at 242 lbs (110 kg) thanks to fat rather than muscle, his appearance was described by match commentator Harry Carpenter as looking more like a wrestler than a fighter. And bear in mind that statement was made in 1987 when the typical wrestler was expected to look like an out of shape, middle-aged, beer-drinking, bar-room brawler. 'He could have done the advert for that tyre company', said Henry Cooper, implying that Gardner resembled the Michelin Man. 'If he's 35 I'm 45', added the 53-year-old retired Londoner. With a bit of all-round improvement, it was possible that Gardner could have one day blossomed into a bum, or a tomato can. Who knows, with real dedication he may have even progressed into a journeyman.

Such was the lack of any quality of Bruno's opponent that the Londoner was in a total no-win situation at a time when he was trying to get back into contention for a world title fight. No form of victory would make Bruno look good against Gardener, whose record was 20-10 (which incredibly means that there were twenty fighters out there worse than big Chuck). For some odd reason, venues like Wembley Arena, Yankee Stadium, Atlantic City, Caesar's Palace and Madison Square Garden didn't play host to the fight. So it went to the Palais des Festivals et des Congres, in the great and legendary fighting city of…Cannes. The indoor arena is where films are screened at the Cannes Festival and in Bruno-Gardner they had a contender for Best Farce, Best Comedy and Most Overmatched bout. The fight started. Less than 60 seconds later the fight ended when Bruno left hooked (at first glance it looked like a jab) Gardner, who then fell through the ropes head first and totally sparked out. 'All the suggestions that this was not a good match, I'm afraid have been proved right…It's a pathetic sight at this festival hall in Cannes', said Harry Carpenter as Chuck Gardner was being scraped up from the canvas.

A concerned-looking Frank Bruno stood by Gardner's side hoping that he hadn't seriously hurt his opponent. In his autobiography, Bruno described the fight as, 'The biggest farce of my career. Chuck Gardener was a middle-aged man—some said he might have been fifty—with some great one-liners and no boxing ability'. Bruno's manager Terry Lawless thought it would be good for him to fight in an environment outside the pressure cooker of the UK. But the move backfired and Bruno's credibility was going to take a hit no matter what happened in the fight. 'I was beating up a fat comedian old enough to be my father. What good was that doing me? I was embarrassed, and disgusted'. As Frank Warren said: 'Chuck Gardner? He couldn't beat my gardener'.

After the match, TV presenters Des Lynam and Henry Cooper slammed the boxing authorities for putting Chuck Gardner's life in danger and Cooper hit out, 'I want to know how these guys get licences to carry on boxing. Who gave him a licence?'

In the same post-fight discussion, Lynam got Cooper to admit that, like most boxers, he and his manager would pick fighters who suited their style

Tim Witherspoon defeats Frank Bruno at Wembley Stadium in 1986. (Getty images)

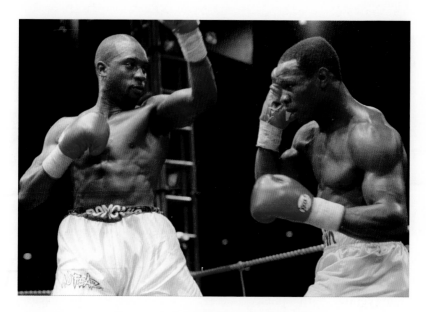

One of the greatest rivalries that did happen. World champions Nigel Benn and Chris Eubank do battle in 'Judgment Night' at Old Trafford in 1993. (Getty images)

However, both Benn and Eubank managed to avoid their fellow super middleweight champions—Michael Nunn (above) and James Toney (below). (Getty images)

Battle of the dodged—Britain's Herol Graham (blue shorts) v Jamaica's Mike McCallum (yellow shorts). (Getty images)

'Have you got anyone other than Burley?' Top of the Black Murderers' Row list, Charley Burley was too good for his own good. (courtesy of Harry Otty)

Riddick Bowe looks dejected as Lennox Lewis wins gold at the 1988 Olympics.
In the coming years the heavyweight super fight of the 1990s went to the doomed
podium of great lost matchups. (Getty images)

Sam Langford, the most avoided man in heavyweight boxing history, takes on
'Iron' Hague. (Courtesy of Clay Moyle)

Jack Johnson, one of the all-time greats. But he refused to give Langford a shot at his title. (Courtesy of Clay Moyle)

George Foreman versus Larry Holmes—enough said. (Getty images)

The opposite of a great fight that never was. Ali v Holmes tops the list of fights that should never have happened. (Getty images)

The post-fight press conference of one of the greatest matches that did happen. A dejected Thomas Hearns stands next to his rival Ray Leonard. Moments later 'The Hawk' Aaron Pryor took centre stage and challenged Leonard to a showdown. (Getty images)

The two most influential and controversial match makers in boxing history stand together in 2006. By this point in time Don King's influence had faded, but Bob Arum still controlled some of the sport's biggest names. (Getty images)

The Greatest finally do battle. Ali spars with Teofilo Stevenson in a Havana ring. (Getty images)

Friends don't fight? Rocky Graziano pretends to hit his buddy Jake LaMotta.
(Getty images).

The match that thankfully wasn't. Hogan v Tyson would have been farcical.
(Courtesy of Kyle David)

Will they or won't they? Floyd Mayweather and Manny Pacquiao face off, but only in a photo manipulation. (Getty images)

Ali-Marciao was never feasable, however in 1969 the two met in the ring in a tale with a contriversial ending.

and would occasionally duck and dodge. Cooper's manager's code for a potentially dangerous opponent was, 'He's a bit too ugly for us. We want good-looking fighters'.

Chuck Gardner isn't going to be in the boxing Hall of Fame anytime soon. However, there is a man who makes Chuck look like Rocky Marciano; a fighter so poor and a match so disjointed and scandalous that the footage became a YouTube hit with nearly 2 million views to date. Kenny Rainford from Liverpool was not a top contender, but he retired on 11-3, which shows he was a capable enough professional. His opponent in March 1993 was Brian Sutherland from North Carolina, and a man who made Rainford look like Roy Jones Jr. If ever there was a match that should never have happened, then it was putting a professional boxer like Rainford in with a man who I could have beaten. I honestly think I could, and I'm a writer not a fighter. However, Rainford-Sutherland is the only professional boxing match I've ever watched where I think I could have knocked out one of the opponents. How Brian Sutherland was given a licence and allowed to compete in a professional boxing ring is intriguing and scandalous. Sutherland came into the Rainford fight with a record of 0-1, having a month earlier been knocked out in the first round by a fighter called Danny Wofford. No footage of that match survives, but the Rainford match held in Mississippi is in the public domain and thrives. The commentary is in Spanish, which is not a problem because the laughter from the two Mexican commentators is in a universal language. Sporting a classic 1980s moustache and mullet haircut, Sutherland provided the world with the most inept, effeminate comedy performance in a boxing ring since Charlie Chaplin in the 1931 film *City Lights*. The bell rang and Sutherland threw a few comedy slaps before Rainford caught his opponent with a right cross. Sutherland, stunned, comically spun around then flopped to the floor as the Mexican commentators chuckled in approval. As Sutherland was falling to the canvas Rainford held out his arms as if to say, 'What the fuck?! That wasn't supposed to knock him out!'

Sutherland was billed as a street fighter turned boxer and retired with a record of 0-2, his dreams of being the next Willie Pep in tatters. I'd be curious to know what neighbourhood Sutherland made his name as a street fighter, because I'm fairly confident that even my mum could beat up everyone who lived there.

Continuing on a theme highlighted in the first chapter, Jake LaMotta versus Billy Fox in 1947 was a fight that should never have happened. But then you could say that about virtually all of Fox's matches. Billy Fox was an average fighter at best, who was controlled by the mob. There was certainly no other explanation as to why he was able to go on a winning streak of 36 fights—winning by knockout on each occasion!

The mob gift-wrapped him victories by paying off opponents to take falls. Fox was supposedly unaware of this and believed his wins were on the level. When he found out he wasn't the man he thought he was, the realisation mentally destroyed him and Fox died penniless.

For years, Jake LaMotta was frozen out of the world title scene by the mafia for refusing to take falls. Eventually, in order to get a shot against the legendary middleweight champion Marcel Cerdan, 'Raging Bull' took a dive against Fox in one of the most blatantly fixed fights of all time. More people were convinced that Vanilla Ice was from the hood than bought into LaMotta-Fox being clean. It was a fight that should never have happened, but taken by a fighter in order to allow a title fight that should have happened. Before the bout, fans and the media had strong suspicions of the stench that would transpire. Regarding the thrown fight, LaMotta recalls in his autobiography, 'The guy you're throwing against has to be at least moderately good. I mean this fight is in Madison Square Garden, and all the writers are there, plus a big crowd, so this little scuffle has got to look like a fight. But the mob guys, like a lot of others, are just plain stupid'. So overmatched was Billy Fox, even in a fixed fight, that soft punches thrown by LaMotta were staggering him. 'The first round, a couple of belts to the head and I can see a glassy look coming over his eyes. Jesus Christ, a couple of jabs and he's going to fall down?' said LaMotta, who added, 'I don't know how we even got past the first round without me murdering him. Sometimes I thought the air from my punches were affecting him, but we made it to the fourth round. By then if there was anybody left in the Garden who didn't know what was happening he must have been drunk'.

In round four the 'Restrained Bull' pretended to be poleaxed and leaned against the ropes to let Billy Fox hit him with about 15 punches that, in reality, did little damage. The referee stopped the 'fight' as the crowd chanted 'fake!' It was not convincing; this was a warrior who Sugar Ray Robinson could not put on the canvas, and yet Billy Fox was able to beat him. One reporter told LaMotta that his performance was so bad that he was surprised that the actors' union didn't picket the event. In 1960, LaMotta testified to the American Senate that he accepted a bribe. He was not on trial, but his testimony was one of many used against Frankie Carbo and Blinky Palermo who were found guilty of conspiracy and were imprisoned. In his autobiography, LaMotta spoke out on his reasoning for accepting $100,000 to lose to a fighter who wasn't in his league. 'Yes, I was ashamed when it was all over, but I did get the chance at the title and I won it…I was warned that I would never get a chance to fight for the title unless I agreed to their proposition. So what could I do? With my career and my life in jeopardy, how could I fight the mobsters?' After the admission of taking a fall in the Fox fight, LaMotta was ostracised from the sport. When Sugar Ray Robinson retired he was given a grand send off at Madison Square Garden. Many of Sugar's old foes were introduced, with the notable exception of the first man to beat him. 'Raging Bull' recalls, '[It] really hurt deep… So I threw the Billy Fox fight—okay, that's the cardinal sin in boxing, and it should be. But did anyone think about the cardinal sin that was being committed against me for so many years? I couldn't get a title shot unless I threw the fight'.

On a similar theme as an average fighter like Billy Fox being propped up by the mob, there are countless title fights that have taken place over the years where bum of the month has been given a shot at the belt because of the corrupt ratings system. Someone like Don King may never have been found guilty of match fixing in the traditional sense, but manipulating ratings can be a form of fixing fights. It's usually done to keep a boxer champion by fighting weak opponents, or to get a sub-standard fighter a big money title shot. For a perfect example we have Peter McNeeley, who moved up in the ratings by fighting tomato cans in the 1990s. To quote Jack Newfield in his biography of King:

> McNeeley was a white heavyweight who had built up a 32-1 record by beating a string of hand-picked losers and retirees who

had a combined record of 301 defeats in 424 fights. McNeeley's opponents had been knocked out a total of 152 times before they were judged incompetent enough to be matched with McNeeley. But King staged a press conference with McNeeley in Manhattan, promised him a championship fight and got him rated in the top ten, even though he did not deserve it.

Peter McNeeley was Mike Tyson's first opponent after coming out of jail in 1995. This was the boxing version of Burton Albion taking on Barcelona. As the two fighters entered the ring the contrast could not have been starker. Tyson was calm and looked like an assassin. McNeeley bounced up and down in his corner like a kangaroo about to take on a T-Rex. The master of ceremonies, Jimmy Lennon Jr., announced McNeeley as the WBA number-seven-rated heavyweight. Thanks to Don King. His record stood as a seemingly impressive 36 wins and only one loss; 30 by way of knockout. Again, thanks to Don King. As the two men faced each other in the stare down, McNeeley swayed from side to side while laughing as if he were at a comedy show. Tyson's expression simply stated 'You won't be laughing in a minute'. Actually, this was a comedy show. On the bell, McNeeley came flying out of his corner and swinging at Tyson. With nine seconds of the match gone, McNeeley hit the canvas. He quickly got back up and referee Mills Lane gave him a standing count. McNeeley proved that his head was clear by running round Mills Lane like he was playing Ring a Ring a Roses. McNeeley kept on swinging and showed plenty of heart. But he was down on the canvas again halfway through the second minute. He had the guts to beat the count but his corner stepped in to the ring to stop the fight. The crowd in unison chanted 'Bullshit!' People in their living rooms were probably also chanting the same at the outcome of a match billed as the largest viewed boxing event in history. The pay-per-view income for Tyson-McNeeley was $96 million, which is a lot of money for a two-minute comedy show. The fans had come out in force for the sport of boxing and were provided with a farce.

'What a letdown', protested the commentator. 'How utterly predictable', is what he should have said. A second-rate brawler had been falsely propped up the rankings to face one of the deadliest pugilists of all time. Nobody should have been remotely surprised with what transpired. Did anyone really believe Don King when he told the world, 'This is going to be the biggest event in the history of the world! That is a fact. This is not a fight, this is a global happening'.

McNeeley being a top ten-ranked boxer is like Peter Andre being rated in the top ten greatest solo artists. In the post-fight interview McNeeley had no regrets and said, 'I'm very satisfied with my performance. I made him miss some punches. I rocked him. I put up with all the media BS. I showed up. I was in the best condition in my life'. When asked if he would be returning to the ring, McNeeley replied, 'Fucking right I am!', before the interviewer informed him that men punching each other in the face is a family show. All the post-match pundit discussion directed venom at McNeeley's corner for stepping in and ruining the fight. Yet no focus was put on King or the WBA for not providing the fans with a more worthy opponent. As far as the Don was concerned the night was a success, and he beamed, 'Tonight I gave you sensation! Spectacle…It was the most terrific altercation mankind could wish to see! Who cares how long it lasted?'

So how can the ratings system get it so wrong? Perhaps in some cases, in the same way as the ratings system in the financial sector gets it 'wrong'—a conflict of interest. For example, in the financial sector the ratings agencies were funded by the banks. In many cases the same banks were selling dud products which had undeservedly good credit statuses. Triple-A ratings were given to companies just days before they filed for bankruptcy. The banks themselves were rated by the agencies which they funded.

In boxing, one common accusation is that some ratings have been manipulated by promoter influence as well as those who set the ratings.

Fights happen that not many people are interested in other than the promoters and a few individuals at a world title body—some of whom might every now and then receive a wad of undisclosed cash. In the 1990s the IBF got taken to court by the FBI, for ratings manipulation after an undercover investigation. Doug Beavers used to be in charge of the ratings system at the IBF and came clean on its methods of operating, after the FBI paid him a visit. 'What took you so long?' said Beavers to the FBI. He was the man who would admit to collecting the cash from the promoters, rate the fighters, and then pass on the money to the IBF. After being approached by the FBI, Beavers then complied with their investigation by going to IBF meetings with a hidden recorder. The tapes showed that at meetings to discuss ratings, money changed hands from Beavers to IBF President Bob Lee and politics was the main topic of discussion as opposed to the form and talent of the boxers.

Underhand dealings seemed widespread and one such bout that came about through alleged bribery was George Foreman's IBF title defence against Axel Schulz in 1995, a year when there were far more deserving title contenders than the big German. The fight only happened because Foreman's promoter Bob Arum is said to have paid $100,000 to the IBF to secure the easier opponent. Foreman beat Schulz on points, though most people watching thought the big German had clearly won and was robbed. Therefore a rematch was ordered, but not before $100,000 went under the table to the IBF, this time from Axel Schulz's promoter Cedric Kushner. Foreman, however, refused the fight and Kushner wasn't reimbursed—no receipt no refund. According to Doug Beavers testimony, the culture of rating's bribery was widespread. 'You paid them money and you got the advantage. It only takes one person to corrupt the whole system because the other people gotta pay just to keep the playing field level…It was like extortion…'.

In court, the promoters Cedric Kushner and Bob Arum both testified that routine pay offs were normal. Despite presenting hours of videotape evidence, the FBI's prosecution against IBF president Bob Lee ended with an acquittal on the racketeering charges (though he was found guilty of money laundering and tax evasion). Lee's defence team had accused Doug Beavers and the FBI of racism, as Lee was the only head of a boxing sanctioning body who was black. The evidence that promoters Arum and Kushner gave - was argued to be a conflict of interest because their rival promoter Don King was named by the prosecutors as a key benefactor to the IBF's ratings corruption. The defence also argued that Lee had every right to accept gifts and thank you payments from his business partners. In football, cash gifts are called bungs and are illegal (though probably more widespread than anyone dare imagine). In 1995, George Graham was sacked as Arsenal manager because he was caught receiving £450,000 by an agent in return for signing a player. Graham called the payment a gift and a thank you, but the conflict of interest issue is clear in that a player must be signed without any financial incentive to the manager.

Beavers reacted to the outcome of Bob Lee's trial by saying 'on the videotape I'm handing him money and talking about the specific fighter that he's taking the money for. Sounds like a bribe to me.'

Also surprised at Bob Lee's acquittal, Jack Newfield said 'Even though there was a mixed verdict you have the undercover surveillance videos and tapes that showed that people paid money for ratings. People paid money for sanctions. What did Cedric Kushner pay all that money for? What did Bob Arum pay all that money for? It's now a proven fact, despite the mixed verdict, that promoters and managers pay for ratings. Ratings are for sale. The definition of a contender is - for sale. Bobby Lee took that money.'

Let's create a new category: fights that didn't happen, but were claimed to have happened in order to create fights that should never have happened!

In 1977, Don King set up a 'super' tournament for the TV channel ABC. The tournament supposedly involved the best boxing talent America had to offer. Apart from the odd name like Larry Holmes and Willie Monroe, it didn't; in fact, some of the fighters were unaware they were contenders, let alone the public. Nigel Benn used to mock Chris Eubank for fighting 'road sweepers', and in the case of King's ABC-TV tournament, such an accusation wasn't that far off the truth. One of the entries was a man called Ike Fluellen who ended up in *The Ring's* top-ten ratings for junior middleweight. That must have been a tremendous shock to both him and his colleagues in the Houston police force. Fluellen was a journeyman and had not fought since October

1975. However, he made the top-ten ratings off the back of fictional matches that did not happen in 1976. He even got mentioned in *The Ring's* Progress of the Year section for his phantom wins. King had been dealing with a corrupt journalist at *The Ring* called Johnny Ort (aka Johnny Bought), who was in charge of the magazine's ratings, which were, and still are, seen as a standard bearer for fair and unbiased rankings.

King's ABC-TV tournament used Ort's corrupted ratings as the yardstick for the scheduling. Of the 60 fighters in the tournament, 11 had manufactured records with phantom bouts that nobody apart from Ort can recall happening. It would appear that such a bad effort was made to conjure up fake opponents that Ort used comedy names or the names of retired boxing legends. Opponents who were supposedly on the end of defeats in fictional fights included one fighter with the surname Bagelman (who we assume was flying the flag for Jewish fighters in the late 1970s) and a chap from Africa called Muhammad Wee Wee. It was recorded that Wee Wee had beaten Tommy Farr in 1974. A tremendous feat considering that the Welsh legend retired in 1953.

Ike Fluellen telephoned *The Ring* and told Johnny Ort that he had not fought at all in 1976. Ort, realising his mistake, took immediate action and moved Fluellen up to third in the rankings for the next month. Fluellen recalled to *Sports Illustrated,* 'I saw the March edition of *The Ring* and noticed that I was ranked third in the US and that I had also been added to the world rankings as No. 8 in group 2. That meant I was the No. 11 junior middleweight in the world. The only American listed ahead of me in the world rankings was Emile Griffith'.

Because of just one rogue journalist propping up weak fighters, the tournament was given credibility and the boxers who beat these 'contenders' would also be given higher rankings. King could then claim that the winners were beating top-ranked names, which might then help put them in the frame for future title shots. A genuine talent like Marvin Hagler was not allowed into the tournament because he and his management refused to sign for King, meaning he would have no control over Hagler after the ABC-TV tournament. Only fighters who would sign deals with Don King were considered the best boxing talent America had to offer.

Rather than highlighting just a few fights from this tournament as matches that should not have happened, it's better to put the whole tournament in a category on its own as a bum-fest which should never have been. The ratings scandal was uncovered by an ABC worker called Alex Wallau. He, along with the help of a boxing stat fan and expert called Malcolm 'Flash' Gordon, managed to prove that some of the fights that influenced the ratings were made up. Thanks to their findings, the tournament was scrapped before the heavyweight final could take place, which was to feature Larry Holmes and a fighter called Stan Ward (who retired with a record of 21 wins 7 defeats and 2 draws).

In the ABC tournament, King favoured white fighters, not because of their talent, but because he more than anyone was on the lookout for American great white hopes. But that didn't stop King from playing the race card for the show being scrapped: 'There is only one thing wrong. They got a spook running the tournament'. Had King replaced the first two letters of 'spook' with a C and an R, he would have got to the main reason.

Before the ABC-TV tournament, *The Ring's* ratings had so much credibility that fighters depended on them for title matches. The aftermath of this scandal transferred power to governing bodies who set ratings and sanctioned title matches. In the coming years this resulted in the formation of bodies like the WBO and IBF, who then flooded the sport with title belts and devalued the prestige of being a world champion. It was a missed opportunity for boxing to at least attempt to come clean and set up a single world governing body that dictated ratings and created matchups that were solely in the interest of the sport. King denied all accusations of corruption and put the blame solely on Johnny Ort. Even though King had paid $5,000 in cash to Johnny Ort he was not found guilty of ratings manipulation. 'I am shocked, saddened and appalled that *The Ring* is no longer the bible of boxing', proclaimed King Don the Innocent.

Let's wind the clock forward a bit. In 2012 there was a fight in London that many people were crying out loud should not be happening. Indeed, when mentioning the theme of this chapter to boxing fans the most common response I have received is, David Haye versus Dereck Chisora at Upton Park (or as it became known in the pre-match build up, 'The Sham at West Ham').

This fight came about off the notoriety of a brawl at the post-fight press conference of the Chisora-Vitali Klitshcko bout in February 2012. Chisora lost on points and at the press conference David Haye showed up and began rowing with Vitali's manager Bernd Bonte. The two men disputed whose fault it was that talks broke down to prevent a Vitali-Haye title bout. Bonte then cleverly manipulated the two British fighters to start on one another, 'Fight against this person [points at Chisora]. He showed heart, contrary to you. You showed us your toe!'

Del Boy chipped in with a message to Haye: 'Me and you will get it on in London. Be quiet'. Chisora then accused the south Londoner of being an 'embarrassment' to boxing. As David Haye went on a rant, Frank Warren, pound signs flashing in his eyes, suggested that Haye fight Chisora and the winner then get a shot at Vitali. Haye didn't seem interested in that proposal and carried on with the shouting match. As the trash talking continued, the tipping point for Chisora came when Haye reminded him, 'You lost to Tyson Fury'. That was too much to take and Del Boy walked over to the Hayemaker for his second fight of the evening. Haye hit him with a glass bottle before the two rolled around for a bit while being surrounded by manic photographers. Up on the press conference stage Vitali Klitschko calmly watched on. When the camera turned on him he couldn't resist a cheeky smile, which told everyone watching he was enjoying the entertainment. Vitali has a habit of looking well behaved and dignified when brawls break out, like the time in 2012 when a bundle between politicians took place in the Ukraine parliament. The one politician not involved in the fighting was the world heavyweight champion, who looked on in contempt at the mess that was transpiring before him.

Many accused the Haye-Chisora brawl of being contrived and one does have to question why the bottle that Haye used a weapon seemed to smash into tiny bits, as if it were a film prop made out of sugar glass.

The confrontation caused outrage and there were calls for both fighters to be banned, which they were by the British Boxing Board of Control. The easy way round this problem was to still hold the bout in England, but have it sanctioned by another European Union country's governing body. In this case that powerhouse of world boxing, Luxemburg, came to the rescue.

On reflection, this brawl was no more shameful than the countless press conference tear-ups there had been over the years. For example, it was no worse than Herbie Hide and Michael Bent wrestling in a puddle on the roof of a London hotel. As Barry Hearn helped pull Hyde off Bent, you could see a subtle gleam in his eye which suggested, 'box office gold!'

Or how about the Trevor Berbick-Larry Holmes post-press conference street fight that looked so staged it could have been used in a Hollywood film. Holmes jumped on top of a car roof and dived upon Berbick in a manner which should have immediately got him signed up by the World Wrestling Federation.

Mike Tyson and Lennox Lewis famously had an unsavoury press conference scrap in which Tyson's overall behaviour and use of language had sunk lower than anything ever publicly seen in the sport. Tyson was heavily condemned, but there were no credible calls for the fight to be called off.

The Haye-Chisora match at Upton Park was the biggest British showdown of 2012 and was high profile enough to warrant Michael Buffer as the master of ceremonies. To quote Steve Bunce, 'The Buffer only comes to town when it matters'.

The fight itself only lasted five rounds, but it was a good, well-fought contest that was met with sportsmanship and harmony once it was all over. Chisora took the fight to Haye and looked dangerous at times, but he was knocked out by a Hayemaker in the fifth round. By the end of the whole saga the opinion seemed to be along the lines of, 'well it wasn't a bad contest, so maybe it was okay for that fight to have happened'.

A lot of people say that David Haye versus Audley Harrison in 2010 was an embarrassment to the sport and should not have happened. But

I don't know what they're talking about because I don't recall that fight ever happening. I do recall a huge promotional campaign involving both men (not sure why or what it was about) and I do remember both Haye and Harrison in a boxing ring together at the O2 Arena in November 2010. But a fight, when? Although, as the two were standing in the ring together, there was an unsavoury moment when Haye, for some reason, threw a few punches at Harrison, who fell over.

1. There's an interesting irony to Berbick's career. In 1981, he was the man who finally finished off the main man Muhammad Ali. In 1986, he was the man who made way for the new main man, Mike Tyson, who flattened him within two rounds, becoming the youngest ever heavyweight champion. In 2006, Trevor Berbick was stabbed to death at a church in Jamaica over a land dispute. The man charged with murder was his 18-year-old cousin Harold Berbick.
2. On Antonio Tarver's Wikipedia page, unlike boxrec.com, his official fight record lists a win against Rocky Balboa in Las Vegas from 2006!

ROUND 10

Ten Crackers Not to Go Off

'I thought I was going to sign the contract…We sat in the home of his manager and the people who guided his career. I even climbed into the ring when he fought an ex-policeman who was 41 years of age.' **Steve Collins talking to *Sky Sports*.**

1. TONY ZALE-JAKE LAMOTTA

Adolf Hitler was an evil man. In the early 1930s he trampled on democracy and freedom in Germany and reigned as a murderous dictator. In the late 1930s his forces marched on Austria and Czechoslovakia who were then merged into the Third Reich. Invading Poland in 1939 resulted in a world war in which tens of millions of people were killed. On top of all of that, it ultimately denied boxing fans a Jake LaMotta versus Tony Zale contest.

Zale-LaMotta was a natural matchup in 1940s middleweight boxing. The son of Polish Americans, Tony 'Man of Steel' Zale was born Anthony Florian Zaleski in the year 1913. He was from the impoverished steel city of Gary in Indiana and as a boxer he gained a reputation as a hard hitter, as well as having solid punch resilience. LaMotta himself describes 'Man of Steel' as 'one of the toughest middleweights ever'. Zale's legendary rival Rocky Graziano described him as 'tougher and faster than anybody I ever fought in my life'. Part of his resilience would no doubt be attributed to impoverished early beginnings where he was subjected to child labour in the factories of Indiana. Zale died in 2006 and in his obituary the *Independent* stated: 'Unlike Graziano, who was a likeable rogue, Zale was a dignified, reserved man who treasured his privacy'. Jake LaMotta, who is still alive at the time of writing, will not have an obituary that praises his personality. Born in 1921 he was portrayed in the film Raging Bull as a moody and violent bastard; yet nobody will ever doubt his toughness and determination as a fighter.

The subject of a Zale-LaMotta dream match was discussed in a 1991 edition of *The Ring* by Angelo Dundee, Teddy Brenner and Hank Kaplan. They were asked to make a prediction of the outcome and all three men tipped a tough fight and favoured LaMotta for the win. Predicting who would win in a Zale-LaMotta fight is a regular debate on Internet boxing forums. A common consensus seems to be that if the fight happened in the early 1940s, when La Motta was a novice, then the current champion Zale would carry the edge. However, by the late 1940s the younger LaMotta would be the favourite against Zale who was near the end of his career. The two men could not feasibly have fought for a few years during that decade and some order of events are as follows:

1934: Tony Zale begins his professional career.

1939: World War II kicks off. America stays neutral.

March 1941: Jake LaMotta begins his professional career and by the end of the year would have a record of 17 wins and three losses.

November 1941: NWA middleweight champion Zale becomes undisputed world middleweight champion by beating NYSAC middleweight champion Georgie Abrams.

December 1941: Ten days after Zale wins the world title, the Japanese air force bombs Pearl Harbour. America declares war on Japan and her ally Germany.

1942: *The Ring* editor Nat Fleischer declares Jake LaMotta the best middleweight in the division. *Boxing* magazine journalist Billy Stevens picks LaMotta as the fighter of the year.

1943: Zale is enlisted in to the US Navy and sent to war. This puts him out of professional boxing action for three years. LaMotta is spared a global conflict and fights his wars in the boxing ring.

1946: The war is over and Zale returns to boxing. He begins a legendary title trilogy with LaMotta's friend Rocky Graziano. Meanwhile, LaMotta continues to build up an impressive winning record.

1947: LaMotta takes a dive to the mob-controlled fighter Billy Fox. By finally bowing down to the mafia it puts him in line for a shot at the title.

1948: After beating Graziano to win the trilogy 2-1, Zale then defends his title against French fighter Marcel Cerdan. A headline reads: 'ZALE TO FIGHT CERDAN FOR TITLE; LAMOTTA

NOW NO.1 CONTENDER FOR 4 YEARS'. LaMotta is in line to take on the winner. Zale loses the title to the French fighter and retires with a fight record of 67-18-2.

June 1949: LaMotta beats Marcel Cerdan and wins the world middleweight title.

Even if Zale had not served in the war, the mafia stood between him and LaMotta. Those who 'played ball' got title shots. Those who didn't, didn't. LaMotta for many years didn't. One headline from the time reads: 'ROCKY AND ZALE IN THIRD TITLE GO. WHY NOT LAMOTTA NEXT?' In his biography LaMotta says, 'My old friend Rocky Graziano was off fighting Tony Zale, but was I going to get a crack at the winner? You can guess the answer, free'.

So to blame for a non-contest between Zale and LaMotta, we have to thank Adolf Hitler, the Japanese air force and the mafia. What a lovely bunch.

2. VITALI KLITSCHKO-NIKOLAI VALUEV

To say that the Klitschko brothers, Vitali and Wladimir, have faced absolutely everyone out there during their era is not 100 percent accurate. In boxing there's always someone who slips through the net, which in this case would be the Russian giant Nikolai Valuev, the biggest heavyweight champion of all time and a man whose title reign coincided with the dominance of the two Ukrainians. The retired Beast from the East was born in Russia 1973, and at 7'1 and 323 lbs (146.5 kg) goes down in history as both the tallest and heaviest world champion, not to mention being the most incredible- and intimidating-looking man in boxing history. Since his retirement in 2009, the 'Beast' has worked in film. When Hollywood needs a monster Nikolai is the man to call, considering he makes Godzilla look cute and cuddly. Valuev however, does go down in history as probably the least skilled champion since Primo Carnera held the heavyweight title in the mid 1930s. Standing at 6'6" and weighing in at 266 lbs (120 kg), the 'Ambling Alp' Carnera was the biggest heavyweight champ in history until Valuev arrived on the scene seven decades later. One thing that the two men did not share in common was that Carnera took some brutal beatings in the ring, while Valuev never took a mauling by anyone. The Russian lost just twice by way of close points decisions to fellow countryman Ruslan Chagaev and Britain's David Haye, losing his WBA title on both occasions.

It does seem farcical that neither Vitali nor his fellow brother and champion Wladimir faced Valuev in a title unification, considering the lack of marquee fight prospects there were in the heavyweight division. A Valuev-Klitschko bout would have caught the attention of the casual boxing fan, which cannot be said of most of their other opponents. Such a contest would not have been hard to promote, especially when you take into consideration the rivalry between the two nations, Russia and Ukraine. Before his retirement in 2009, Valuev had accused the Klitschko brothers of not wanting to take a risk against him and said, 'I have a feeling that my bout against one of the Klitschko brothers will only take place if I lose one of my legs or something. In a word, during telephone conversations they are ready to fight, but it's different in practice'.

Nikolai Valuev was Don King's last meaningful claw hold in boxing.

The Klitschkos wanted nothing to do with boxing's pantomime villain but that didn't stop King from trying to sign them up when they were emerging stars. Initially, the brothers were flattered and excited that the man who promoted Mike Tyson and Muhammad Ali was showing an interest in them. King invited both brothers to his mansion to lure them into contract deals. King told them they would be part of one big happy family and to further impress them strolled over to his grand piano and played Mozart's 'Don Giovanni' like a master pianist. Vitali was impressed and thought, 'What a multi-talented person', before seeing the real artist that King was. 'I walked around the table and saw it was all a fake. The piano was playing itself! I could see one of the pedals moving without him touching it!' Returning from the piano a pumped King hollered, 'Ain't no other promoter who can play like that'. Not wanting to be played by King, the Klitschkos turned him down to be their own bosses. Valuev deep down has some admiration for that and said, 'If my career to some extent depends on my promoters, Wilfried Sauerland and Don King, the Klitschkos have a thousand times repeated that they themselves are the masters of their fate. They own the K2 production company, which organizes all their fights. The brothers are good businessmen; they carefully plan their each and every move, and they don't want to take unjustified risks'. He added, 'It is clear that commercial interests prevail when the Klitschkos choose their opponents...Who between them is stronger? Each has his pluses and minuses, so both boxers Wladimir and Vitali are approximately equal...I have a normal attitude towards Vitali and Wladimir, furthermore—in their previous fights I wanted victory for the brothers and not for their competitors'.

In 2009 it was reported that Vitali-Valuev had been agreed by both men and was on. Writing for Boxingnews24, reporter Matt Stein covered the story and wrote: 'In facing Vitali, the seven foot, 320 lbs [145 kg] Valuev will easily be getting the biggest payday of his long 16-year pro career. It's unfortunate that it has taken this long for Valuev to get a career-defining fight, however. But as the saying goes, better late than never'.

Better late than never was the view in 2009 and as it turned out 'never' prevailed. Valuev went on to lose to David Haye in late 2009 and retired soon afterwards. The following year in 2010 Vitali made an offer to Valuev which was down from the initial $2.5 million previously on the table and insisted, 'I'm offering him $1.5 million. Now it's around $1.2 million. He can accept that or not. He is not a mandatory challenger. So if not, they might have to wait for eternity for a world title shot against me'. By 2012 there were still talks of a possible Vitali-Valuev fight. However, the big Russian wasn't prepared to come out of retirement, as, like Vitali, he too has political aspirations. Dr Iron Fist spoke of the missed opportunity with the Beast from the East and said, 'It would have been interesting to see where we [could] find sparring partners for this fight. I'm 6'7" and Valuev is [7 foot]. I never fought against such a big fighter and this fight would be interesting for me, [and] especially for all the audience...I have a dream to fight Nikolai, but he decided [that] because of a lot of injuries, to retire'.

By 2012, Vitali was past 40 years of age and Valuev only a few years younger and so it would have been a typical case of the fight that no one cared about anymore. Valuev and Vitali Klitschko were not blood brothers, nor close friends; but it was more convenient not to fight and to remain champions, in what is a classic example of too many title belts ruining the sport.

What's interesting about the heavyweight division in recent years is that it's been dominated mostly by white men, and yet public interest slipped under the radar. For years, charismatic black Americans had dominated the division while promoters were scrambling to find a great white hope to catch the public imagination. Early 21st Century heavyweight boxing was ruled by white Eastern Europeans, and nobody west of Ukraine and Russia seemed particularly excited. After all the 'hope' of a great white hope, we discovered that many boxing fans were more colour blind than anyone gave credit. It's the country where the fighter came from which was what mattered more. In the second decade of the 21st Century we have a situation where the heavyweight division is now looking for a whole host of great hopes and nobody remotely cares what skin colour they are. How different from the second decade of 20th Century when Jack Johnson reigned supreme…

3. BILLY WELLS-JACK JOHNSON

Winston Churchill was a supreme wartime leader for Britain, but his greatness as a saviour ends there. His domestic record as a politician, before and after the Second World War, portrays an aloof elitist who had contempt for the working-class struggle for better social conditions. He turned the guns of the army on striking miners. He campaigned strongly against the concept of a national health service and a welfare system. And if that wasn't bad enough, he also cancelled a boxing match that people wanted to see.

To describe Wells-Johnson as a potential 'cracker' is not at all justified, and it was an example of poor matchmaking at a time when better fighters were denied shots. But the reasons for its cancelation were not justified either, because they were born out of prejudice rather than concern over the sport. 'Bombardier' Billy Wells was described by one British journalist of the time as a 'good second-rater', so there should be no illusions that the British champion could have remotely troubled the great Jack Johnson at the height of his powers. But if a fight is going to be cancelled, then it should be for better reasons than a religious puritanical dislike of the sport, along with political paranoia regarding maintaining a colonial empire.

Organised championship boxing originated in Britain in 1719 with the emergence of the first ever champion James Figg. In the early part of the following century, African Americans Bill Richmond and Tom Molyneux had both fought for the heavyweight title in the UK and lost against Tom Cribb. The colour line was not put in their way. In the 20th Century Sam Langford was paid more by UK promotions than back in the US. There was a degree of acceptance and respect towards black fighters in the UK—but, all is relative—the forces of racial prejudice were still very strong. British society at large was racist; it just wasn't as racist or violent as America.

Jack Johnson sailed to England in June 1911 to be present at the coronation of King George V. He was a figure who drew intrigue on these shores and generated huge crowds for his public appearances. When asked if he had come to the UK to fight for America he responded, 'Well I should say not. What has America ever done for me or my race? Here I am treated like a human being'.

On 2 October Johnson was booked to defend his title against Billy Wells at Earls Court. Johnson complimented the ability of Wells in order to build up interest in what was a clear mismatch. When talking off the record about why he wasn't bothering to train properly Johnson would admit, 'I'll beat him easy'.

The Earl of Lonsdale called for the match to be scrapped because it was a mismatch, but that didn't stop the 10,000-capacity Empress Arena at Earls Court from selling out. Johnson was a name who put bums on seats no matter who the opponent was, not to mention Billy Wells being a good looking local boy who some fans would have carried a fantasy belief of being able to win.

Enter the Reverend F. B. Meyer, a campaigner against many of the world's evils, which included boxing. The British magazine *Boxing* described Meyer as the figurehead of the 'No Fight Brigade' and gave the reverend a platform on which to give his reasoning for campaigning against a sport which he described as 'inconsistent with the manhood that creates a great nation'.

Revered Meyer disapproved of fighting for money and recommended to young people that they focus instead on 'boxing the devil'. He was out to make a name for himself by banning something and had already tried and failed to criminalise the selling of Karl Marx literature. He was more puritan than many leading voices of the church and called on rebel clergyman to hold sermons which denounced Wells-Johnson. The fact that Wells-Johnson was interracial was in the eyes of Meyer even more reason to ban this match and he told *Boxing:*

> So far as battles between coloured men and whites are concerned, I am absolutely opposed to them…When white opposes black it is not a game of skill, for the black nature has more fire in the blood than the white and has more passion. The reason men like to see blacks fighting whites is because the black men fight so

passionately; it introduces the element of animalism which you do not see in the case of two white fighters.

According to Johnson's biographer Geoffrey C. Ward, 'Johnson was disgusted. English preachers knew nothing about boxing, he said, and even less about black people. Boxing simply pitted one individual against another. It had nothing to do with race'.

Boxing magazine was a keen supporter of the fight going ahead and predicted, wrongly, that Meyer's campaign would be doomed to failure and that pugilism was, 'The best possible test of British manhood'.

The very heart of the No Fight Brigade's crusade was to prevent the humiliation of British manhood in a spectacle which contradicted the Empire. In 1911, Britain ruled lands in all corners of the world. Johnson-Wells had only one realistic outcome: a black man easily knocking out a popular white fighter who had once served in the British army. What message would this send out to those under the rule of Empire? The worst fear was that British vulnerability would be exposed and that the repressed people would rise up against the rule of imperialism. All that was on show was a mere boxing match, but this fear of damage to the Empire was unashamedly aired by a writer for the *Times* who warned:

> Surrounded, as we are, by natives in all stages of civilisation, from the sea to the Zambezi, we seek to establish our supremes, by force of character and by codes of conduct…based upon principles that we can stand up for and defend. To attempt to do this by precept, if not backed by example would be futile, for we should be held

up to scorn and derision by the natives who think-and there are many such-and who draw conclusions and comparisons. How can we look them in the face when such a fight is permitted to take place in the heart of the Empire? Why pit black against white at all, and why do so with all the odds in favour of the black man? And why permit the contest to take place in London before a European audience and with official sanction? The baneful effects will be felt far beyond the spectators who witness the fight. It will make the position of the white man more difficult still in distant parts of the Empire.

The highest religious leader in the land, the Archbishop of Canterbury, now supported Reverend Meyer and came out as an opponent of Wells-Johnson. He wrote a letter to Churchill calling on the fight not to happen, and his message was supported by other powerful church leaders, including Sir Baden-Powell. What had started as a campaign doomed to failure by a fringe religious sect now had mainstream Church of England backing! Winston Churchill believed passionately in the Empire and if anyone was going to sympathise with an argument that a mere boxing match could undermine queen and country, he would.

The future of the fight lay with the future prime minister, who one month before the fight, took a puff of a cigar, sniffed his lip north and said, 'I have made up my mind to try and stop the Wells-Johnson contest. The terms are utterly unsporting and unfair'.

A few days later, Johnson and Wells stood next to each other in Bow Street Court in one last bid to save the fight. Reverend Meyer was in attendance and he along with everyone else in court was won over by the charm and charisma of Johnson, who represented himself and cross-examined witnesses. In one brilliant moment, Johnson cross-examined a police chief who claimed that the outcome of the fight would cause a breach of the peace. Johnson reminded the court that not so long ago Sam Langford had beaten a white fighter called Bill Lang in London. Johnson asked him if Langford-Lang had caused a breach of the peace. The officer could not answer. 'Have you ever seen any championship contest?', asked Johnson to which the answer was, 'No'. Johnson got the officer to admit that had no knowledge whatsoever of boxing, yet despite such an impressive performance in court the match was still cancelled. Once Churchill got involved, the wish of two boxers was not going to override the will of a leading figure of the world's largest empire. 'Unsporting and unfair' was Churchill's reasoning, but that is also how you could describe soldiers firing bullets at striking workers—but that was one mismatch to which Churchill did give the go ahead.

4. CHARLEY BURLEY-THE WORLD

'The finest all round fighter I ever saw.'

Eddie Futch, Boxing trainer of legends shares his thoughts on Burley

Racial apartheid in boxing was not always limited to the heavyweight division. In the 1940s the boxing writer Budd Schulberg used the term 'murderer's row' to describe a group of black boxers who were denied fights that should have happened. Top of the list on murderer's row was a man named Charley Burley who was born in Pittsburgh in the year 1917 to a white mother and black father. Regarded as one of the most unrecognised all time greats, Burley's name is always accompanied by that sad phrase, 'the greatest fighter never to be a world champion'. Much like the dodged middleweight Mike McCallum, Burley's fight record is most noticeable for not listing the great middleweights of his era.

Avoided like a carrier of the bubonic plague, the fighters that stayed clear of Burley read like a who's who of 1940s middleweight boxing: Tony Zale, Marcel Cerdan, Rocky Graziano and Jake LaMotta to name just a few. It's said of Charley Burley that his biggest mistake was being black and far too good for his own good. *Boxing News* noted, 'It didn't take too long for him to be considered persona non grata'.

Burley's easy first round knockout of Phil McQuillan in 1942 was a major turning point in his career. People saw what happened, turned around and said 'not for me'. At that time an overtly dangerous black fighter was still easy to shun and the notorious Jim Crow Laws that legalised discrimination and segregation would remain in American law for another two decades until the civil rights movement broke it down in 1965.

'No! No! No! I don't want Burley. You can have him for Christmas, for New Year's, or your Aunt Tillie's birthday. But never mention his name again'.

Those were the words of Johnny Ray, who was manager of Billy Conn, the world light heavyweight champion. Billy Conn, like Burley, was also from Pittsburgh and gave the heavyweight champion Joe Louis one of the hardest fights of his career and nearly won, until he was knocked out in the

13th round (in today's time stipulations Conn would have won a 12-round decision). Yet when offered to Conn, the dangerous middleweight was run from like a zombie in *28 Days Later*. Even the great Sugar Ray Robinson's management steered their man clear of the dangerous Burley. Robinson's manager George Gainford told matchmakers that Burley was not right for Robinson's style and asked, 'Have you got anyone else other than Burley?' In the November 1946 edition of *Boxing News*, Burley was featured on a front page that carried the heading, 'Long Rated Pittsburgh Middleweight Menace Dares Zale, Graziano, LaMotta to meet him'.

Dare they did not, even though magazines such as *Boxing News* and *The Ring* did push the case for Burley and apply pressure. The public knew very little of him, to the frustration of *The Ring* which in December 1946, published, 'To boxing authorities, particularly managers of middleweights, Burley needs no introduction. They know him well. But to the public at large—and, after all, it's the public who pay the freight, Charley is practically unknown'.

The Ring's ratings in 1946 had LaMotta and Burley as the top two contenders to Tony Zale's middleweight title, and suggested that instead of waiting for a train that wouldn't come, they could fight each other. The magazine stated, 'There are those who feel that Burley could do no worse than an even money proposition in a showdown with Jake. They are about on a par in fighting ability'.

Not only did the fight not happen, but Burley didn't even get a passing mention in LaMotta's autobiography *Raging Bull*. Just like Jake LaMotta, Burley was in part kept out in the cold for not dealing with the mafia and taking a dive. It wasn't just about race and being too good; Burley's career coincided with the most notorious years of the mafia having a major influence in fight scheduling. Harry Otty, author of the acclaimed book *Charley Burley and the Black Murderers' Row,* wrote:

> It has been reported that, after seeing the Pittsburgh master in action, Sugar Ray Robinson said 'I'm too pretty to fight Charley Burley'. The real truth was that Burley was far too honest to fight Ray Robinson—he was offered a series of three fights with the Sugarman, with a provision that he lose the first. He wasn't interested. Throughout his career Burley refused to 'play ball' so was ostracised by the powers that be and never received a shot at any title.

Charley retired with a record of 83 wins, 12 losses and a draw. For a man spoken about with such awe, 12 career losses may seem like a contradiction, but many of those losses were to bigger opponents. Just like Sam Langford who was really a middleweight, his reputation preceded him, so he was forced to fight above his weight class. In an article on Burley in 1946, *Boxing News* said:

> A guy's got to eat…Lack of work in his own weight forced him into the ring with Jimmy Bivins Cleveland heavyweight ace…And don't let anybody tell you that 'Cleveland' James didn't have his hands fuller than full in winning a tight ten-round verdict over li'l Charlie!. . .Easy fight just isn't in the lexicon when you're in there with Burley—regardless of your weight.

Another two of Burley's losses were against the legendary Ezzard Charles, who would go on to win the world heavyweight championship. Both matches were roughly in the space of one month and in-between those bouts, Burley still found time for a match against Holman Williams for the revived World Coloured Middleweight Championship. In 1942, the American forces were fighting against Nazi ideology, yet back home the World Coloured Championship and Negro Baseball League were still considered acceptable. Burley and Holman fought each other six times with each man winning on three occasions. Holman got a given shot at Marcel Cerdan and Jake LaMotta and lost against both men in July and August of 1947. Burley, who had beaten Holman three times, was not granted the same opportunity.

Early on in his career, Burley's path was held back in part by him standing up for principles. He had the chance to fight for a spot on the American team for the 1936 Olympics which were held in Nazi-controlled Berlin. America was quite happy to give black athletes an equal platform to compete if it meant bringing home gold medals. Burley, however, sidestepped the chance to travel to Germany because he disagreed with Nazi politics and racial prejudice. Instead, he agreed to fight in the People's Games, which were to be held in Barcelona in the same year. With the outbreak of the Spanish Civil War, that tournament became as doomed as Burley's future chances of getting a middleweight title shot.

5. RICKY HATTON-JUNIOR WITTER

'If Junior was fighting in my back garden I'd draw the fucking curtains.'

Ricky Hatton

During an amateur boxing event in 2012 at the Emirates Stadium I ended up having a chat with former fighter turned TV pundit Richie Woodhall. I mentioned the theme of the book and that I'd be interested to know a lost fight that he thought should be included. Woodhall had a long think about it and replied, 'In terms of domestically, I would say Hatton v Witter'.

I was delighted to hear him say that because it was on my list to be mentioned. Woodhall continued, 'For me, that fight would have been 50-50'.

That statement, however, did surprise me, simply because in the eyes of many, Hatton would be the favourite. I asked Woodhall if he really believed that it would have been that close and he was insistent. 'Absolutely. I don't know why they didn't get it on. Maybe Hatton was just too big a star compared to Witter, therefore the pay may have been too far in his favour'.

This is a matchup that resonates strongly with boxing folk from these shores. While in conversation with retired Irish heavyweight Joe Egan I mentioned Hatton-Witter, to which 'Big Joe' piped up, 'That was a fight that should have happened, definitely, no doubt about it'.

Not to say however that there isn't doubt out there. For example, when talking to Barry Hearn I mentioned Woodhall's suggestion of Hatton-Witter, to which the Essex promoter laughed and said, 'Why?. . .No one wants to watch Junior Witter. A clever fighter, but you can't hit him. It's like watching paint dry. I think he's [Richie Woodhall] quite sensible normally, but I'll have to have a word with him about that one. He's obviously been taking some pills if he says he wants to watch that fight'.

Hearn added, 'Witter's like Herol Graham—top of the list of Who wants him? Answer: nobody. It's cruel but it's sad'.

Most importantly, that nonchalant attitude towards Witter was shared by Hatton. The 'Hitman' had built up a worldwide reputation while Witter was attempting to do the same. Manchester's finest accused the Sheffield man of 'having no following whatsoever' and said in his autobiography, 'I reckon it couldn't take five Frank Warren's to build him up'.

Whenever Hatton talked about Junior, he did so in a manner that suggested that he was uninspired, and he referred to him as the 'Steve Davis of boxing'.

Hatton's a hard man to accuse of sidestepping a challenge and if anything he's accused more of over-confidence in his own ability. In December 2008 he was in attendance at the Oscar De la Hoya-Manny Pacquiao bout at the MGM Las Vegas. He witnessed the complete destruction of the legendary 'Golden Boy' as the 'Pac Man' terrorised his older opponent in eight brutally one-sided rounds. The 'Pride of East LA' may have been past his prime by this point, but Pacquiao's speed, class and firepower were still clear as daylight and Hatton saw the destruction firsthand. While many world titleholders would have run a mile from the prospect of fighting such a chilling opponent, the 'Hitman' put his name to the fight. The rest his history; and for Hatton, it's horrible history.

Hatton's dismissive attitude towards Witter was born from an incident directly after the 'Hitman' beat Jon Thaxton at Wembley in 2000 for the British light welterweight title. After a tough 12 rounder, Witter approached Ricky and challenged him to a match. Thaxton and Witter were both stable mates of the Ingles and Hatton accused the Sheffield-based trainers of dismissing the brave Thaxton to stand by the new challenger Witter. Hatton saw the move as disrespectful to both him and his opponent directly after such a brutal fight. As Hatton was being asked about future opponents Witter chipped in, 'And you've got me of course'. He then praised Hatton on his win, who sarcastically replied, 'Oh, thanks very much'. But Witter warned him, 'I'm gonna take that belt off you…I will destroy you'. Throughout Witter's tirade Hatton's expression suggested that he was thinking—this is my moment, now fuck off.

In 2001, Witter beat Alan Temple and this time Hatton turned up at ringside after Junior claimed that he was the best light welterweight in the world. 'Do you think you can beat me?' asked Witter, to which Hatton replied, 'I know I can beat you'. The 'Manchester Hitman' suggested that Witter continue to put in good performances to raise his profile, but warned, 'To be honest you sell no tickets, you've been a little bit boring in the past. But in fairness to you in the last few fights you've been looking a bit more like [you are being exciting]…' Witter then accused their joint promoter Frank Warren of looking after Hatton's interests only, prompting Hatton to say that the fight should go ahead because it was a good clash of styles. The two then stopped arguing and posed together for the cameras. In contradiction to the story the photographs would imply, this would be the one and only time the two men would face each other in the ring.

While backstage with other boxers and waiting to appear on *BBC Sports Personality of the Year*, Witter approached Hatton to tell him, 'One day'.

'One day, what?', replied the 'Hitman', who accused Junior of 'acting like a dickhead'. At the after-show party, Hatton had said that he'd be willing to fight Witter as soon as possible; a statement that the Sheffield man took literally and went out to the car park. The challenges did get through to Hatton who told Frank Warren, 'I want to fight that tosser'. Warren advised that the timing wasn't quite right and to be patient and wait for the demand. In 2003, Sky Sports announced the fight was to go ahead and both Witter and Hatton sat down together for a press conference. Witter boasted that his soon to be opponent had ducked out of fighting him at the BBC car park and that Hatton had generally spent the night avoiding him. Hatton replied that he was more interested in talking to, 'the more important people' of *Sport's Personality of the Year* like Alan Shearer, and told Witter, 'Why would I want to talk to you? You're not exactly Mr Personality'.

Despite holding a press conference, no papers were signed and no match happened. One has to feel sorry for Witter, as it must be frustrating to be denied a sporting opportunity on the basis of lacking charisma and popularity. Other sports don't operate in that manner, as only merit through results dictates scheduling. From Witter's point of view he had merited a fight with Hatton and by 2006 both men were world champions at light welterweight at the very same period in time. Hatton held the WBA and IBF belts while Junior was the WBC champ after winning the vacant title against DeMarcus Corley at Alexandra Palace. The natural matchup at that point had to be to rekindle the lost match of Witter and Hatton and put on a British super-fight to unify the world titles.

Hatton went Stateside to pursuit a dream of total world domination, but famously lost his unbeaten record against Floyd Mayweather in 2007. Speculation remained that a fight with Witter could still happen. The *Daily Express'* Niall Hickman referred to both Brits as the best light welterweights in the world; however the Hitman had signed a deal with HBO and told Witter that he would have to raise his profile in order to get a shot. Speaking to Sky News he said, 'Junior Witter needs to do his part of the deal by fighting some big names. I don't owe Junior Witter anything considering the way he's spoke to me over the years. He can get the fight by proving himself. Even then it will happen if and when I want it'.

In March 2008 the Manchester Mexican faced the real Mexican Juan Lazcano at the City of Manchester Stadium. At the time, Steve Bunce suggested that Witter would have been a more worthy opponent for Hatton considering that in Lazcano's last fight he lost to Vivian Harris, who Junior had beaten. Hatton's argument that Witter had no following held a lot of water, but what kind of a following did Juan Lazcano have? Buncey conceded that Witter had not caught the imagination of the public, but also made the point, 'If Ricky Hatton can sell 55,000 tickets against Juan Lazcano, who's 33 years of age, who hasn't fought for 18 months, what would he sell against a guy who's known as his nemesis? Who's known as his greatest rival in this country. I reckon they could have done Wembley. . .this is the fight the British fans want'.

Buncey then suggested that Witter was too big a threat to Hatton and if he lost then it would ruin his plans for more mega-fights in America.

Junior planned to prove his worth further by defending his WBC title in Nottingham against the emerging American Timothy Bradley. Before the fight, Witter noted that Hatton's army of fans were writing to boxing magazines and demanding that the two meet. He claimed the problem was that casual fans had not seen enough of him and that the Bradley fight (on ITV to a larger than normal audience) would be the turning point in his career. It was, but not in the way that Junior had hoped. Bradley won a split decision to the shock of the Nottingham crowd and from that point on Witter's career slowly faded out into obscurity, unlike Bradley's. Rather than slowly fade out, Ricky's career was blown out of the water in stunning fashion. In May 2009, Manny Pacquiao knocked the 'Hitman' out in two one-sided rounds. The devastated Hatton retired, knowing that even if he remained active his worldwide drawing power was now over. He'd been in too many wars and his punch resilience had gone. To the despair of many, but also to the excitement of many, Hatton came back in 2012 with plans to go out in style and heal old wounds. After beating Vyacheslav Senchenko he had desires to get back in the title scene. Although not drawing much attention to his fights, Junior had remained active. He'd spent a whole decade calling out Hatton and couldn't foresee any realistic direction in which Hatton could now go. 'He should leave it as that, unless there's a purpose behind him coming back—like fighting me. If he came back to fight me then I could see the point in it. But if it is to beat non-punchers like Malignaggi then there is no point'. In the same interview, Junior did praise Hatton for having a fantastic career and not having anything to prove to anyone. To the prediction of many sceptics, Hatton was sadly floored by a Senchenko body shot and retired for a second time. His real victory was getting himself back in shape and challenging his demons of depression and unhealthy living. Perhaps a comeback fight with Witter would have been a better option, as Hatton would not have been the only one in the ring who was well past his best.

In his 2013 autobiography, the 'Hitman' remained unapologetic for his refusal to fight Witter, but conceded that if the fight happened it would have been tough because of Junior's ability to fight both orthodox and southpaw.

Hatton's prediction is that he would have taken Witter apart by getting in close, but there is a doubt, and that's the foundation of a fight that should happen. Witter-Hatton falls into that sad category of bitter feuds that never got settled in the ring. But time is a healer and in Hatton's autobiography he did have the grace to say, 'Now bygones are bygones I can't help but admire Junior for the titles he won…'

6. PRINCE NASEEM HAMED-ARTURO GATTI

'I ain't trying to brag. But I was bloody good!'
Naseem Hamed

Steve Bunce, who rates Hamed as highly as any British fighter, told me that during a fight in Las Vegas in 2001, he spoke to Floyd Mayweather who mentioned Hamed as a possible opponent. 'Pretty Boy' told Buncey that he was a big fan of the 'Prince' and that the two should fight. One of Mayweather's entourage then chipped in and said that Hamed should bring his 'Arabs' over from the UK and they could 'get it on with the brothers!'

Hamed-Mayweather is dream matchup heaven and it was very feasible. However, the prospect of Naseem Hamed fighting anyone was dashed in 2002 when he surprisingly retired at the age of just 28; his reasoning being reoccurring hand injuries and a desire to spend more time with his family.

Some have questioned whether or not the 'Prince' retired with a broken heart. . .Joe Calzaghe used to be on the road with Naseem and in his autobiography referred to him as a 'schoolyard bully'. Hamed had been verbally mocking the laid-back cruiserweight world champion Carl

Thompson and ridiculing his earnings, which were pittance compared to the money-drawing 'Prince'. One day Thompson lost his patience with the Sheffield featherweight, called him a 'fucking dwarf' and offered to take him outside to teach him a lesson. Naz went quiet and Calzaghe claims, 'That's what happens when someone stands up to a bully'. The Welsh middleweight legend then drew a distinction between that incident and the Hamed-Barrera fight. 'A lot of big punchers, deep down are really bullies who rely on intimidation and the fear they instil as much as they do on the punch. Take that intimidation factor away and there's no plan B, which was the case when Naz fought Marco Antonio Barrera in 2001 in Las Vegas… once he was exposed Naz never recovered from what happened in the Barrera fight'.

Naz had taken a big step up in class of opponent when he fought Marco Antonio Barrera and not only did he taste defeat for the first time but he took a comprehensive beating. Chris Eubank had warned Naz early in his career that he would have to learn how to absorb a beating one day as it was the nature of the game. Naz dismissed the warning (and also Eubank's readings of Shakespeare) and told Eubank that such a thing would never happen to him. When it did against Barrera, it was the beginning of the end for the flamboyant featherweight who retired just one fight later.

Hamed called himself 'Prince' because he was destined to be king. That fairytale never happened; whenever people talk about him, the common theme tends to be that it could have been so much more. As great and talented as Naz was, he's the classic example of a fighter who's dogged with legacy issues because of who he didn't fight. He regularly performed brilliantly, but his wins were not against anyone of any great note and people tend to judge true greatness on how you faired against the best of your era.

In the years since Hamed's retirement Mayweather grew into a boxing god, which did not go unnoticed by Naz who said, 'Floyd may go down as the best fighter who ever lived'.

But surprisingly, Sheffield's finest also finds Mayweather's flaunting of money uncouth. 'The only thing that's putting me off him is that it's distasteful the way he's going off before fights and pushing money, pushing dollars to the cameras. I used to say it with a tongue in cheek and feel a bit embarrassed saying it'. Carl Thompson in the limousine obviously never recognised the 'tongue in cheek' manner of Naz's constant bragging of money. If Naz thinks your flaunting of wealth is vulgar then maybe it's time to take account of your personality.

Hamed has also been critical of Mayweather for what he believes is a genuine dislike and arrogance towards his opponents, and said, 'I never had anything in my heart against my opponent. But he seems to have this—I don't know whether its malice or, bad intention, bad feeling, and all that does is take that shine and the star away from him despite how really good he is'.

Mayweather-Hamed at some point in the early 21st century was mouth-watering, but it wasn't particularly talked about to any great degree. Unlike a match against Arturo Gatti, the former double world champion who got inducted into boxing's Hall of Fame . 'Thunder' Gatti, a Canadian with Italian heritage, won the IBF super featherweight title in Madison Square Garden in 1995 against Tracy Harris Patterson. Then in 2004 he won the vacant light welterweight title before losing it to Floyd Mayweather a year later. The legend in the making comprehensively outclassed and battered Thunder whose corner refused to let him out for the seventh round, and resulted in Gatti crying his heart out in pain and frustration. A couple of years earlier, an enthralling trilogy against 'Irish' Mickey Ward cemented Gatti's reputation as one of the most exciting fighters around, but the Mayweather defeat signalled the beginning of the end and he retired three fights later with a record of 40-9.

Before the turn of the century, a leopard-skin-clad Naseem Hamed had strutted into America to make his name, to which Gatti told Sky Sports, 'An offer was made and we want to fight. Since he's doing a tour in America and wants to fight American fighters I should be next'.

Gatti then went on to criticise Naz for his ring entrance and said he shouldn't be allowed to clown around in the manner he does. He claimed that dancing and fooling around should only be reserved for when you win the fight, not beforehand. 'I'll joke around after I knock him out', said the Canadian.

'I'll give him a lot of credit. He's a hard puncher. It makes him what he is. He's a very awkward fighter and I might get punched but he leaves himself open. He's never in balance. Totally opposite to what I am...I think he's a clown. He can't do nothing to me but jump around and he'll walk into my punches which will put him to sleep for a couple of weeks'.

A question mark hung over where a Hamed-Gatti match would take place, Britain or America? Naz, who was promoted by Frank Warren, might have preferred the home advantage, but his main aim was to build a reputation in the US. Gatti said he was happy to come to the UK to fight Naseem but also challenged his potential opponent to prove he could perform in front of an away crowd. 'I'll go England whenever he wants me to...If I get the fight I'd go anywhere to fight him. Once it's in the ring, it's in the ring. He can have all his fans and everybody but it ain't gonna help'. The Canadian added that he would prefer an American venue and said, 'But he thinks he's so bad, coming to America and thinking he can beat everybody, he should try and beat me here. That would be great for TV and for me and him'.

Sky were taking the view that Hamed-Gatti would be the fight of the year and their pundit Richie Woodhall agreed that this was the one that everyone wanted to see. Woodhall was putting his money on Hamed, claiming that he would be too sharp and hard hitting. The former super middleweight contender took the view that the better the opponent the better Naz would perform, despite Gatti's claims that he could handle the punching power of the 'Prince of Sheffield'. 'It's all very well having a good chin but when Naz hits you, you go down and your lights go out', said Woodhall.

The TV network HBO were certainly very excited about the arrival of the Naseem Hamed carousel in America. His contract with them guaranteed six fights as long as he kept on winning. The Prince made his American debut at Madison Square in 1997 against a dangerous and experienced hard hitter called Kevin Kelley. The match was a short and sweet action-packed humdinger and both men went to the canvas three times each before Kelley was stopped in the fourth round. HBO described the bout as the featherweight version of Hagler-Hearns. George Foreman at ringside for HBO gleamed:

> I enjoyed myself tonight…He's gonna shoot everybody he fights!—this guy has power, he doesn't look it—like Muhammad Ali, you're supposed to whip him but for some reason you don't'.

Foreman added, 'We're gonna enjoy watching this guy in years to come and I wanna be at ringside…This guy's the prince of entertainment.

Gatti's manager Pat Lynch was at the Kelly fight and saw dollar signs in Naz, as well as a potential great pairing, and a deal for a Gatti-Hamed showdown was done and dusted. However, Gatti's form in 1998 put pay to the dream matchup. He lost to Angel Manfredy in a big upset and then twice in a row to Ivan Robinson. Before Angel Manfredy was considered a good prospect he had to first develop into a journeyman, as the standout stat of his early career is a bum's record of 2-2-1. In Atlantic City, New Jersey the crowd gave Manfredy a greeting of total indifference before giving a great reception to Gatti who looked happy, calm and confident. HBO reported that Manfredy was facing a dark cloud in Gatti and to make things worse he had suffered a rib injury three weeks earlier. Gatti, at this moment in time, looked like a superstar who would go on to achieve greatness. 'This is the first big fight of 1998. Happy new year', said HBO's Larry Merchant. For Gatti it was a horrible start to a horrible year. He was cut badly on the eyelid from the first round and in the third round Manfredy struck Thunder to the canvas with a stunning left hook. Gatti was facedown on the floor, but managed to stagger up and beat the count. The referee stopped the fight in round 8 due to the damaged eyelid and confirmed the standout win of one man's career and a disaster for the fallen champion. By losing three fights in a row, Gatti's reputation as a rising star had taken a major hit and a super-fight with Naz simply lost its status as a showdown between the top two featherweights. Gatti would go on to blame poor lifestyle choices as to why his form dipped in that period.

HBO still loved Hamed and would pave the way for him just as long as he stayed on form. All the top names between the weights 122 and 130 lbs (55–58 kg) were being discussed. The problem, however, was that Naz would soon develop a lax attitude to training. For a fighter who could have had it all he became his own worst enemy and dropped the basic disciplines that had made him so brilliant. His former promoter Frank Warren looks back on Hamed's career as wasted potential and blames him for 'cutting corners in training'. In later years his former trainer Brendan Ingle told *Boxing News,* 'He'd got the technique perfect. All he had to do was turn up and train. He always used to be the first one in and the last one out. But that changed. He'd turn up when he wanted to and try and dictate who was around him'. Ingle added, 'When he started to make a lot of money his whole family got involved. What experience did they have in boxing?'

Cutting corners would be disastrous against an opponent like Marco Antonio Barrera and in consequence many people will judge Hamed for how poorly he fared in that fight. It was the one and only time that he faced a world-class opponent and he fell well short. Post Brendan Ingle, Naz was taken on by the legendary trainer Emanuel Steward, who in later years said, 'he had so much talent that in preparation for the Barrera fight he just took it real lightly. If he had trained with the same focus and intensity that he had I think he would have beat Barrera'. The Kronk legend continued, 'I think his punching power, his elusiveness, his instincts were just too much. But it was a case of someone not being prepared for a fight mentally'. Steward had warned Naz that Barrera was going to be a very formidable opponent and was urging him to watch videos of the Mexican's last match. Instead of concentrating on the reality of his opponent's menace, Naz would focus on watching videotapes of Barrera getting beaten in a match five years earlier.

Despite a lack of wins against pedigree opponents, *The Ring* still lists Hamed as the 11th best British fighter of all time. Had the 'Prince' gone back to basics and stuck about for a few more years, then fights with Floyd Mayweather, Kostya Tszyu, Enik Morales, Diego Corrales and a rematch with Barrera had the potential to take him to 'King' status.

At the end of the first decade of the millennium, some speculation arose that Naz was going to come out of retirement. In 2008, he hinted of a return and joked that he had never retired and had just been on a long break. If he were to come back he claimed it would be as a super featherweight or lightweight, but Naz had piled on the pounds and looked no stranger to a Mars Bar. According to Hamed in 2008, 'Weight ain't no issue for me. I'm big because I want to be big. Don't ever underestimate the Prince'.

In the end he would stay retired. With Arturo Gatti, regrets over not fighting someone like Hamed, or any boxing issue, are futile compared to how a life ended so early and violently. In Brazil 2009, on the same day as his sister's wedding, Gatti was found dead at in his hotel room in a pool of blood. His Brazilian wife, who had bloodstains on her handbag, was arrested and charged with homicide. She would shortly be released and the police changed the verdict of the death to suicide. In further investigations, detectives in 2011 came to a conclusion of homicide, but nobody has ever been convicted of murder. The reasons for his death remain cloudy and unexplained and this horrible end to an ex-champion's life has parallels with a boxer in the next feature. . .

7. FREDDIE MILLS-ARCHIE MOORE

Upon hearing that I was writing a boxing book, my Aunt Penny informed me that Grandad Bazell was a fight fan and used to go to the odd match. His favourite boxer was the Dorset-born light heavyweight Freddie Mills who during the 1940s and 1950s was a major sporting star and TV personality. An intriguing, controversial and a charismatic character both inside and outside the ring, he was perhaps a boxing version of Paul Gascoigne: loveable but hugely flawed. Mills was a man who seemingly had it all, from sporting success to acting roles after retirement, as well as owning nightclubs. However, he is ultimately remembered for tragedy, and his personal life became surrounded by mystery, horror and the very darkest of allegations.

Freddie Mills' pro career started in 1936 when he fought out of the seaside town of Bournemouth. In 1942, he fought for the British and Commonwealth light heavyweight title at White Hart Lane, the home of Tottenham Hotspur. As Grandad Bazell was a Spurs fan,[1] I'm sure he would have been there if he wasn't fighting a war. His opponent was Len Harvey from Cornwall, and Mills flattened him inside two rounds to domestic acclaim. Harvey retired, while Mills would become a world-title contender.

In May 1946, Mills got a title shot against the world light heavyweight champion, Gus Lesnevich from New Jersey. The bout fought at the Haringey Arena (which is now, depressingly, a supermarket) ended in defeat for the Dorset man when he was stopped in the tenth round. Despite losing three more times over the space of a year, Mills was able to get himself a title rematch with Lesnevich at West London's White City stadium (now, depressingly, a yuppie housing development) in July 1948. In a match that went the 15-round distance, Mills achieved the standout win of his career and was awarded a unanimous decision by the judges. In 2013, *Boxing News* listed Mills-Lesnevich part two as one of the top ten standout revenge bouts and noted, 'A barnstormer of a first fight saw Mills go down four times before being stopped in the tenth round in 1946. Two years on and Mills reversed the roles, putting Lesnevich down twice en route to the light heavyweight title'.

The standout event from Freddie Mills' career that didn't happen was a title defence against the great light heavyweight Archie Moore. Mills never fought once in the US, and his only matches outside the UK were a couple of bouts in Johannesburg. This article is from the *Toledo Blade* from May 1949:

FREDDIE MILLS TURNS DOWN OFFER TO MEET ARCHIE MOORE HERE:

London, May 7—Light Heavyweight Champion Freddie Mills yesterday reported that he is not interested in going to Toledo, for a title shot with Archie Moore. News dispatches said Mills had been offered $50,000 by promoter Pat Thurkettle to fight Moore in Ohio City. Mills manager, Ted Broadribb said he had read of the offer but had not received it. 'But in any case', Broadribb said, 'Our immediate objective is the British heavyweight title match against Bruce Woodcock at White City June 2nd

Yorkshireman Bruce Woodcock had already beaten Bournemouth's finest in 1946, which was Mills' first fight since losing to Gus Lesnevich. Unlike the Lesnevich rematch, Mills would not avenge Woodcock and lost the north v south battle of Britain in 1949. As this fight was for the British heavyweight title, Mills remained the world light heavyweight champ, but the next year in 1950 he was dethroned by the American Joey Maxim in Earls Court, London (which, depressingly, is soon to be a hotel). Freddie was knocked out in the tenth round in what would be his final fight, and he retired with a record of 77 wins, 18 losses and six draws. Joey Maxim held on to his title for a couple of years before losing the belt to Archie Moore in December 1952. Maxim attempted to win the title back from 'The Old Mongoose', but lost on both occasions. Archie Moore never won the heavyweight title and came up short whenever given the chance;[2] but as a light heavyweight he was a king and recorded the longest ever title reign which stretched a decade.[3] The Old Mongoose retired in 1963 with a record of 185 wins, 23 losses and ten draws.

Freddie Mills lost more than just a title. In London's Soho in 1965, at the age of 46, he was found dead in the seat of his car with a gunshot wound in an apparent act of suicide. Many people said it was murder. Mills had connections to London's gangland and the gun found at the scene was said to have been too long for him to have held to his face while being able to pull the trigger. His family claim that he was killed by gangsters who were targeting club owners who refused to pay protection money. The author James Morton claims that fear of the Kray brothers drove Mills to suicide and said, 'The Krays didn't actually kill him, but the threat that they were going to move up against him was enough to push him over the edge'. Mills, who it's believed was bisexual, was also having marital problems at the time of his death and there have been rumours suggesting that he and Ronnie Kray had sexual relations. Author Kate Kray, who married Ronnie, asked her husband about the Mills rumours while he was in prison and he flatly denied it.

In 2001, *The Guardian* reported that a book was due for release claiming that Freddie Mills was the Hammersmith Ripper, which is an unbelievably damning allegation considering that the Ripper was thought to have brutally murdered eight women between the years 1959 and 1965; the last murder coming just a few months before Mills suicide/murder.

The validity of the claims are not strengthened by the fact that the book was never released, probably because of lack of evidence. Whoever the Ripper was remains a mystery, just like the life of Freddie Mills. His life story would make a great film, but the only problem is that nobody knows what a true portrayal of his life would be.

As for Archie Moore, he made the boxing Hall of Fame and died at the age of 81. One of his many claims to fame is that he was the only man to face both Muhammad Ali and Rocky Marciano. One fighter who maybe should have also been granted that honour was Floyd Patterson, which takes us on nicely to the following feature.

8. FLOYD PATTERSON-ROCKY MARCIANO

While Hall of Famer in the making Floyd Patterson was rising through the ranks, his trainer Cus D'Amato would ask him, 'Do you think you can beat Marciano?' This was the benchmark for whether or not you had what it takes to be the man. If Floyd was going to make it as the champ then he'd have to get past an ageing Brockton Blockbuster. Or so they thought. After beating a washed-up Archie Moore, Rocky Marciano retired and told the world that it was time to spend more time with his family. The Moore fight was tough and the old Mongoose even had the champ down on the canvas in the second round. Contributing to Marciano's decision was an injury, plus the fact that he no longer wanted to work for his manager Al Weill, and by quitting boxing it made it easier to break away from Weill with no legal disputes. So when Rocky retired in 1956 at the age of 32, he did so with the plausible intention to come back in the near future and take his unbeaten fight record of 49 to the nice round figure of 50.

According to historian Bert Sugar (who some might say viewed the Rock with rose-tinted glasses), Rocky had cleaned up the division and there was simply nobody left to fight. Floyd Patterson's biographer W. K. Stratton is one to differ on the idea that there was nobody worthy out there and says:

The real reason he quit was the one significant heavyweight in the division he had yet to defeat. Floyd Patterson. Though Patterson had fought just once as a heavyweight, considerable attention had been paid to his prospect of becoming heavyweight champ. He and Marciano were approximately the same size, and both could deliver hard punches. But there was one big difference between them. No one had ever seen a heavyweight with that speed, in particular, hand speed. No one knew how, or even if, Rocky would be able to cope with hands that fast. It was a very real possibility that Rocky could suffer a humiliating defeat against a fighter 11 years his junior. Especially given Rocky's tendency to leave himself unprotected and as he fought close to his opponent'.

Stratton added:

Word spread that people close to the champion feared Marciano risked getting killed in the ring with Floyd. Likewise the Patterson camp was confident its man would win easily. 'It will be a no contest', Floyd's trainer Don Florio said. 'Patterson is too fast. I've trained a lot of old guys. I've trained Joe Walcott. They get tired. And if you get tired in there with Patterson then God help you. I would hate to be that guy.

By the time Marciano's title was vacated in 1956, the young Olympic champion Patterson had built up a professional record of 31-1 and was put in a title eliminator against Tommy Jackson. Patterson won that match and then faced Archie Moore for the heavyweight title. If he were to win then the 'Gentleman of boxing' would make history as the youngest man to win the undisputed heavyweight crown. Patterson, aged 21 years, ten months and three weeks, knocked out Moore in the fifth round to claim that honour. After four successive title defences he lost the belt to the Swedish hard-hitter Ingemar Johansson in 1959, in a match in which he was floored seven times before being stopped. Patterson pretended to look on the bright side of life and noted that, 'I may have got knocked down seven times, but at least I got up seven times'. But deep down Floyd was ashamed of the defeat and when in public he disguised himself behind a wig and sunglasses so as not to be recognised.

At this point Rocky had eyes on a comeback. According to historian Bert Sugar, Marciano wanted a title shot with Johansson in a blockbuster match between two tough-punchers, Rocky's 'Suzie Q' versus Johansson's 'Hammer of Thor'. But first, there was the issue of a Patterson-Johansson rematch in June 1960 and this time 'The Gentleman' floored Johansson in the fifth round to take back the championship. By winning the rematch, once again Patterson created boxing history, as he became the first man to ever retain the undisputed heavyweight title. Marciano didn't want to fight Patterson and so stayed retired. Patterson had wanted the fight to happen and via the promoter Emil Lence offered a $1 million guarantee to Marciano. It wasn't enough and not even Frank Sinatra could get the match on. Old 'Blue Eyes' tried his hand at putting together Patterson-Marciano and offered his fellow Italian American $750,000 plus shares in a telecommunications company. The Rock's answer was not the communication that Sinatra was hoping for and the singer's future role in heavyweight championship boxing would be as a ringside photographer at Madison Square Garden for Frazier-Ali.

Patterson and Johansson fought a decider in 1961. Patterson was knocked down twice and got up to knockout the Swede in the sixth round to win the trilogy. The following year a 'Bear' by the name of Sonny Liston came on the scene to challenge Patterson. Liston was number-one contender, but Marciano was one of many who predicted a win for the current champion. The matchup was a contrast in personality as well as style: a knockout merchant and tough slugger who had mafia connections versus a church-going nice guy and boxing purist. In this case the bad guy came first and it only took Liston one round to knock out the champ. Liston's rise to the top leads to a lot of gossip about whether an ageing Marciano should have come out of retirement for a dream matchup of the 'Rock' versus the 'Bear'. Intriguing as that would be, 1962 was nearly seven years since Marciano's last match. He was too-long retired and most likely too old to take on such an awesome force. Liston's destiny would be to raise hell for a couple of years, then in 1964 make way for a new superstar on the scene called Cassius Clay.

There is a good case for Marciano-Patterson in the mid to late 1950s. Even though Rocky goes down in history as the only undefeated heavyweight champion, he's another fighter whose legacy has always been subject to question because of a lack of pedigree opponents. Not that it was his fault that he didn't reign in a great era of heavyweight boxing, and there's no question that he flattened some great names. The problem was those names were from a previous era and past their time. Ezzard Charles was 33 when Rocky beat him on points (the only man to take Marciano the distance in a title fight). 'Jersey' Joe Walcott was near 40 when Rocky knocked him out in two matches in 1952 and 1953. An old and broke Joe Louis met the young bull Marciano in 1951 at the Yankee Stadium and was horribly knocked through the ropes in the eighth round and counted out.

In the comedy film *Coming to America*, Eddie Murphy played an ageing barber who was championing Joe Louis in a heated debate over the greatest of all time. The Jewish old boy in the barber shop (also played by a whitened Murphy) mentioned Rocky, to which Murphy's barber character fumed, 'Oh der they go...der they go...Why is it every time I talk about boxing a white man got to pull Rocky Marciano out der arse....Marciano was good but compared to Joe Louis he ain't shit'.

'He beat Joe Louis' arse!'

'What! Joe Louis was 75 years old when they fought...Joe Louis always lied about his age. One time Frank Sinatra came in here and sat in this chair. I said Frank, "you hang out with Joe Louis, just between me and you, how old is Joe Louis?" You know what Frank told me, he said, "Hey,

Joe Louis is 137 years old!'"

Marciano's last ever fight was against the great Archie Moore, who was a weight-class lighter and 38 years of age (but a spring chicken compared to the 75-year-old Joe Louis).

In fighting Floyd Patterson in one final battle, Marciano would have been in a reverse role to the pattern of his career. He would be the legend going up against the talented young gun. This one fight, win or lose, could have blown away all accusations levelled at Rocky that he only beat up old men and young bums. In 1969, at the age of 45, Rocky was in boxing terms a very old man, but sadly that's the young age at which he would perish in a plane crash.

And while on the subject of undefeated champions with Italian heritage who couldn't be tempted out of retirement...

9. JOE CALZAGHE-CARL FROCH

The original title of this book was *Fights That Should Have Happened*, before the publisher suggested something different. I was okay with the new title. I always felt a bit uncomfortable with the word 'should', because boxing is a sport where lives can be shortened. Who am I to say that you should get into the ring with that monster?

Just like Marciano-Patterson, it's tricky to label Calzaghe-Froch as a fight that 'should' have happened, as you have to respect one's right to stay retired. It's a great fight that never was, and no one has the right to use the term 'should' in a case like this. The Welshman proved himself to be one of the greatest ever British fighters in an undefeated career that ended with victory over Roy Jones Jr. in November 2008. Jones knocked down Calzaghe in the first round, but from that moment on was out-boxed and lost 118-109 on all three scorecards. Calzaghe officially retired a few months later, just as Froch emerged into a clearer and more visible light.

There has never been any shortage of speculation regarding a Calzaghe-Froch matchup, along with plenty of ill feeling. The first credible rumblings of the two meeting were in 2008 when Froch became number-one contender to Calzaghe's WBC super middleweight title. At the time, pundit Steve Bunce correctly predicted that the fight would probably not happen because Joe had big dreams to pursuit in the USA. Calzaghe therefore vacated the WBC title, which was won by Froch in a classic war against the Canadian Jean Pascal. Calzaghe remained unapologetic about turning down Froch's challenges and said, 'At that stage Mikkel Kessler was 39-0 and held the WBC and WBA titles, so no offence to Carl but Mikkel Kessler's a much bigger fighter. After Mikkel Kessler, Bernard Hopkins was the big fish…and number-one in the world. I just wanted to fight the best'.

During that era, speculation regarding Froch-Calzaghe was a mirror image of the Hatton-Witter out-of-ring feud which was going on at the same time. Like Hatton, Calzaghe was a name, while Froch, like Witter, was dismissed on the argument that he wasn't enough of a name.

Calzaghe told reporters that he didn't like Froch and asked, 'Why should I give him a pay day?'

After fighting Mikkel Kessler in 2007, Super Joe had made a decision to retire in the near future, and once out he kept to his word.

In April 2009, a couple of months after Calzaghe retired, Froch travelled to America to defend his WBC super middleweight title against the former undisputed middleweight champion Jermain 'Bad intentions' Taylor who was once on Calzaghe's list of potential opponents. The 'Cobra' was put down by Taylor in the third round and was behind by four points on two of the scorecards at the start of the final round. To win, Froch needed a big round, and with less than two minutes left on the clock he stunned Taylor with a right hook. Still on his feet, Taylor desperately kept his distance to see out the round but was floored by a brutal Froch attack with just 40 seconds remaining. 'Oh my God', gasped the American commentator as Taylor was given a generous long count and rose to his feet in time. It didn't matter; Froch finished him off moments later with just 16 seconds remaining. Directly afterwards, the 'Cobra' called for Calzaghe to come out of retirement and said:

> I'll tell you what's top of my agenda…Joe Calzaghe was using the excuse that nobody knows who I am in America. Now everybody in America knows who I am. So he's got no excuse now. Joe Calzaghe's next. If he gets himself out that armchair and gets himself back in the gym let's have a fight for the British fans and the rest of the world. Let's do it'

When asked if he could get the Welshman out of the armchair Froch responded, 'I think I can get him out of there. But I don't think he's got enough bottle. I'm there. I'm champ. I'm now a big name in America. I've shown people what I can do, so where's Calzaghe? Get yourself out that armchair and come and have a fight. It's only boxing, don't worry about it. Let's get it on'.

The Italian Dragon stayed in the chair of retirement, but even before his title unification bout with Andre Ward in 2011, when asked about his ideal opponent Froch spoke of his desire to meet Calzaghe. By this point in time Froch acknowledged that it was now very unlikely to happen and when asked why he wanted Joe so badly, he replied,

> Because he's undefeated. A brilliant super middleweight world champion, the best on the planet. When he retired I was coming through and just won the WBC world title. But until you beat the man you don't feel like you deserve your number-one spot. I do at the minute because Joe Calzaghe's retired. But if he was still an active fighter that's the one I want…but he's been retired for too long now and chilling out and relaxing like he should be.

It was a more respectful tone than Froch had previously used when talking about Calzaghe and once the possibility of the fight happening faded, so did some hostilities. Froch told Steve Bunce that he had the chance to talk to Calzaghe at *Sports Personality of the Year* and thought he was 'actually a lovely bloke'.

In turn, Calzaghe said that he understood where Carl Froch was coming from. He acknowledged the methods of an up-and-coming fighter's intentions to brashly call out the established big gun. A young Joe had done the same with the likes of Chris Eubank. When asked by Sky Sports if he was ever tempted to come out of retirement, the 40 year old replied, 'Not at all. After Roy Jones Jr. I'd had enough of boxing. The injuries…I achieved everything I wanted from boxing so I feel blessed'.

Before Froch fought Yusaf Mack in 2012, the American challenger got under his skin by calling the 'Cobra' a 'Fake Calzaghe' and would be made to pay for that remark with a third-round knockout. Before the fight, Froch responded to Mack's taunt by praising Calzaghe, but also claiming he would have beaten him:

> Joe and I have become good friends now. He is a gentleman and I regard him with dignity. But I have told him to his face that while it would have been very difficult for me to outpoint him, I am sure that I would have taken him out inside the twelve rounds. It would have been a fantastic fight, which I would have loved. Joe nicked a lot of his wins because of his terrific work rate. He was extremely fit and threw a lot of punches, which caught the eyes of some of the judges. Some people accuse him of slapping but that was really only later in his career when he had brittle hands and needed to work a bit with the inside of the glove. I, for one, can excuse him of that. I know I would have had to knock him out to win but I do feel I would have done that. He was vulnerable to a big shot and was put down by fighters who were not as good or heavy hitting as me. It's just a pity that we never got it on. It would have been one of the great nights in British boxing.

Naturally Calzaghe would disagree and in 2013 he told *Boxing News* that had he not retired he would 'love to face Froch or [Andre] Ward'. He added, 'Froch was just coming through the ranks when I was at the top. Since I've retired, he's established himself as one of the best fighters in the world. If we met at our peaks, I'm 100 percent confident that I'd win with my hand speed'.

Later that year Joe's father and trainer Enzo Calzaghe laid into Froch after the 'Cobra' won a controversial stoppage against the unlucky George Groves, and slammed, 'Carl Froch has finally convinced me that he is an average world champion. All the hype was fake. No more talk about him boxing Joe. It would have been a lamb to the slaughter'.

Harsh words, perhaps, considering that Froch had beaten some top names while being the underdog, and a questionable performance against George Groves doesn't discount the good things he had done previously in his career. In May 2014 there was no question or controversy about Froch-Groves 2, as the 'Cobra' won via a stunning one-punch knockout in round 8 which was anything but average.

The question of a Froch-Calzaghe fight is whether or not Joe should have taken the up-and-coming star instead of fighting Roy Jones. After all, in his autobiography which was published in 2007 Calzaghe dismissed the idea of Jones and said, 'I have no interest anymore in Roy Jones…Jones is washed up'.

With the benefit of hindsight, a win against the emerging Froch would have been a far bigger scalp on Calzaghe's record than a washed-up Jones, assuming of course that he would have won. Before fighting Mikkel Kessler in May 2013, Froch claimed to have surpassed the achievements of Calzaghe and questioned his legacy. 'I don't like to talk Joe Calzaghe down but when you look at his career and the people he has beaten, I've fought more unbeaten fighters, more than anyone in Britain at world champion level'. The Nottingham native added, 'Calzaghe has two or three names which stand out on his record, I've got 10 or 12 that stand out. So as far as I'm concerned my legacy has already superseded Joe Calzaghe—and I've got to call him the great, phenomenal Joe Calzaghe, who is retired, unbeaten in 46 fights'.

The Warrior Froch could have provided the war that Calzaghe never wanted. In his autobiography, Calzaghe admitted that had no interest in a battle of attrition and regarding Hearns-Hagler said:

> I don't crave to be involved in that kind of fight. I don't want to be in a Muhammad Ali-Joe Frazier scenario where winner and loser both end up in hospital and the winner describes it as 'the closest thing to dying'. When I get in the ring I just want to beat the guy in front of me and come out unscathed myself. I don't want to be remembered as a crowd pleaser, if it means some day someone will treat me like a punch bag.

Whether or not Froch could have engaged the elusive and fast Calzaghe into a war will never be known and like Hatton against Witter, one of Britain's biggest feuds remains a hot topic of 'what if?' and 'who would have won?' debates that can never be decided and answered, as for every person who claims Calzaghe would have won, you'll find a person who will argue the case for Froch.

Another missing fight from Calzaghe's career was a showdown with Irishman Steve Collins in the mid to late 1990s. Collins was an established ageing champion, while Calzaghe was young and up and coming. But when Collins looks back at his career, there's only one fight that stands out as the one that went missing…

10. STEVE COLLINS-ROY JONES JUNIOR

While writing this book, I was aware that one of the featured chapters involved a fight that could still potentially happen; that bout being Floyd Mayweather versus Manny Pacquiao.

Every other chapter was safe, or so I thought. That was until I spoke to a contact in boxing who knows Steve Collins and asked, 'Can you get me in touch with him, I'd like to talk to Collins about the book'. The man replied, 'He's a bit busy at the moment, he's training for Roy Jones'.

'What!?' I replied, as I checked that the year really was 2013 and that I had not been transported back to the 1990s. Yes, Collins-Jones is a match that should have happened, but, needless to say, many years earlier.

Speaking in 2013 a defiant Collins said, 'There was something in my career that wasn't finished and I never thought it would pop its head up at this stage of my life. But the opportunity has come again to settle an unsettled score going back many years'.

Jones did not dismiss the suggestion and replied, 'We do have fires that are lit. That got lit from birth. If you pour a little gas on that fire then whoosh…he says he still wants some. I was a giver. If you wanted it I gave it to you'.

When it mattered, Jones didn't give anything to Collins apart from a cold shoulder. A Jones-Collins match in the year 2013 all depended on a backer putting up enough money. A promoter who was prepared to take a leap of faith that the public would respond and come out to see two men who were past their prime give us a fight that should have happened.

In the 1990s this would not have been a difficult sell for any half decent promoter. Roy Jones was hotter and more sellable than any super middleweight on the planet, and WBO champion Collins was a more than worthy name who had twice beaten British heroes Nigel Benn and Chris EubankSky boxing pundit and ex-cruiserweight world champion Johnny Nelson calls this, 'the fight that should have happened', and in 2013 he interviewed both men on *Rivalries* to ask what went wrong. The 'Celtic Warrior' Collins responded, 'There was no one left to fight. Both me and Roy had beaten everyone on both sides of the Atlantic and the natural fight to then happen was Roy and myself. And I went to Pensacola and I chased Roy down. But he was too busy to fight me!' The Irishman added, 'I wanted to fight, but Roy just wasn't interested. But it could still happen and I've got my licence'.

Jones Jr., looking almost apologetic, had said, 'We never got to be rivals. We did discuss trying to fight a couple of times. Then he got [into a feud] with Reggie Johnson, and it never happened. But he says he's got a licence for a year...'

In 2012, Collins was less pragmatic when talking about Roy Jones. He told the radio station ATG that Jones 'was a coward for not taking me on'. Collins was looking for one last big payday before retiring and scorns Jones for not giving him a chance. 'He ran, he wouldn't have it and that's my big regret...and I don't forgive him for that'.

In 1999, Jones beat Rick Frazier in his hometown of Pensacola in a mismatch which was later described by HBO commentator Larry Merchant as 'junk'. Post-fight, Merchant interviewed the victorious Jones on credible future opponents and put Steve Collins' name in the mix. Jones' response was brash towards any future opponent, but as he tried to continue, Collins stepped into the ring and spoke over him. As Jones shouted in the direction of the camera, Collins put his arm round the IBF champion and said, 'I'm Steve Collins from Ireland'.

'If you want some, come get some', boasted Jones, still looking into the camera, and paying no acknowledgment to the 'Celtic Warrior' who was standing beside him. 'I'm here Roy', said Collins, but to no avail, Jones didn't even look in his general direction.

'We were the last two left in our era…you were the one who could have made it happen, I came to your yard', said Collins to Jones in 2013. Jones was lost for an answer and looked a bit uncomfortable about the subject.

Jones ducked Collins, but was it fear or was it financial? Neither reason seems to make sense. As far as promoting the fight and making money goes, a white Irish hope based in Boston would not have been a tough sell in America. If there is one thing to resonate with white America's interest in boxing then you can't go wrong with a Celtic warrior. Like Hatton-Witter or Vitali-Valuev, the ducker was the one who most people would have expected to win the fight; but the guy they were expected to beat was just that little bit too tricky for comfort. Collins may have been a decent enough fighter, but Jones was nicknamed 'Superman' for good reason and surely would have beaten the tough Irishman.

As far as Steve Collins is concerned it was down to fear, and he told ATG radio, 'People say that Roy Jones is a great fighter. But I said all along that Roy Jones doesn't have a great chin. If I'd of got a fight with him. I'd get so close to him I guarantee I'll catch him on the chin and he'll go down'.

What would be a bigger shame than the fight not happening is if both men one day turned it into a fight that should never have happened. Jones Jr. vs. Collins was what you could call a super middleweight lost war. And that leads us to Round 11…

1. I take no pleasure in revealing that kind of dirty laundry.
2. Bruce Woodcock also defeated Gus Lesnevich in 1946 by way of an 8th round knockout. The one and only time the American was counted out. But just like his win against Mills, Woodcock didn't become a world champion because Lesnevich's world light heavyweight title was not on the line. Heavyweight Bruce Woodcock never won a world title belt, but the Doncaster man had a Ricky Hatton-style fan base and had no trouble filling an arena with his army of fans.
3. From 1958, Moore was stripped of titles by governing bodies, but was still recognised as the legitimate champion.

ROUND 11

BENN, HEARNS, JONES: THE LOST WARS

'I wanna go to war with Roy Jones!'
Nigel Benn

'Me and Benn—enough said. I like Benn that's why I want to fight him.'
Roy Jones Jr.

'I'm ready when he's ready. Bring it on, Roy!'
Thomas 'Hitman' Hearns

In his autobiography, Nigel Benn makes a couple of passing references to Thomas Hearns being considered a potential opponent for him while he was fighting out of the US between 1989 and 1990.

I'm pretty sure that that teaser was subconscious inspiration for writing this book, as Nigel Benn and Thomas Hearns were my favourite boxers on either side of the Atlantic. It's a dream fight that, more than any other, I wish had happened, and I know I'm not alone in this; when I mention Benn-Hearns to people it creates a keen reaction, because the immediate feeling is that such a contest was unlikely to have lasted the distance. For the most part these two men knew how to win decisively, but they also went out on their shield. It's certainly of great importance whether or not a fighter wins or loses, but being involved in something that people remember and talk about for years is also what legends are made of. The best football match I ever attended was an Arsenal-Manchester United semi-final at Villa Park in 1999. My team lost 2-1 and I was devastated, but I'll always appreciate having been at such a great game. I knew that my team gave everything and went down fighting. That match was an end-to-end equal battle and could have gone either way. It was, in football terms, the closest thing to a war. So, a devastating defeat goes down in my mind as one of the most profound football memories that I cherish. And in a similar nature, Thomas Hearns is celebrated in memory of his brutal third-round loss to Marvin Hagler in 1983. That fight was an epic collision that lives in the psyche of boxing fans as the epitome of the sport at its most exciting. At the end of the first round the commentator noted, 'That was an entire fight accomplished in three minutes'. Boxing historian and author Ted Sares noted, 'His [Hearns'] three rounds of unmitigated fury with Marvellous Marvin Hagler will always remain a part of his legacy as one of the most exciting fighters I have ever seen'.

In parallel, 'Satan's Right Hand Man' Nigel Benn should feel a sense of accomplishment for his loss against Chris Eubank in 1990. He may not feel that way, but as a fan of his I feel an accomplishment on his behalf. Despite being on the other end of victory he was involved in a classic war that became a measuring stick for future domestic matchups. If a British fight enthralled us then it will be described as being like Benn-Eubank. There are fighters out there of whose wins make little to no impression on us, let alone their losses. We don't know who would have won a Hearns-Benn bout, but we can assume that the loser would have gone down swinging to the last.

Although the mention of Benn-Hearns evokes a very keen reaction, the common response is for people to question if such a matchup was feasible. Hearns was five years older than Benn, however they were both competing at the highest level in the super middleweight division during the same period of time. In 1989, Hearns was 31 while Benn was 26. Benn's reference to Hearns was regarding the era when he was fighting out of Miami and rebuilding his career after the devastating defeat to Michael Watson in 1988. American super promoter Bob Arum had taken him on and described Benn as the 'British Marvin Hagler'. Arum's main plan for Nigel Benn was to pit him against Thomas Hearns and Mike McCallum, both from Emanuel Steward's legendary Kronk stable. Hearns' form during that time was inconsistent, although he did register one of his best ever career performances, which was the drawn rematch against Ray Leonard in 1989. After the Leonard rematch, a boxing TV bigwig called Lou Falcigno had dismissed the idea of Hearns competing in more matches with the golden generation of 1980s middleweight stars. He said, 'I think we have to wait for some new and exciting fighters'. If that were the case, where better to have looked than the great young middleweight Brits of that era, none more exciting and fierce than the demonic 'Big Bad Benn'.

In April 1990, Benn took on WBO champion Doug DeWitt in Atlantic City and before the fight Arum told him that if he won, a fight could then be set up with Hearns. DeWitt, for his part, was hoping to beat the perceived British novice in order to get a rematch with the 'Hitman', who had beaten him on a points decision four years earlier in Detroit.

DeWitt, nicknamed the 'Cobra', knocked Benn down in round two, but he was disposed of by the 'Dark Destroyer' by the eighth round and a new WBO champion was crowned. However, no fight with the 'Detroit Hitman' emerged. Instead, there was far more talk of matching him up with Roberto Duran. Benn had accepted an offer of £650,000 to fight 'Hands of Stone', but the bout was sabotaged by the British Boxing Board of Control who expressed doubts over the fitness of the 37-year-old Puerto Rican. The deal fell through and Benn-Duran will certainly be considered by some as a great fight that never was. We do have a teaser to what might have been, as on the Internet wonderful footage can be found of Benn and Duran sparring together in an eight and a half minute session from 1988.

In the biography of Thomas Hearns, entitled *Hitman,* there is no reference to a possible fight that never happened with Nigel Benn. I spoke to the book's co-author Damien Hughes, who implied that Benn was very briefly mentioned when they interviewed Emanuel Steward during research, and the impression given was that Benn wasn't considered big or credible enough.

The most notable comparative link between these two fighters is Iran 'The Blade' Barkley. In June 1988, Hearns fought Barkley in defence of the WBC middleweight title in the Hilton Hotel in Las Vegas. Hearns was the firm favourite and his trainer Emanuel Steward had predicted that his man would win by knockout within two rounds. Hearns did dominate the first two rounds and Barkley got cut below the eye and was also bleeding from the mouth. However, the predicted knockout didn't come. In round three, Hearns stepped up the pace and caught 'The Blade' with a number of great shots and the commentator noted that the crowd were sensing a knockout. The crowd were right and what followed was one of those special moments in the sport when a fighter on the brink of defeat managed to turn it around and snatch victory. With less than a minute remaining in the round, Barkley, to everyone's amazement, caught Hearns with a devastating right hook which sent the 'Detroit Hitman' crashing to the canvas. Hearns just about beat a slow ten count from referee Richard Steele. But he was knocked down again within a few seconds and fell through the ropes. Barkley was crowned the new WBC champion. 'That guy's the winner!' remarked the stunned commentator, in reference to Barkley's battered and bloody face.

'The Blade' would then lose his next two fights in hard-fought contests. The first was a split decision against Roberto Duran and the second was a majority decision against Michael Nunn, but on both occasions he put up a good fight. One year later in August 1990 Barkley was pitted against 'Big Bad Benn' for the WBO belt, which the Englishman had won from DeWitt. In the stare down, Barkley, whose Father had died just a few days beforehand, looked down to the floor and not into the 'Dark Destroyer's' glaring and vexed eyes. Benn's eyes alone could have done further damage to one of Barkley's retinas, which was suspect enough for the British Boxing Board of Control to refuse to sanction the match. The State of Nevada gave the go ahead and Benn looked so furious anyone would have thought Barkley had pick-pocketed him on the way in to the area.

The American commentator noted that, 'Under no circumstances will this be a beauty contest. These are two of boxing's better brawlers. When you have two bombers it's often the man who lands his bomb first who comes out on top'.

Benn came out like a possessed wild man and landed the first major bomb in just two seconds. A few punches later and Barkley was down with only 16 seconds gone in the contest. 'The Blade' responded well and hurt Benn, before being put to the canvas with 28 seconds left in the opening round. Not that Barkley being down was going to stop Benn from swinging, and in a moment of madness he clumped Barkley in the head directly after he hit the floor.

The American commentators cried out for Benn to be disqualified. Interestingly, if you watch the fight with British commentary, Reg Gutteridge suggested that Benn should be docked points! Benn won on the three knock down rule when Barkley fell for a final time with just a few seconds remaining in the first round. Speaking to Reg Gutteridge directly after the contest Benn said, 'I've done what I wanted to do, beat Barkley and beat him bad!'

Everything about the interview made it clear that the British boy was staying in America to cause more havoc, and he expressed a desire for British fans to come to the States to support him in his future battles. Barkley by that point was a wounded soldier who was past his best, but the ferocity of Benn's victory against such a name could not be ignored. A huge statement had been made and from that moment on the obvious thinking would be that Nigel Benn was going to be put straight in the mix for the biggest fights on American soil. Instead, that win against Barkley in August

1990 turned out to be the last time that he would ever fight in the United States. His brief American adventure between 1989 and 1990 was successful and undefeated, but rather than staying and pursuing bigger scalps, Benn returned to fight out of England and began an unforgettable feud with Chris Eubank. Benn's former manager Ambrose Mendy had designs on Sugar Ray Leonard and wanted Benn to stay put. Mendy told the writer Ben Dirs:

> It didn't make sense to me…He was a superstar in America, feted by absolutely everybody—Mike Tyson, George Foreman, old timers like Jersey Joe Walcott, Kid Gavilan and Beau Jack. Everywhere we went, everybody knew who he was. He should have never left the United States, he should have stayed out there, because all of his weaknesses and frailties were here in the UK. And so was Chris Eubank.

Returning to England didn't mean that a Benn-Hearns showdown was totally out of the question. In his autobiography, Chris Eubank claims that the winner of the first fight between himself and Benn in 1990 was going to be lined up to fight either Michael Watson or Thomas Hearns. The underdog Eubank won and went on to begin a brilliant and ultimately tragic feud with Michael Watson. Had Benn beaten Eubank then we may very well have seen that dream matchup between the 'Dark Destroyer' and the 'Hitman', considering that Benn never expressed any great desire to fight Watson again, probably because Watson's style was wrong for him. Nigel Benn was always on the lookout for opponents to come at him and engage in a full on war of attrition.

Hearns only contest in 1990 was against the defensive Michael Olajide who he comfortably beat on points, despite an average performance. Olajide only took the fight to Hearns in the final rounds after he spent most of the contest as far away from the 'Hitman' as possible, much to the vocal frustration of the crowd. Later in 1990, Hearns was being lined up to fight Michael Nunn in a huge deal worth $10 million. But the offer was scrapped when Nunn put in a poor performance against the unrated Marlon Starling.

1990 was also a period of time when many were questioning whether Hearns should fight anyone at all, and there were calls for him to retire. Comparisons were being made to his earlier years and concerns were also being raised about hints of a slur in his speech. To put in a defence against those concerns, it had only been a year since 'Hitman' had produced a world-class display against Sugar Ray Leonard, and Emanuel Steward conceded that his fighter didn't perform well when he takes on weak opponents. He needed someone like Michael Nunn, Mike McCallum or, of course, Nigel Benn.

There may not be any mention of Nigel Benn in the biography *Hitman*, but there is a passing note of a chap called Roy Jones Jr. Also known as 'Superman', Jones has always had his doubters, due mainly to the perceived quality of his opponents, but that didn't stop boxing writers from voting him the superstar of the 1990s. Emanuel Steward was never one of the doubters and claimed that Jones was the only boxer he knew of who didn't need a jab, because of his lethal knockout ability with either hand.

In 1991, Jones and Hearns held amicable talks about a fight in Las Vegas. What got in the way of this dream war was that the negotiations caused a further rift in the fragile relationship between Hearns and Emanuel

Steward. Their partnership had become strained due in part to financial disagreements and the boxer had a desire to conduct his own negotiations, which was partly to prove a point to Steward. The only point proven was that their relationship was irreparable and Hearns and Steward bitterly parted ways. The 'Hitman' then opted to have the convicted fraudster Harold Smith as his adviser, who had once served time for the crime of embezzling millions of dollars from Wells Fargo bank in order to promote boxing matches. Harold Smith was not able to help matchup his newly acquired legend with the top marquee names. Instead of a mega-fight with IBF champ Roy Jones, Hearns' opponents in 1991 at super middleweight were Kemper Morton and Ken Atkins, both of whom he knocked out within three rounds. Later in the year he moved up to light heavyweight and fought the respected Virgil Hall, who he defeated on points in a fight in which Hearns turned back the clock and put on his best display in years. 1991 was a year when Nigel Benn fought four non-names and this is a time when a strong argument can be made of a Benn-Hearns contest had the American not opted to move up a weight class at the end of the year. Between them, Hearns and Benn fought seven matches against weaker opposition, when just one fight against each other would have caught the imagination of boxing fans worldwide. Since his match against Ray Leonard in 1989, Hearns never again featured in a big time bout, with the arguable exception of a rematch with Iran Barkley in 1992, which he lost on points.

By the mid 1990s the 'Hitman's' star had faded, while Roy Jones Jr. was establishing himself as the most destructive pound for pound man in boxing. But that still didn't stop speculation of a matchup between two men from different generations. After Hearns beat Karl Willis in 1996 he said in the post-match interview, 'Roy Jones said that he would demolish Thomas Hearns…Bring it on, Roy, bring it on! I'm here. I'm putting out a challenge to you. All you have to do is accept'. The interviewer asked Hearns when he would be ready for such a matchup to which the Kronk legend replied, 'I'm ready for him when he's ready'.

Hearns by this point was undoubtedly past his prime and there were continued concerns about his slurred speech. People were urging him to retire; but that wouldn't have stopped Jones-Hearns being a hit at the box office.

Hearns took a dig at Jones and claimed that had he been around in the 1980s he would have been 'chewed up and spat out' by the superstars of the day. Jones responded by saying that the same thing would have happened to Hearns if he had come along in the 1990s. The fight never transpired and years later in November 2012 the two men came together in harmony for an Emanuel Steward tribute night. Both Jones and Hearns got up on stage to praise one of boxing's legendary trainer/managers who had died in October of that year aged 68.

During the mid 1990s Jones Jr. was a wanted man and seen as the measuring stick against whom to measure yourself as the best in the super middleweight division. In the year 1996 one match in particular involving Roy Jones would have caused a stir among boxing fans on both side of the Atlantic. At the tail end of Nigel Benn's career he openly stated on a number of occasions that he desired to fight Captain Hook, in order to go out in style. By the mid 1990s Nigel Benn was no untested novice. In 1995 he'd beaten Gerald McClellan in one of the most dramatic and tragic fights in the modern era. Before the fight Roy Jones had predicted a win for McClellan and said, 'I think McClellan beats Benn. But, maybe, just maybe it's gonna be tighter than some people expect. Nigel's a real warrior. He can still bang a bit. And I think McClellan's jaw is kinda suspect when he gets tagged'.

When asked by the writer Donald McRae if Benn could absorb McClellan's power, Jones replied, 'No, probably not. Eventually he will go'. Jones had his eyes firmly on Benn-McClellan and at the end of it he was expecting to be matched up with the American. He told McRae, 'I don't see a problem with Gerald McClellan—he's just another fighter I'll beat. Sure, Gerald McClellan's a good boxer. Sure Gerald McClellan can knock anybody out. But, after four rounds, Roy Jones kills Gerald McClellan'.

In hindsight, these are chilling words, but the destruction of the 'G Man' would come via Benn not Jones.

In a major upset, Benn raised his status to an indisputable top name. The next natural showdown in the super middleweight division had to be a collision between Benn and Jones Jr. Directly after the McClellan war, Benn was being interviewed for American TV by Muhammad Ali's former doctor Ferdie Pacheco and called out Jones Jr. there and then: 'The one person I'd like to say hello to back in America is Roy Jones because he's the top boy. If I want to class myself as the best super middleweight in the world I have to beat Roy Jones. Roy Jones, I'm very happy for you beating the mouth James Toney'.

While McClellan lay unconscious in a critical condition in the corner of the ring, his promoter Don King was primarily concerned with sidling up to Benn. He insisted to the 'Dark Destroyer', 'Let's unify. Let's do the WBA title, then you have two and Roy has one. Then we'll go for Roy'.

In a post-match interview against Danny Perez in 1995, Benn stated, 'I wanna fight Roy Jones. Everyone talks about Roy Jones being this and that…and he is bad…fighting Roy Jones will be my last fight and I ain't even gonna box him. I'm gonna get fit for 12 rounds and just have it with him…I don't care if I win, lose or draw I'm gonna go out there and have a war with him. No boxing'.

This was the third post-match interview in a row in which Benn put out a challenge for Jones. In his previous fight against Vincenzo Nardiello a couple of months earlier, he challenged Jones, but did so in a way that's very rare for boxers; he was humble, and his respect for his potential opponent was evident. Benn said, 'I don't mind being number two to Roy Jones I think he's a class act. He'll frighten me and that's what I need, someone to really frighten me. I'd be up for that fight like a mother! Please God, Don King, Frank Warren, HBO, if you can get that fight on I'd fight him in his back garden…He's the only one that can give me that real fear…he'll put the fear of God up me'.

Jones was more than aware of a lurking Benn menace and after beating Tony Thornton warned, 'If a guy makes a mistake against me it's ding dong…Be careful, Benn, I'll get you like that'. Jones later respectfully added, 'You go tell Don King I'll take that fight anytime. Nigel Benn's a great warrior that's why I want the fight'.

Jones boldly proposed a mouth-watering Britain vs. America showdown featuring the best of Frank Warren's stable of talent. Jones and Benn would headline. On the undercard Naseem Hamed would fight Derek Gainer and Frank Bruno would take on Alfred Cole. Jones claimed that the event should happen in the UK and that he wanted his fellow American fighters there as moral support. 'My bros must come with me. I must have cover if I go to another country…Let's make it a great night'.

For just an evening of Jones-Benn, a Don King offer of $25 million was being floated about, but Jones and his management would not accept any proposal that gave King any future decisions over Jones' career. Jones claimed to have been happy for the combined purse to be $20 million as long as King stayed clear afterwards. A common theme throughout his career was the absence of King as a promoter. King though was the Wizard of Optimism. 'We are going to travel down the yellow brick road to the city of Oz. Dodge the scarecrow [why, he's simple and harmless?], Tin Man [why, he's made of tin and harmless?] and the Lion [why, he's a coward and harmless?] and bring back Roy Jones'.

Regarding the UK pool of talent, Jones said that their problem was:

> They can't make their own decisions without King. We can. They don't have the power. They're denying the public of some great fights…people want to see something which is intriguing to their minds. Something which will look good…I really like the biggest challenge out there. When I fought James Toney, it was a project. Benn is a project because he's a warrior and he will be a tough fight for me. I really believe Benn wants to fight me. I have a lot of faith in him. I respect him.

In contrast to that claim, a few months later Jones claimed, 'The only challenge is Nigel Benn and he won't return my phone calls. He doesn't want to fight so there's no challenge'.

Frustratingly, we'll never know just how tough a challenge Benn would have given 'Superman'. One factor to take into consideration is that post-McClellan, Benn was in the process of passing his prime, while Jones was still lethal. The East London war machine had gone through so many battles and now he had to face the trauma of nearly killing a man in the ring. He would shortly lose his edge in a way similar to Chris Eubank after the second Michael Watson fight. Eubank became a man content to win on points rather than knock opponents out. Benn clearly wasn't the same fighter after the McClellan epic, which was just one war too many, both physically and emotionally. A pre-McClellan Nigel Benn? Now had that guy fought Roy Jones it would have been even more interesting. Boxing writer Bert Sugar went so far as to rank Benn as his fifth favourite super middleweight of all time, one place behind Roy Jones Jr. Sugar's analyst buddy Teddy Atlas from ESPN ranks Roy Jones as his fifth favourite super middleweight and Nigel Benn as his third. Despite being so closely rated, Roy Jones would have been a clear favourite in this matchup. But you could certainly make a case for Benn having an outside chance, purely because of his warrior's heart and punching force. Taken from his intriguing autobiography, below is Chris Eubank's almost poetic assessment of Benn's power:

> In my opinion he was equal to what Tyson was reputed to be. Benn's power was simply astonishing. Fight fans ask me which punch of Benn's is the hardest - I say 'simple, all of them.' Every shot. The jab to the head was like a huge battering ram, his left hook was devastating…When Benn hit you, it was a lucid, lingering punch; it was almost like a living entity whose sole purpose was to wreak havoc inside your skull. That degree of

shocking power cannot be trained into someone, it's just within them...He is by far the hardest puncher I have ever come across.

To address the balance of Eubank's opinion, here is his assessment of Roy Jones Jr.:

> He was, pound for pound the best fighter on the planet; in regards to his style, his devastating punching ability, the whole repertoire, he had it...Had he been [number-one contender to Eubank's title] I would not have dodged. I would have taken the fight. Would I have won the fight? Highly unlikely...he would have come away from the fight and got hurt, and I would have been hurt probably far more than he was.

It's also worth noting that Eubank claims to have heard rumours suggesting that he himself was the only fighter who Roy Jones Jr. had reservations about facing. That's questionable, as when the writer Donald McRae asked Jones about his thoughts on Chris Eubank, Jones wasn't informed enough to make a judgement as he knew little about him. In recent years however Roy Jones had this to say about the two Brits:

> Nigel Benn was a wonderful fighter, people didn't give him the credit he deserved. Benn beat a very good friend of mine, Gerald McClellan, so you can't say those guys, Benn and Eubank, weren't great fighters or just as good as the top fighters in the United states at the time...The mistake McClellan made against Benn is he went

out and slugged with him and that was Benn's favourite thing. So I wasn't going to slug with him, I was going to soften him up, get some of that power out of the system and then step in for the kill. Like Michael Watson did.

Despite Benn being past his prime in the late 1990s, a credible performance against Jones would have been the icing on the cake on a fantastic career. It's the only fight he wanted and it's possible that he could have raised his game just one more time. The key word in this instance is 'fulfilment', which is central to the whole subject matter of fights that should have happened. After the McClellan tragedy Benn took part in a live studio debate on whether or not boxing should be banned—a popular topic in the 1990s. Benn stated that he had thought about retiring after the McClellan fight but didn't because 'I love boxing...I still had the animal inside me. I have to carry on'.

The host of the debate, Darcus Howe, pressed Nigel Benn to say if he would retire in the manner in which Jeremy Paxman would press an MP. Howe asked, 'Why do you keep putting yourself at risk? I can't believe you'd put yourself at risk because of a Porsche. There is something else that is firing you?'

Benn finally cracked and admitted, 'Maybe I just want to go down as one of the best super middleweights in the world...I feel like I still have something to prove and I think fighting Roy Jones [will do that]. I just don't feel fulfilled yet, I really don't'. Darcus Howe conceded that fighting Roy Jones could make Benn as much as $15 million, but even with such a huge sum would the risk of fighting such a dangerous man be worth it? 'Yes, most definitely. That's the fight I really want. Then I would retire. I've said that if I get the Roy Jones fight I will donate one million dollars to Gerald McClellan'.

Benn did not get the 'fulfilment', he sought, and in contrast, he ended his career losing his last three fights: one of them against Thulani 'Sugar Boy' Malinga, who he had already beaten earlier in his career (and who Jones had knocked out by round six in 1993). Benn announced to the crowd that he would retire. That decision didn't last long and he came back for two fights, both of which were losses against Steve Collins. In the second Collins fight, Benn retired after round six while sitting on his stool. Former world champion Johnny Nelson recalls, 'Did anyone ever expect that from Benn, ever? The kind of fighter he is? The kind of person he is? No. But his body said, "I can't do this, I can't fight at this pace", so he quit'. It wasn't the 'out on the shield' manner in which anyone would have expected Benn to go out, and this time no one had any doubt, himself included, that there were any more wars left in one of sport's most fearsome soldiers. Benn conceded, 'Can't do it no more and I know it's time to call it a day. Thank you all for supporting me'. Steve Collins described Benn as, 'The most exciting fighter in the history of British boxing'. The fact that so many people will agree with that statement should be enough to silver line the career legacy of the 'Dark Destroyer'.

Despite being one of the most exciting fighters in the history of the sport, Thomas Hearns' search for total fulfilment kept him boxing way past the majesty of his prime; the same with Roy Jones Jr., who is not officially retired at the time of writing. For a man who should have retired by the early 1990s, the 'Hitman's' last bout wasn't until 2006 at the age of 47. Seven years previously he had fought in England for the very first time, on a Prince

Naseem Hamed undercard in which his biographers Brian and Damian Hughes recall:

> It was a sad footnote to that night, long before the conclusion of the 12 rounds, many spectators chose to leave the arena rather than watch their memories of a once-great champion being tarnished. The crowd did not heckle or boo; their respect was too sincere for that. But the contrast between the warrior who had been involved in some of the sport's greatest tussles and the pale shadow before them seemed even starker given that it had been seven years since one of his fights had last been broadcast in the UK.

Nigel Benn and Thomas Hearns both retired with five losses to their names. Had war commenced at any time in the late 1980s to early 1990s, then one can only speculate on whose record would instead read six.

INTERLUDE

THE WASTED ONES

Top-rated talent that gets wasted equals great matches that never were. Kirkland Laing, who was featured in the previous interlude, wasted his own career, but in doing so was never a severe menace to society. This is unlike Tony Alaya Jr., who by the end of 1982 had built up an impressive record of 22-0 and was scheduled to meet the WBA junior middleweight champion Davey Moore in 1983. That fight never happened and Alaya's liberty was to be taken away at the age of just 19 after being convicted of a brutal rape offence. Sentenced to 35 years behind bars, the severity was due to two previous rape assaults for which he got away with probation. The decision to let him walk free from the first two convictions was highly questionable considering that one of his victims was left with a broken back. Alaya was rated very highly and expected to win a world title, but by the time he resumed his career after release in 1999, it was too late to make a meaningful impact. In 2004 he was sent back to prison for speeding and being in possession of heroin.

When Alaya was originally released from jail in 1999, another man considered an up-and-coming star was heading the other way. Between 1994 and 1999 the Nigerian heavyweight Ike Ibeabuchi built up a record of 22-0 and was strongly tipped to dominate the future heavyweight division. Outside of the ring 'The President' was in need of professional mental treatment and was said to have severe bipolar disorder. He once kidnapped a 15-year-old boy and drove a car into a wall, which caused the boy lifelong injuries. He escaped a custodial sentence because it was deemed that he was trying to commit suicide. Ibeabuchi was a destructive force inside the ring and even more dangerous outside of it. Ike's demon's were never helped or repressed and in 1999 he raped a stripper in the Mirage Hotel in Las Vegas. The city that should have made him millions of dollars became the venue of his self-inflicted downfall. This time the justice system sent him to prison, which put pay to any boxing career. Ike would be aged in his 40s by the time of release.

Even if we are not a menace to society most of the time, we can dig our own grave with one act of stupidity. In 2007, Diego Corrales was killed in Las Vegas when his motorbike collided with a car he was trying to overtake. Corrales, a world champion at both featherweight and lightweight, was said to be speeding and also three times over the Nevada State alcohol limit.

The fight that would have happened had Corrales not been killed was a trilogy decider against Jose Luis Castillo. Their first fight is rated the best of 2005 and famous for having one of the all time great comebacks. Castillo had twice knocked down Corrales in the tenth round and was seemingly on the way to victory. Corrales rose to his feet in time and got a one minute extra breather due to his mouth guard needing to be washed after it touched the canvas. As Castillo went to finish him off, a refreshed Diego caught the Mexican with a right hand and won by TKO.

No talent was ever more wasted than that of the amazing featherweight Salvador Sanchez, who, just like Corrales, also died after trying to overtake another vehicle at high speed. In August 1982, the 23-year-old Sanchez was driving a Porsche in Mexico and collided after trying to overtake a lorry on a motorway. Two months earlier, he had beaten the awesome Azumah Nelson to retain his WBC featherweight title, but he was dethroned as champion through losing his life. Before his death Sanchez was tipped to become one of the greatest featherweights of all time. The match that many believe would have happened had Sanchez not died was a super-fight with the legendary Alexis Arguello.

Pre Manny Pacquiao, the number-one rated Filipino boxer was the flyweight Pancho Villa. Promoted by Tex Rickard, Pancho won the world flyweight title in 1923, but the following year disaster struck. At the age of just 23, having never been knocked out, a tooth infection spread to the throat and sent Pancho into a coma, from which he never awoke. Villa was ultimately to blame for his own death, because against his medic's advice he boxed with the infection, which spread the infection from one tooth to three. He then ignored the doctor's advice to stay in bed and get better. Instead, he went out and socialised and within days he was dead before a quarter of a century of his life had passed. Despite dying at such a young age, Pancho still fought 107 times and had a career record of 92-9-4. The 23 year old had fought a lifetime of bouts, and his defining victory was the knockout of the Welsh legend Jimmy Wilde in 1923.

One man whose career and life were wasted and destroyed due to the fault and malice of others was Billy Collins Jr. from Nashville, a prospect in the early 1980s. Collins' career ended brutally at the age of just 21 after his face was pummelled to a swollen wreck in a match with Luis Resto in 1982.

Resto was known as a tough guy, but also as a bona fide stepping-stone verging on journeyman; the type of fighter who a hot prospect like Collins was expected to beat on the way up. Much to the surprise of the Madison Square Garden crowd, Resto was the man doing all the damage and won a ten-round decision. 'He's a lot stronger than I thought', said Junior in-between rounds. Collins looked like he had been a car crash and it certainly seemed strange that Luis Resto, who was not rated as a hard puncher, could have inflicted such damage. At the end of the match, Junior's trainer and father Billy Collins Sr. went to shake the hand of Resto and as he did so, held on to the gloves, much to the distress of Resto who wanted to walk away. 'Hold it, commissioner. All the padding's out of the damn gloves', cried out Collins Sr. The alleged culprit was the trainer Panama Lewis who Resto instantly looked over to with an expression that stated, 'We've been caught'. 'Those are the gloves you gave us', insisted Lewis, who always denied knowledge of the removed padding. In the same year Lewis had been accused of doping Aaron Pryor in between rounds during his win against Alexis Arguello. 'Give me the bottle I mixed', said Lewis, and in the following round Pryor found a new burst of energy and stopped Arguello.

With his boxing career over due to a torn iris, a demoralised Collins Jr. turned to the bottle and within a year he was dead. Drunk at the wheel and in a suicidal state of mind, Junior died when his car swerved off the road and crashed into a creek. The episode also destroyed Luis Resto's state of mind and he went on to admit, 'Because that thing happened, I wanted to commit suicide. I didn't care if I died or not'. Denial of the crime from both Resto and Lewis didn't stop them from being prosecuted in 1986 for assault, conspiracy and possession of a deadly weapon and they both served two and a half years. In 2007, Resto finally admitted knowledge that Lewis had removed the padding and had also soaked his hand wraps in Plaster of Paris to harden the material. He also claims that Panama Lewis, on occasions, gave him spiked water which opened up his lungs and eased exhaustion. In the documentary film *Assault in the Ring*, Resto confronted Lewis with his claim but the banned trainer continued to deny that he removed the padding.

Birmingham's Rob McCracken was an up-and-coming name in 1990s British boxing whose appeal to top promoters was not helped by football hooligans. In 1994, McCracken was enough of a name to have Nigel Benn fight on the undercard of his championship bout with Steven Foster in Birmingham. During the Benn-Gimenez bout, Birmingham City and Manchester United hooligans clashed in the stands in a brawl involving around 200 people. Benn was not in his usual ferocious mood, but outside the ring there was chaos in scenes bad enough to force McCracken to ringside and plead for the fighting to stop. 'Eh eh…stop fighting', begged McCracken though the ringside microphone while Benn and Gimenez impressively remained focussed while surrounded by mayhem.

Frank Warren at ringside called it 'a rotten night for boxing', and asked about the conclusion the American audience would make on the culture of British boxing. (To be fair, the Americans put on their own riot in Madison Square Garden after the conclusion of Bowe-Golota)

Warren's co-promoter for the event, Don King, looked fascinated and almost entertained at his first experience of football hooliganism, and compared the rioters to Vikings. The Zulus of Birmingham City were supporters of McCracken and the *Independent* reported that this was a concern for the British Boxing Board of Control. Having a following with a potential to cause a mass riot did for the future of McCracken about as many favours as The Clash getting an endorsement from Simon Cowell. However, for McCracken there was light at the end of the tunnel as he's ended up as one of the most prominent boxing trainers in the UK for both Olympians and professional world champions. To get McCracken as a trainer would most likely reduce one's chances of being wasted talent.

ROUND 12

THE CUBANS ARE NOT COMING

'We always put our revolutionary principles first. No amount
of money can stand between us and our principles. They're
incorruptible.'
Rolando Garbey, Cuban Olympic double medallist

'Cuba has given the world cigars rum and salsa, but the most
amazing product are the Olympic boxing champions. Dozens of
them, a seemingly endless line of first class fighters, they are the
undisputed kings of the ring.'
Steve Bunce

After the 9/11 World Trade Centre terrorist attacks in 2001, President Bush
listed three enemies of freedom and potential terror. Those countries were
Iran, Iraq and North Korea, with, of course, no mention of free and liberal

states such as Saudi Arabia, UAE and Bahrain. Two of Bush's colleagues in the government, Condoleezza Rice (in-coming Secretary of State) and John Bolton (in-coming Undersecretary of State) then added more evil to the list: Libya, Syria and Cuba.

I visited Cuba for a holiday in 2007 so that I could experience evil firsthand. The evil Fidel Castro was still officially in power, but his age and ill health led most to believe that he was unofficially retired. Therefore his 'evil' brother Raul was thought to be the person running the country.

After being in Cuba for a week, the main evil I encountered was their cooking, but when a country is bound by US-led trade embargos, then one cannot expect Michelin standards on every corner.

My overall impression was that Cuba is a bit like the small kid at school, who fearlessly throws punches back at the big bully who pushes his weight around; and if there's a country in the world who knows how to throw punches it is this little Caribbean island 220 miles from Miami.

In the early 20th Century, American sailors introduced boxing to the docks of Havana. Before the 1959 revolution, not only had Havana been a venue for big fights (most notably Jack Johnson-Jess Willard), but Cuban boxers were a credible force in mainstream professional boxing, especially in the lighter divisions. The two most famous names were Gerardo 'Kid Gavilan' Gonzalez, who was a world welterweight champion between 1951–55, and Eligio Sardinas 'Kid Chocolate' Montalvo, who held featherweight and lightweight titles between 1931–33.[1]

Once in power, Fidel Castro put sport on a pedestal as a state ideal and said, 'The revolution must concentrate on sport. It is of vital importance to the country. Youngsters of outstanding talent will be picked from the masses. They will be given the best possible training. On the front line of sport the revolution will advance. Fatherland or death, we will win'.

Professional boxing played no part in the importance that Fidel Castro spoke of. Two years after the 1959 revolution, Castro banned professional boxing, claiming that, 'Athletes are being exploited by parasites'.

From 1961, fights that should have happened involving top Cuban stars didn't happen, unless a fighter defected, a decision which could involve a dangerous sea crossing to Florida. Cuban boxing historian Elio Menendez recalls, 'Cuba's new government gave professional boxers two choices. They could either stay at home and work for the state as boxing coaches. Or they could go abroad and pursue their boxing careers'.

Those who did defect in the 1960s were already established professionals who were used to making money from boxing both in Cuba and abroad. Luis Rodriguez, Jose Legra, Benny Paret, Ultiminio 'Sugar' Ramos and most famous of all, Jose Napoles, became world titleholders after the ban in 1961. At the time of writing, Sugar Ramos and Jose Napoles are still alive and may not regret the decision to have stayed professional. Benny Paret, however, died at the age of 25, ten days after a brutal beating by Emile Griffith in 1962. The footage of the match is damning, scandalous and gave justification to Castro's argument that professional boxing was immoral. The referee Ruby Goldstein was mostly to blame for the tragedy as he was far too slow in stopping the onslaught from Griffith who wanted to hurt the Cuban for his homophobic pre-fight taunting.[2] The conclusion of Paret-Griffith saw one fighter resembling a punch bag and being pummelled to death, before the ref saw fit to stop the fight.

Benny Paret chose a brutal and ruthless profession, but he had no financial incentive to stay in Cuba. Post-1961, if a Cuban desired to make money then boxing has been the wrong profession to choose. In recent years, an amateur fighter has had to get by on just $13 a month, the same salary as the typical street cleaner, road painter or teacher. The hotel worker or cab driver will earn more money than a boxing star as a result of tips from tourists. 'Kid Chocolate's' ownership of 150 custom-made suits and love of spending money in the 1930s was not compatible with the lifestyle on offer in his homeland in the decades to follow (as a result of a home burglary, the 'Kid' was robbed of 130 suits and only left with 20).

Cuban boxing is a microcosm of what is good and bad about the country. On the bad side, there is no freedom of independent enterprise. In Cuba you cannot set up an ethically run business and then sell your products and make a profit. Everything is controlled by the government and has to be in line with the regime's barriers. That, of course, includes the career options of a boxer who has no independence in his career path. One can understand Cuba for rejecting the neo-capitalist free market, because what we have in the Western-style economy has become a plutocracy that has allowed big business to dominate and own too big a slice of the pie. Countries are not run for the greater good, but by millionaires for the benefit of other millionaires. A far worse extreme of that divide was life in Cuba before the 1959 revolution. The country was ruled by a US-friendly military dictatorship and turned into a gangster's playground, which effectively enslaved the masses. Castro claimed that the revolution was not to oppress the people, but to oppress the exploiters of the people.

Cuban boxing prospers through collective endeavour and a common struggle for the greater good. Cuban boxers are not wealthy but the standard of training they get is second to none. Talent is recognised at an early age and developed at the cost of the state rather than the individual's family. Through this collective, a small third world country has produced more boxing Olympic medallists than any other nation besides America. The boxing coach and father figure of Cuba's boxing revolution Alcides Sagarra explained, 'The key to victory is the fighter goes into the ring thinking not only on the technical aspect of boxing, but also in his mind he is representing all that Cuba stands for'.

Perhaps flexibility in the good and the bad might have allowed Cuba to prosper so much more in both work and in sport whilst maintaining its core principles? Perhaps Cuba could have allowed its fighters the chance to win world titles and to bring them back to Havana on an open-top bus to cheering crowds? The millions of dollars its boxing superstars would have earned could have found a way back to the Fatherland to care for the poor and vulnerable, which, after all, is the cornerstone of the socialist philosophy. Instead, some of the island's finest became outcasts. Cuba's heyday in professional boxing was in the years following the revolution, but the revolutionary forces back home were not celebrating. If champions like Jose Napoles were to ever have come home they were to face hostility rather than open-top bus parades. The middleweight world title contender Florentino Fernandez decided to stay in Miami, rather than return home. In 1961 he narrowly lost a title fight in a split decision against Gene Fuller, leading to speculation of him being granted a rematch in Havana. No such happening transpired and *The Ring* had warned:

Fighting Fernandez in Cuba would hardly be an enjoyable experience except for another Cuban, a Russian, or a red Chinese. A Fernandez-Yankee battle in Havana would be put in a military atmosphere and amid turmoil. It was recalled that one Rocky Kalingo knocked out Fernandez in one round in Caracas and then let the Cuban have a return fight in Havana. Kalingo knocked Fernandez down in the first and then appeared to be heading for another victory. The mob wouldn't have it. Kalingo was threatened to the point at which he was scared into near-paralysis. He was stopped.

In recent decades there have been appearances in the professional sport from Cuban nationals who have been able to make a home in the United States. For example, there was the unspectacular Jose Ribalta whose biggest claim to fame was when he fought and lost to Mike Tyson in 1986.

The 6'7" giant Jorge Luis Gonzalez reached America from Havana in 1991 with a reputation of being Cuba's top amateur. He would also gain a reputation for being a poor trainer who believed that he had nothing to learn as he was already so brilliant. He knocked out a few bums before facing Riddick Bowe for the world heavyweight championship in 1995. The lack of preparation and discipline took its toll and Gonzalez was battered to a six-round stoppage. The Cuban would then lose seven of his next 15 fights before retiring.

After defecting in 1996, the talented Joel Casamayor became a world champion at super featherweight in 2001. In the following years he both won and lost against quality opposition and is rated as one of Cuba's all time great boxers.

Rene Arevalo who is a Cuban national coach says of defections, 'It's true that some of the boxers there have earned millions. But they are only a few. The vast majority of them are living in very difficult conditions. And some of them are even trying to return to our country'.

That statement will almost certainly not be inclusive of Guillermo Rigondeaux, a two time Olympic champion who defected and went on to become a formidable world champion at super bantamweight. 'The Jackal' won Gold at the 2000 and 2004 Olympic Games and left Cuba in 2009, 50 years after the revolution. The defection of the brilliant Rigondeaux may have been the tipping point for the Cuban authorities to be open to the idea of change. Without a slight change in philosophy, more defections would keep on happening, which is no good for the fighter or for Cuba. The state trains a champion, only to be abandoned by someone whose ambitions force him to make a heartbreaking sacrifice. As with the great Cuban champions of the 1960s, all the recent defectors became outcast in their homeland and cannot return to see their families. One Cuban boxing trainer summed up the impossible dilemma that his countrymen face by saying, 'All Cubans are cursed from birth. Cursed if you stay, cursed if you leave'.

In 2013, the Cuban national team trainer Juan Hernandez Sierra came out and said that the strain and sacrifices that boxers make in the ring should be rewarded with more than just national prestige. A five-decade-long ban was in the process of being partially lifted and in 2013 something remarkable happened: Cuban boxers represented their state in a tournament, fought without head guards and vests, and received prize money. Cuba was now part of professional boxing via the World Series of Boxing, which specialises in country against country competition. The head of Cuban boxing Alberto Puig de la Barca endorsed the competition's safety standards and said that his nation will 'bring the WSB to a higher level'.

The prize money Cuba gets from the World Series of Boxing has a corporative philosophy to it, because being in line with their 'evil' principles the cash is split between everyone, from the trainers to the team cooks. This professional participation will not totally stop defections, but it is a step that will persuade some to stay. In the decades before the ban was partially changed, the very best stayed loyal, leading one to wonder what might have happened if they hadn't.

Despite success in the lighter divisions, the country has never had a professional heavyweight champion, which surely would have changed had their best heavyweights been allowed to compete post-revolution. If world politics were different, then two of Cuba's finest would have most likely collided with the two most famous heavyweights in boxing history.

TEOFILO STEVENSON-MUHAMMAD ALI

'I always liked to face the best. And for me fighting Ali would have been the thing to do because he was a great boxer.'
Teofilo Stevenson

'He was Cuba's answer to Muhammad Ali.'
Steve Bunce

Over the span of his career, 'The Greatest' fought pretty much everyone credible there was available to him, and so did Muhammad Ali. The 1970s is considered a golden era for heavyweight professional boxing and this is despite the absence of the decade's golden boy. To a Cuban fight fan 'The Greatest' is Teofilo Stevenson; the winner of three Olympic Gold medals between 1972 and 1980 and who sadly passed away in 2012 at the age of 60. A country mourned the loss of one of its favourite sons, and around the world the boxing community also acknowledged the death of a legend. But to the mainstream media there was no major story to cover. When Muhammad Ali passes there will be extensions to the news and other scheduled programmes will be cancelled. Quite rightly so, yet they reserved little to no acknowledgment for the man who in the 1970s was offered $1 million to fight Ali in what would have been the boxing event of the decade. Stevenson would have been only the second man in history to have gone straight from amateur status to the position of fighting for the world title. Straight into the deep end perhaps, but if ever a man was ready for knockout action then it was Stevenson. His fights were not the decision wins that we are generally used to seeing in Olympic amateur boxing. Stevenson didn't hang around to hear matches get decided by judges and preferred to leave his opponents lying on the canvas. Before Teofilo faced the American John Tate in the 1976 Olympic semi-final, he was personally introduced to George Foreman and asked if he would like to fight him. Stevenson responded bluntly, 'George Foreman is professional and I'm amateur'.

Stevenson then went on to knock out John Tate in a manner that even Big George himself would have been proud of. A single right cross sent Tate staggering to the corner in slow motion, like a drunk trying to walk home from a heavy night out. Tate then dropped in a heap and the fight was over. This was normal routine for Stevenson whose first two Olympic campaigns in 1972 and 1976 went by with a 100 percent knockout ratio. In the 1980 Olympic Games the Hungarian Istvan Levai managed to take Stevenson the distance in the semi-final but still lost by five rounds to nil.

In 1974, Stevenson was courted separately by Don King and Bob Arum to sign a deal and fight Ali. Don King offered the $1 million with a footnote to Stevenson that there would most likely be more riches further down the line.

Ali-Stevenson is perhaps the greatest fight that never was, but it would have had to happen before or during 1975. Any time after the brutal Thrilla in Manila would have tipped the edge too far in the Cuban's favour, who was ten years Ali's junior.

Greatness v Greatness, Hero v Hero, and just like Muhammad, the 6'5" Stevenson had the appearance of a boxing god. He wasn't the typical, brutish-looking 1970s heavyweight demon and had this match happened Ali would have been facing someone nearly as pretty as him! If Stevenson had defected, then a fight with Muhammad would have been as big as the Rumble in the Jungle, but therein lay the problem. The shenanigans surrounding the Rumble would have only strengthened Cuba's stance against the professional sport. On show was what many perceived as the exploitation of a third world country. A handful of people made millions of dollars out of a country where the people had nothing. It was a throwback to the days of Batista in pre-1959 Cuba. Post-revolution, the people were still poor but they were not starving, and they had good education and medical care.

Stevenson put national self-esteem ahead of money and asked, 'What is one million dollars compared to the love of eight million Cubans?'

In 2012 Don King said that if he had the chance to have spoken to Stevenson personally, he'd have pointed out to him that, 'Eight million people would mean more, along with the one million dollars. You [with the money] can help those who are the down trodden and denied, those who are underprivileged…So let's do it for the people'. King's argument that Stevenson could have had both the people and the money is a strong one, but the great convincer never got the chance to hold face-to-face talks with the great Olympian.

Even Cuba's great boxing coach Alcides Sagarra agrees that, 'The world would have loved to see them fight. It would have been the greatest amateur in the world against the greatest professional. But that's the problem. There was a congress in boxing that set the rules and these rules forbade amateurs and professionals from fighting eachother'.

In 1996 and 1998 Ali travelled to Cuba and met Stevenson. They built up a friendship and Teofilo said of the man whose framed picture hung on his wall, 'Ali was an idol. Not only to me but to the whole world. He was an inspiration to many sportsmen around the world. Not only for amateurs but for professionals as well…Ali is much the greater as a person than as a boxer'.

In a wonderful and unique moment the two ageing legends got into the ring and sparred together for the cameras. Both wearing black trousers and white shirts they circled one another without connecting any punches. Moments before Stevenson stepped through the ropes, Ali had already comically taken a dive against a Cuban kid who was able to land a few soft body shots and floor the champ!

Speaking to the BBC a couple years before he died Teofilo said of his idol, 'They used to call him big mouth but I thought it smart the way he used the press. This was a smart guy inside and outside the ring. That is why he achieved so much in boxing and in life'.

Cuba's boycott of the 1984 Los Angeles Summer Games denied Stevenson the chance of more Olympic glory and a fourth gold medal. On the way to the podium he may very well have met a young Lennox Lewis, before facing the eventual winner Tyrell Biggs. Stevenson and Biggs had already fought earlier in the year with the Cuban winning on points. The home crowd in America booed the decision as the Cuban team danced around the ring in celebration.

Throughout the 1960s, America's Olympic boxing heroes included Cassius Clay, Joe Frazier and George Foreman. Of their era, one great world champion never found a way to the Olympics. Larry Holmes versus Teofilo Stevenson in 1972 was a classic dream matchup that would have happened had Holmes been picked for the American squad. Instead the place was taken by the white heavyweight Duane Bobick, who Holmes remembers as being someone he used to box circles around. In his autobiography Holmes recalled, 'US amateur officials wanted a white hope to represent America after all those years of black Olympic heavyweight champs…there hadn't been a white US Olympic heavyweight since 1956'. Holmes also claims that along with race, other elements played a part, such as Bobick coming from what he describes as, 'established programmes with deep pools of talent'.

Bobick beat Holmes in the amateurs when the referee disqualified the 'Easton Assassin' for clinching. But the story that would emerge from this match was that Holmes had a panic attack and crawled under the rope and out of the ring. Holmes insists that the tale is farcical and that no such thing happened. But what was for certain is that, truth or lie, people believed the story. The accusations of being a coward and yellow would taint the image of Larry Holmes throughout the 1970s. The only way he could overcome the sneers and doubters was to become world heavyweight champion and beat everyone put in his way. Luckily, he did just that, unlike Duane Bobick who was knocked out in round two of the 1972 Olympics by Stevenson. To the backdrop of a Cold War stalemate, the USA v Cuba gold medal match was so one sided that Harry Carpenter in the commentary box noted, 'The legend of Bobick is being absolutely destroyed here…completely shattered'.

FELIX SAVON v MIKE TYSON

'In order to be an athlete you have to be disciplined. You have to be honest. You have to have integrity. That's what the young people need to learn.'
Felix Savon, three-time Olympic champion

'My dream is to be like Felix Savon.'
13-year-old Cuban schoolboy Rulan Carbonell

Rural country boy Felix Savon may not be anywhere near as famous as superstars like Tyson, Lewis, Bowe and Holyfield, but he was a colossus in the amateur division during the same era. No man could have done a more perfect job in taking the torch from Teofilo Stevenson as Cuba's heavyweight golden boy. Standing at 6'5" Savon won gold medals at the 1992, 1996 and 2000 Olympic Games as well as six World Amateur Championships. He could not compete in the 1988 Olympics in Seoul due to a Cuba boycott that was related to South Korea's Cold War with Cuba's ally North Korea. If he had competed in those games then a showdown with

Riddick Bowe and Lennox Lewis would have been a reality. Savon and Lewis once sparred together when they were both amateurs and the Cuban recalls 'He asked me to take it easy. I showed him some boxing; he showed me some dance moves [gyrates, reggae style]. Nice guy, humble'.

At that point in time Savon was at the beginning of his career. Today he is regarded as Cuba's greatest living sporting legend after Stevenson died in 2012. What's striking about Felix Savon is that when interviewed, it appears that his brain has never been pounded. His face doesn't resemble someone who has been beat up too many times. He doesn't slur, sound tired or look beyond his years. The contentment he speaks with doesn't sound like someone who has been screwed over by dodgy managers or promoters. Savon doesn't talk like an embittered man who has regrets about not competing in fights that would have earned him millions of dollars. Speaking at the National Hotel by the Malecon Promenade, Savon said, 'Cuba is the heart from where I was born; it's my own heart. Cuba for me is the best of the world…And if it weren't for Cuba and its revolution I wouldn't have had success, glory; the world wouldn't know me'.

In a 1992 amateur championship held in America, Savon knocked out his South Korean opponent in just 13 seconds. The reigning World Heavyweight champion Evander Holyfield was at ringside for HBO and looked impressed, although he did question Savon's ability to improve by not facing better opponents. The HBO commentator Jim Lampley had asked Savon if he would like to come back to America and meet Evander Holyfield, to which the Cuban replied, 'I've already met him!' When Larry Merchant interviewed Savon after the fight the Cuban gentleman expressed only a desire to keep on fighting to win gold medals.

Savon's appearance on the pro heavyweight scene during the 1990s would have been fascinating. In an era filled with flawed champions, Savon, like Stevenson, could have become the first ever Cuban heavyweight champion of the world. If there was talk of Savon fighting anyone then it was Mike Tyson and Don King had reportedly offered Savon millions to make the fight happen. In 1995 Savon said that he was open to the idea and had 'no fear', but that it should be an amateur rules fight. He told the *Daily Granma,* 'We do not back out from a fight against anyone. The better prepared will win'.

The insistence not to box professionally put pay to any possibility of the fight happening. In later years, however, Savon told the journalist Brin-Jonathan Butler that if the fight had gone ahead Tyson would have been defeated. When Butler related Savon's prediction to Tyson the American dismissively replied, 'Next question'.

Brin-Jonathan then asked Tyson if he would rather fight for Fidel Castro or Don King to which Mike responded, 'Cubans aren't fighting for money. They're fighting for glory. They're saying they're better than money by turning it down. They're better than us as human beings. All that stuff'.

The only place to prove who was best was in the ring, but even if Cuba became flexible and allowed a prize fight in Havana, Tyson would still not have been allowed to go there and fight Savon. An American citizen who travels to Cuba is not allowed by US law to spend money there because it's seen as enhancing an evil regime. This law only applies to Cuba and an American citizen is free to go to North Korea and spend money. Trade with Cuba is sanctioned, so this clearly prohibits professional boxing as a fighter would effectively be selling his combat skills to make money. Journalists are allowed to travel to Cuba, as are amateur boxers who represent the United States. However, an American citizen who goes there for a mere holiday, or to earn money, can receive a prison sentence and a $250,000 fine. Tyson's not a man to let anyone tell him where he may roam and in 2002 he flew from Jamaica to Cuba, apparently so that he could meet the great Teofilo Stevenson. He didn't get the chance, and claims that he got himself in trouble and had to leave the country: only to then face interrogation from American home security.

Savon would have had to leave Cuba to fight the great 1990s heavyweights such as Tyson, Holyfield, Bowe or Lewis, there was no other option. He recalls, 'They were trying to get Don King on the phone with me, and get me a helicopter [to defect]. But I said "no" to imperialism'. When asked what he thought about Tyson's career Savon admitted that he never got the chance to watch professional boxing but noted, 'I remember him biting a guy's ear off though'.

When Brin Jonathan asked Tyson if he could make such a sacrifice as to defect from a nation and never to return he answered, 'Where I am at now. No. I couldn't leave my family. But I was born here. They'll put me in the ground here. Those Cubans like Stevenson or Savon represent all that insane stuff over there, I represent all *our* insane stuff'.

The best professionals of the 1990s were spared from facing Savon, but the Cuban did meet the future world heavyweight champ Shannon Biggs in Havana in 1991 for the Pan American tournament. Shannon Biggs was knocked down and then stopped by Savon inside of the first round and the Havana crowd went delirious, as they normally do when Cuba beats an opponent with USA written on his vest.

Savon retired in 2001 with a record of 362-21 . Of his 21 defeats, each one was avenged and just like Lennox Lewis, he never fought a man he didn't beat. On his retirement, the BBC boxing journalist Jim Neilly felt that had Savon gone pro then he would have more than held his own as a multi-million earning prize fighter and wrote, 'His strength, speed and power would have compared him with any of the great professionals in his era. His style was very much a professional one from the start. As Lennox Lewis has demonstrated, it takes several years to make the transition from a top amateur to a world champion and any judgment on how Savon would fare against Lewis or Holyfield is speculative'. Neilly added, 'Had he gone professional after Barcelona [1992] then there can be no doubt that he would have been on par with either of them especially if he had gone to America at the start of his career. I'm not sure he would have beaten Tyson when the American was at his peak but the same could be said for most boxers at that time'.

The version of Mike Tyson in 1995, however, was beatable, but Savon never took a chance on worldwide fame and millions of dollars. It's a great fight that never was, but for Savon there are no regrets. 'Making a million new friends for every million dollars I turned down...There is nothing greater than the love of one's countrymen'.

1.   Despite being Cuba's first ever world champion it's said that 'Kid Chocolate' became a forgotten champion after 1959 and was overlooked by the government. He had returned to Havana in 1934 and it took until the 1970s until he received acknowledgment and granted a pension to live on.
2.   Emile Griffith was gay, but during his fighting career he never came out. In the 1990s he was attacked outside a gay club in a homophobic assault, which left him injured for the rest of life. He died in 2013.

ROUND 13

FRIENDSHIP AND BROTHERHOOD

'That's family, there's no amount of money that would ever get me to fight family.'
Adrian Broner on whether or not he would fight his friend and idol Floyd Mayweather

'I look at Adrian Broner like Daniel-san and I'm Mr Miyagi. We never see Daniel-san go against Mr Miyagi!'
Floyd Mayweather

'Brothers don't fight. I don't fight my wife. That never happened. That was a big one.'
Bert Sugar

In 2000, an excellent wrestling documentary was released called *Beyond the Mat,* which featured an insight into the real lives of American pro wrestlers. One of the issues that the Director Barry Blaustein tried to get to the bottom of was: how could men kick the crap out of one another in the ring and also be friends outside of it? On this issue, he focussed on the wrestlers Terry Funk and Mick Foley who, although good friends in real life, committed sadistic deeds on one another in what were some of the most violent matches in history. A typical Foley-Funk 'wrestling' bout would involve barbed wire ring ropes, nail tacks, chairs and fire. Their matches were explosive, literally, as actual bombs went off in the ring. In looking for an answer to Blaustein's question, Terry Funk remarked, 'You know, what's so stupid about it, is that the worse you hurt each other the more money you make, and the more money you make the better friends you are!'

From the late 1980s and beginning of the following decade, the British heavyweight scene had an obvious matchup that would have been guaranteed to draw attention, but friendship and a duty of care took precedence.

'Just a diamond guy, good boy, nice person; he was a legend in his own right', were Frank Bruno's words at the funeral of his friend Gary Mason in 2011: a life that tragically ended at the age of 48 when his pushbike was hit by a van in South London. Born in London in 1962, Mason was the son of Jamaican immigrants and started boxing professionally in 1984. He built up an impressive unbeaten record and defeated some credible American names along the way, including James 'Quick' Tillis and Tyrell Biggs, leading him to become a world top-ten-ranked contender. The big man was respected and popular within the boxing world and there was something about him that was instantly likeable. Like many fans, I know that the first time I saw Gary Mason fight on the TV something straight away told me that I wanted that guy to do well and he'd have my support. Maybe it was because he reminded us of Big Frank who so many people loved?

Bruno-Mason at the tail end of the 1980s was a happening that may not have caught the imagination of a worldwide audience, but at home both were popular personalities. Their place of work was the Royal Oak boxing stable, run by trainer Terry Lawless and which had strong links to Mickey Duff's promotional umbrella. Lawless had a reputation for protecting his boxers against risks they didn't need to take, which often caused him to fall out with Mickey Duff who naturally wanted his fighters to be involved in tough and potentially dangerous money-drawing matches. Lawless passed away in 2009 and at his funeral the boxing journalist Colin Hart described him as, 'Without doubt, the most caring boxing manager there's ever been'.

Speaking a couple of years short of his own funeral, Mason also had kind words for his former manager and said, 'He was compassionate. He had empathy with his fighters, which is unique'. Bruno gives Lawless the credit for teaching him respect and referred to him as a, 'special human being, a one off'. With Lawless as trainer for Bruno and Mason the chances of an in-stable showdown were slimmer than the prospect of Rage Against the Machine being invited to perform live on *X-Factor*.

As understandable as that duty of care is, it prevented a match of like for like. The two South London heavyweights shared a resemblance in look and physique and gained reputations for being hard hitters. With infectious, larger than life, humorous personalities they seemed to share much in common, however, a significant factor that set Mason and Bruno apart was that one was a household celebrity and one of the most recognisable men in the country. Gary Mason was well known in the boxing world, but most of the time he could have walked down the street and not be recognised. Despite the disparity in their celebrity status, an interesting element of such a fight is that it would have been the only Bruno match held in Britain where there would have been significant split loyalties in the crowd. Thousands of fans would have been rooting for Mason and such a divide would have been alien to a typical Big Frank contest. One classic example of Bruno's degree of support was in 1987 when he fought Joe Bugner to a crowd of 35,000 at White Hart Lane. In what was the biggest domestic British heavyweight showdown of the decade, hardly a soul supported 'Aussie Joe'. Bugner, born in Hungary in 1950, formerly represented Britain, but by 1987 he was now Australian, which did little to endure him to the British fight fan who still begrudged him for his points win over Henry Cooper in 1971. By the time he boxed Big Frank in 1987, the tail of the tape was a man in his prime against a man who had peaked in the previous decade. Bruno took out the big Aussie/Brit/Hungarian in the seventh round when the referee stopped the fight after a Bruno onslaught. Such was the support for Big Frank that after the bell ended the first round the crowd began a rendition of the football chant 1-0 – 1-0 – 1-0, along with chants of 'You Fat Bastard'.

The crowd support in a Bruno-Mason clash would have been far more even-handed, as would the fight itself as both were top-ten-ranked world title contenders and only a year apart in age.

In March 1990, Mason beat Everett 'Bigfoot' Martin to take his tally to an impressive 34-0, but he suffered a detached retina, which was the beginning of the end of his career. Mason retired, but received surgery on the eye and came back at the tail end of 1990 and beat the American world title contender James Pritchard. This set up a British super-fight with the latest emerging world title contender by the name of Lennox Lewis. At Wembley Arena in March 1991, Mason hit Lewis with some good bombs but the 'Lion' look them well and was in the leanest shape of his career. Overall, the future champion was a class above the brave Mason, who faced a Lennox Lewis that was slimmer and faster than the one who would go on to dominate the division in the following years. Lewis' future rival Frank Bruno was a TV pundit that night and noted at the end of round two, 'I'm very impressed by Lennox Lewis because a lot of people were saying he wasn't ready, but he looks very ready to me, very confident'. At the time of the fight, Mason was the seasoned pro and 2/3 bookies' favourite, while question marks hung over Olympic Champion Lewis whose record at the time was 14-0. Mason came out strong in the third round and hit Lewis with some great shots, but the strength of his opponent's jab further hurt the eye which had already been damaged in the Pritchard fight a year earlier. Commentator Harry Carpenter wisely noted, 'This is going to be no 12-rounder'. Mason continued to fight hard in the fourth and fifth rounds but his eye was closing at an alarming rate. One man had to lose their unbeaten record and Lewis stopped the hearty Mason in round seven, just seconds after the South Londoner had Lewis on the back foot with a last desperate attack. Even though Mason still had some fight left in him, the referee decided that his eye was too damaged to carry on. In later years Lewis would go on to say about his old foe, 'You may be surprised, but of all my opponents, Mason hit the hardest'. Losing brave battles to Lennox Lewis was another thing that Bruno and Mason would share in common. As a result of the eye injury, Mason was forced into early retirement, but he came back briefly in 1994 to fight two matches in America against journeymen. He won both matches with early TKO's but then retired once again with an overall record of 37-1.

Whether or not Bruno-Mason is a fight that should have happened is all down to perception. There is no doubt that it would have been an intriguing domestic matchup between the two equals. It all depends on how traumatic it would have been for either fighter to go out to hurt a friend. For some it wouldn't be a problem. In 2012, the *Evening Standard* asked Ricky Hatton if fighting Amir Khan one day would be a problem for him as the two were friends. The 'Hitman' replied, 'Everyone in boxing are mates and you can knock the shit out of each other for 12 rounds and still be mates. Whether you've won or lost—you have this bond. You know how hard your opponent has worked and the time he's spent away from his family to prepare'.

Mason and Bruno did regularly spar together, and in his autobiography titled *Frank*, Bruno briefly mentions his former stable mate:

> Gary Mason joined us at the Royal Oak. He was a talented fighter and an obvious rival. Gary's a funny guy. He worked as a jeweller and opened a shop called "Punch and Jewellery". But he didn't like training as much as I did. I think Terry [Lawless] was frustrated with him because he had so much natural talent. He had quick hands and moved well, even if he did carry a bit extra most of his career. I always thought if he put in a little more effort, he could have gone further in the game…I still see Gary now and again. And he is still a joker…We gave each other some excellent workouts,

without ever trying to knock the bark off. The big guys can't afford to unload too much in the gym against fighters from the same stable. For serious sparring, Terry used to bring over guys from the States. I gave them hell.

Had Bruno-Mason happened, the Royal Albert Hall in Kensington would have been a fitting venue as both men had fought there so many times and built reputations as emerging contenders. When they became bigger stars, Wembley Arena would be the typical Bruno/Mason place of work. If the two were matched up, and had the promotional marketing been good, such a contest would have been held in a football stadium, given the popularity of both fighters.

With Gary Mason, however, there are far bigger regrets which make not winning a world title and not fighting Bruno seem totally insignificant. Today, when people think of Gary Mason they just regret that he had that accident and that he's no longer alive.

From the 1970s there's a gaping hole in the scheduling for a heavyweight fight that didn't happen for the same reason as Mason-Bruno. Joe Frazier and Ken Norton shared much in common and were world champions during the early 1970s. Both men fought trilogies against Muhammad Ali. Both men beat Ali once and lost the other two in close contests. They go down as the only two men to have beaten Ali before 'The Greatest' was considered old and washed up. Both men lost their heavyweight title against George Foreman and were floored inside two rounds against the emerging superstar in the division. Both men were friends and from the same stable. Both men were trained by the legendary Eddie

Futch. Both men died less than two years apart from another, Frazier in November 2011 and Norton in September 2013. 'Smokin Joe' and 'Black Hercules' fought against one another on a regular basis as sparring partners, but never in a sanctioned bout. It would have been billed as one of the biggest of the decade, but the two friends vowed never to do battle, unless the money was simply too good to turn down. The only realistic chance for this fight to have happened was if George Foreman were to have stayed champion for longer than his reign of 21 months. Therefore Frazier and Norton may have had to compete in a form of title eliminator. Foreman wouldn't have needed need to fight them both again as he had already beaten them so convincingly the first time around. But a title rematch with at least one of them one would have been expected. As it happened, Ali beat Foreman in the Rumble in the Jungle and both Frazier and Norton got a shot at the new champion, considering they were the only two men to have beaten Ali.

When the subject of great fights that never were comes up, it's not uncommon to hear the names Jake LaMotta and Rocky Graziano pitted together in what would have been the battle of the silver screen icons. Historian Bert Sugar lists it in his top two lost bouts along with Norton-Frazier. The two fought many times, they just never had managers or promoters. Their bouts were usually in the slum streets of the Bronx where the two kids grew up in poverty. LaMotta claimed that he and Graziano invented rock and roll: First we'd hit you over the head with a rock and then we'd roll you!' When they weren't fighting they'd help one another steal and as teenagers they were reacquainted in the State Reform School in New York for young offenders. '

Jake…Hey Jake, it's you, bullhead! I didn't know you were here.

Whaddaya do? How long you here for?'

This was where the two struck up a good friendship that continued after boxing.

'See you on the outside', said Graziano who was released from reform school first.

Along with being residents in a young offenders home, LaMotta and Rocky shared a lot in common: Both from Italian heritage, they were from the same tough Bronx neighbourhood. They started boxing as welterweights and moved on to middleweight. They both had an aggressive brawling style and became world champions. And on a wonderful note, they were two former slum kids who had Hollywood films made about their lives. Paul Newman starred as Rocky Graziano in *Somebody Up There Likes Me* and Robert De Niro portrayed LaMotta in *Raging Bull*.

The perception is that the two men never fought in a sanctioned bout because they were good pals. But according to LaMotta in his autobiography he desperately wanted the fight, but Rocky was lukewarm. After beating Marcel Cerdan for the world middleweight title, 'Raging Bull' offered his friend a shot at the title (Cerdan had beaten Tony Zale, who in turn had beaten Rocky for the title). He claims:

> There was a lot more dough to be made, was my feeling. For all concerned, if I fought Rocky Graziano and then Robinson. I had wanted a Graziano fight before Mitri. All the fans knew Graziano, Robinson and me. And, as impartial as I can be, I would say that any one of us at the top of our form can probably take either of the others. . .The minute I even mentioned a Graziano fight, all I got

was static—first of all from Rocky of all people. I couldn't figure him out. I told him he had the chance to win back the title he lost to Tony Zale, and what did he say? 'I don't want no title. I had too much trouble when I had it'.

The prospect of this fight wasn't helped by the fact that *The Ring* magazine only ranked Graziano as number-nine contender for the title, to which the champion LaMotta queried, 'I couldn't understand because he'd won every fight since he lost to Zale, except for a draw with that kid Tony Janiro'. Despite that, LaMotta's persistence in wanting the fight seemed to bear fruit:

> I was convinced that a LaMotta-Graziano fight would be a natural, and would also make a fortune. And just personally, it was the kind of fight I'd like after all those kid-stuff slugging matches we'd had back on the East Side. This would be a real fight. Finally, to set it up, I offered Rocky 30 percent of everything, instead of the 40-20 split that was natural between a champion and a contender, and finally the contract was signed.

LaMotta got his wish, but the prospect of this super-fight was dashed when Rocky broke his hand in training and the bout was sent to the golden scrap heap of lost matchups. LaMotta blamed himself for wanting the fight too much and didn't sound like a man who had a dilemma about punching his pal. 'There was a curse on that fight. I was always a great believer in the play-it-cool-bit if it was to happen. And maybe the fact that I wanted it so much and did so much to swing it put the curse on it'.

In the years to come, the two men would headline bills together, but it would be for TV and film skits. After retiring from boxing, Graziano became a small-screen celebrity and LaMotta would occasionally get the chance for a cameo. In a 1970s talk show the two men were asked if their lost bout was one that was wanted by the fans of the time. 'Oh yes', insisted LaMotta. Rocky replied, 'My wife wanted me to fight him so bad. She hated him, she wanted me to bust his head!'

They were then asked how the fight would have gone, to which Graziano replied, 'It would have been a rough tough fight but I know I would have licked him'.

To which Jake hit back, 'You sure what he's smoking is not just cigarettes?'

I spoke to the retired Irish heavyweight 'Big' Joe Egan on the dilemma of fighting a friend. He said, 'All fighters wear their hearts of their sleeves and it's hard to get up for a fight if it's your mate. I boxed friends. It's better to take other options than to fight your friend because even if you win you're gonna lose'.

Friends fighting in the ring takes some argument, however, a case can usually be made. When good pals Richie Woodhall and Joe Calzaghe fought it wasn't a unique scenario or anything unusual. At the end of the contest the two men embraced and raised the other one's hand in a show of friendship.

Blood brothers however is a no-go in a zone exclusive to boxing. Jedward aside, most people do not wish for two blood brothers to brutally pummel one another.

Not competing against a family member because of a duty of care is something that once again is unique to this combat sport; no other sport has this dilemma. Tennis legends Serena and Venus Williams have played against one another countless times on the grandest of stages, while their mother portrays a look of non-emotion so as to remain neutral. When one of the Williams sisters beats the other, pride may be hurt but neither one of them will risk a life-threatening injury. Bobby Charlton regularly competed against his older brother Jack as the two played for bitter rivals Manchester United and Leeds United respectively. Having the tough reputation, which Jack Charlton did, I'm sure that he might have clumped into Bobby in a less than gentle manner on more than one occasion. A bit of bruising or a sore leg might have been at risk here, but not irreversible brain damage or a dislodged retina. In professional wrestling, the Hardy brothers Matt and Jeff would violently compete against each other, but the art of that 'sport' is to look like you've hurt somebody while doing your best not to.

I asked fight historian Miles Templeton if there is any significant boxing heritage of battling siblings and he told me:

> There is no meaningful history of brothers fighting one another in a sanctioned bout. For a start, a body like the British Boxing Board of Control would not sanction a fight between two siblings. As far as America goes, each state has their own commission, and hypothetically if brothers were willing there would always be one state that would give the green light. There are some state commissions in the US that would put on a fight between a

Grandmother and Grandson if there was money to be made. And the Grandson could be armed with a baseball bat while Granny just had a knitting needle but that wouldn't matter either.

Fights that could have happened if the two boxers were not siblings include Leon Spinks-Michael Spinks, Max Baer-Buddy Baer, Gaby Canizales-Orlando Canizales, Roger Leonard-Ray Leonard, Ricky Hatton-Matthew Hatton, Donald Curry-Bruce Curry and Randolph Turpin-Dick Turpin the two British middleweights from the 1950s.[1] Miles Templeton went on to add, 'Aside from serious sanctioned bouts, brothers fight all the time in boxing. For example it wouldn't be unusual for boxing brothers to be sparring partners. Randolph and Dick Turpin would have sparred together many times, along with fighting the odd casual exhibition bout for a few quid'.

Vitali Klitschko, born in 1971, against Wladimir Klitschko, born in 1976, is a fight that did happen in Ukraine in the mid 1980s. Vitali suggested to his younger brother that they box and the two put the gloves on and squared off. Wladimir was ten years old at the time of that domestic super-fight and recalls, 'it made me scared of boxing', drawing us to the conclusion that Vitali won.

Without question, the fight that would, or should have happened, had the two boxers not been siblings, was Vitali-Wladimir as adults: the two dominant forces of 21st-century heavyweight boxing. The Ukrainian brothers have an incredible combined record of wins and up to the time of writing have lost just five fights. But the brothers will always be dogged by the fact that they have prospered during the weakest and most uneventful era in heavyweight boxing history by beating opponents who, to coin the classic phrase, 'aren't even household names in their own household'.

If ever a weight class needed a high-profile contest like Vitali-Wladimir then it was the post-millennium heavyweight scene. In recent years the division has been moribund, to the point where at the tail end of Joe Calzaghe's career he claimed in his autobiography: 'The heavyweight division is so bad that if I were a stone heavier, I would give away the rest in weight to fight some of those guys. James Toney was once a middleweight but now fights with his belly out over his shorts. How can a blown up middleweight become a heavyweight contender?'

The biggest name Vitali ever fought was Lennox Lewis in 2003. Since that time he's not had the chance to fight a marquee name because, with the exception of his brother (and maybe Nikolai Valuev) there aren't any. To quote the boxing journalist Dan Rafael, 'People complain all the time that they [Wladimir and Vitali] don't have top opponents. But you cannot manufacture a top-class opponent for them to fight. They can't fight Muhammad Ali. They can't fight Joe Frazier. They can only fight the guys from their era...they've done that and beaten all them mostly decisively...I don't know what else they can do'.

Lennox Lewis has an answer to that question and on the documentary feature film *Klitschko* he cheekily said, 'Somebody said, I think it was me, that the two brothers should fight each other...Boxing is like the king of the hill. Only one champion...Then you have two brothers who each control a title, which kind of devalues it to a certain degree, because everybody wants only one champion'.

Both sons promised their mother Nadeshda that they would never box each other, not even for a bit of fun. Which brother would reign supreme can be argued either way, and is debated on a regular basis. An interesting comparative link between the two champion siblings is the former heavyweight title-holder Chris 'Rapid Fire' Byrd who has faced and lost to both men. Along with Lennox Lewis, Byrd, however, is one of only two men to register a win against Vitali, although it was a victory obtained because 'Dr Iron Fist' injured a shoulder and retired on his stool. Byrd claims that both brothers are heavy hitters but that 'Dr Steelhammer' Wladimir is by far the harder puncher.

The Lennox Lewis-Mike Tyson bout in 2002 grossed $106 million, which to the time of writing stands as a pay-per-view record for a heavyweight fight. Since that time, the division had had no major worldwide draws. David Haye is a big name in Britain and Wladimir Klitschko is a big draw in parts of Europe, but when the two faced in 2011 in the biggest heavyweight showdown for years the viewing figures were still dwarfed by fights in lower weight classes. The only fight in the heavyweight division to generate a major worldwide interest during that time would have been Vitali-Wladimir, but here the sport has to put on a self-imposed straight jacket. Being a boxing fan can sometimes be hard to justify at the best of times, as essentially we are cheering violence and brutality, which can cause lasting damage to other people's lives. The comedian Billy Connolly once said that he was a fan of the sport but it went against everything that he believed in. He had a moral dilemma, but Connolly came to the conclusion that it was the bravery and heart of the fighters which meant that he could justify being a fight fan. Like many boxing fans I'd be curious to find out who would win a bout between the Klitschkos, but to watch and cheer two brothers punching one another would have plummeted boxing to a new all time low.

1. Warwick's Randolph Turpin's best win was against the great Sugar Ray Rob-
    inson for the middleweight title, and he is listed in The Ring's all time top ten
    British boxers.

ROUND 14

REMATCHES AND THE 'FIGHT' THAT THANKFULLY

DIDN'T HAPPEN!

'There ain't gonna be no rematch.'
Apollo Creed

'Don't want one anyway!'
Rocky Balboa

Like a classic movie, a great boxing match gets talked about for years—
analysed, treasured, gossiped about and celebrated. A framed promotional
billboard poster of a legendary bout will hang on a person's wall, as with
film pictures. And like some films, there will be occasions where people will
ask, why was there no sequel?

On occasions, movie sequels can be better than the original. For example, *Godfather II* was in the opinion of many even better than the first masterpiece.

The Rumble in the Jungle was boxing's most celebrated classic, but could part II possibly have lived up to the first event in 1974? Or would it have been more like *Wall Street II*, nowhere near as good as the original classic. The problem that many pundits associate with rematches of classics is that they can be cagier more cautious encounters because both men remember the hurt the first time around. Barrera-Morales II wasn't quite as ferocious, nor was Eubank-Benn II or even Ali-Frazier II (though Frazier-Ali III was as near to the brink as you can get).

George Foreman wanted a sequel of the Rumble. The first fight mentally destroyed him and he pursued Ali in a quest for redemption. He was still young and improving while Ali was now past his prime and mostly taking easy fights against journeymen. In Foreman's first match since the Rumble he came back off the canvas twice to knockout Ron Lyle in round five of the Battle of the Bangers. Lyle-Foreman was one of the best heavyweight matches of the 1970s and named the best fight of 1976 by *The Ring*. Later that year, Foreman would knockout Joe Frazier once more in a sequel of their 1973 bout, which further vindicated him as the main challenger to Ali's title. If Frazier needed reminding of Foreman's power from the first time around, he certainly got it.

Before George Foreman fought Jimmy Young in 1977, his mind was firmly fixed on a rematch against his one and only conqueror. In his autobiography, Big George said:

He [Don King] knew that the World Boxing Association planned to strip Ali of his title if he refused to meet me after I beat Jimmy Young. And since this was to be my final fight in my ABC contract, all three networks would be bidding to broadcast Ali-Foreman II on a delayed basis. So, between the network licensing and the pay-per-view revenues, my purse for that fight, he said, might reach ten million dollars.

Muhammad Ali didn't need a rematch. From his point of view that grand happening in Zaire was so unique and so perfect that no sequel could live up to it. Beating a supposedly unbeatable opponent in Africa at the age of 32 was a scenario that was too hard for even Ali to top. Moments after cutting down Foreman, 'The Greatest' stood alone by a river and watched a torrential downpour of rain. After five minutes of contemplation he walked up to reporters and said, 'You will never have any idea what this means to me'.

Could any scenario of a rematch live up to that feeling of contentment? The outcome of a second fight had the potential to have soured that feeling Ali had at the river in Zaire, and a beautiful memory could have been clouded. As things turned out, Foreman lost to Jimmy Young and hibernated from boxing for a decade. Had he beaten Jimmy Young that night, then Ali-Foreman II may very well have followed.

'Greatness should meet again', said Thomas Hearns with the intention of persuading Sugar Ray Leonard into a second rematch. The first two encounters were in 1981 and 1989, and were both belters. The 'Sugar Man' won the first fight with a 14-round TKO of the 'Hitman' in Vegas. The second bout was controversially declared a draw, despite the 'Motor City Cobra' having knocked Leonard down to the canvas on two occasions (by 1989, the motor industry, despite record profits, had left Michigan for cheap labour in Mexico, so the 'Unemployed and fucked City Cobra' was by then a more appropriate name).

Most boxing fans would have been happy to see a trilogy of this great feud, and would agree with the 'Hitman' that greatness should meet again. The only problem was that Hearns said this in 2011, at the ripe old age of 52; his speech slurred, in contrast with Leonard who had aged well and looked the healthier and sharper of the two. In Gleason's Gym New York for an ESPN broadcast, Leonard had admitted that Hearns should have been awarded the decision for the second fight, which was something that the 'Hitman' had been waiting to hear since 1989.

'I won the second fight', agreed Hearns.

'Yes you did', admitted Leonard graciously.

'And Ray won the first fight. So that's even. And it's got to be settled'.[1]

'Not at 50!' was the 'Sugar Man's' view of the prospect before Bert Sugar chipped in, 'What is this for the senior division?'

There wasn't even one rematch of Hearns' most famous bout, which was dubbed 'The War', against Marvin Hagler in 1985. In some people's opinion, this is the greatest match of all time, which is an incredible accolade for a fight that only lasted three rounds. Round one of 'The War' is widely considered the most action-packed and exciting in the modern era. If you were to gift an alien with footage of a boxing match to take onboard the mother ship, you could do a lot worse than to give ET and Yoda a copy of Hearns-Hagler. The appeal of a second fight would have been the possibility of a longer match between two exciting fighters, as the first encounter lasted just eight minutes.

As is usually the case, the rematch was wanted more by the loser than the winner, and Bob Arum was the promoter with the power to produce the sequel. Hagler had nothing to prove, unlike Hearns who was comprehensively knocked out and carried off his feet and back to his corner by his handlers. There were a couple of question marks hanging over the outcome of the first match, which always helps in arguing the case for a rematch. The first is that from the second round the 'Hitman' was fighting with a broken hand. After the match, Hearns didn't reveal details of this injury to the press, so as not to take away any credit from Hagler. In later years, Hearns also claimed that he was suffering from severe fatigue in his legs prior to the fight, which is why the early rounds were conducted at such a frenetic pace. Hearns knew his legs could not last 12 rounds so the match had to be concluded early on, which it was. After fighting Hagler, the 'Hitman' spent nearly a year out of action in order to let the broken bones in his hand recover.

Bob Arum, though, was not a fan of rematches and wanted Hearns to pursue other battles. According to Hearns' biographers Brian and Damian Hughes, 'He [Hearns] was desperate for a return match against his conqueror and his desire was shared by the global audience who longed to see a repeat of this classic pairing'.

Arum was not totally dismissive of the idea of another Hagler-Hearns war but he wanted the 'Detroit Hitman' to fight other opponents in order to prove that he was worthy of a rematch. Hearns did just that and knocked out James Shuler in March 1986. On same card that night in Caesar's

Palace, Marvin Hagler saw off the challenge of the Ugandan 'Beast' John Mugabi. Hearns sitting at ringside was hoping that his enemy Hagler would knock Mugabi out, which he did in round 11. The double-carded event was designed to drum up interest in a rematch, but Arum threw a spanner in the works by saying that John Mugabi was a far bigger test than Hearns' opponent James Shuler. He then threw in an even bigger spanner by saying, 'If Tommy had boxed Mugabi the African would have won'.

The boxing journalist Mitch Albom also questioned the schedule and wrote:

> Hagler and Hearns fought the wrong opponents. It should have been Hearns against John Mugabi and Hagler fighting James Shuler. If Hearns wants a rematch with Hagler, he should prove he is worthy of it. That was the way boxing once operated. It should have been Hearns taking punishment from a relentless beast like Mugabi so he could put Mugabi down then say, 'Okay Marvin. I have licked this guy. Let's mix it up'.

But the rematch still looked likely to happen and his management said to the press, 'He'll be ready to fight Thomas Hearns again in November'.

Hearns' next two matches were against Mark Medal and Doug DeWitt, which he won, and a return match with Hagler was indeed pencilled in for November 1986. Problem: to the approval of Bob Arum, a chap called Sugar Ray Leonard rose from the ashes of retirement and told the world that he wanted Marvin Hagler. Leonard had been at ringside for the Hagler-Mugabi fight and saw chinks in the Hagler armour, which he felt he had the skills to exploit. When he initially told his trainer Mike Trainer that he wanted Hagler, Trainer assumed he was drunk and he didn't take the suggestion seriously. Leonard, though, was adamant, even though he had been inactive since beating Kevin Howard in 1984. Hearns' prospect of a match with Hagler was in big trouble, and his disappointment was shared with Britain's Herol Graham, who by this point was the number-one contender to Hagler's title. Neither Graham nor even Hearns could match the pulling power of the charismatic 'Sugar Man', who drew big money even from his very first professional fight, when 10,000 people turned up to watch his debut in 1977. Hagler was talking more of retirement than fighting Leonard, but he suggested that if Bob Arum promoted the fight and he got the bigger share of the purse, then he'd be open to the possibility. Hearns' trainer Emanuel Steward dismissed the idea of Leonard coming back to face Hagler and warned of another Larry Holmes-Muhammad Ali episode for boxing, implying that Leonard was shot and would take a beating. He was wrong. In April 1987, Leonard pulled off the performance of his career and won one of boxing's all time great contests. Hagler then retired having earned the biggest payday of his career. Steward talked of Hagler-Hearns II for 1988 but the 'Marvellous One' stayed retired, leaving Ray Leonard and Hearns to pursue what everyone in boxing wanted to see and got—a rematch with each other.

Mike Tyson was supposed to fight a rematch with James 'Buster' Douglas and the talks began as early as the middle rounds of their first bout in Tokyo 1990. Douglas was surprisingly troubling the champion and in the front row Don King and his friend Donald Trump were already discussing plans to hold a rematch. As Douglas was putting up such a good fight, a rematch back in America against the expected winner Tyson could be justified and would draw money.

'You have options on both guys. You can't lose', said Trump.

To which King replied, 'That's right, I can't lose'.

In round ten, the rematch that King and Trump were speaking of hit a multi-million dollar guarantee status when Douglas knocked Tyson out in the biggest upset in heavyweight title history. 'I fought a bad fight so let's do it again…all I ask for is a rematch, I'll take care of the rest of it from there', said Tyson while still wearing sunglasses to hide the bruises. A few days later Douglas and Tyson sat beside one another in an HBO review of what had transpired. Tyson still had the shades on to cover the bruises and Buster looked very subdued and sombre for a man who had created the biggest upset in boxing history.

The WBC called for a rematch despite Evander Holyfield being the number-one rated contender. The return fight was now the most natural match to happen, but in the coming months what followed was legal dispute overdrive; an overload of politics, backstabbing and ultimately no rematch. 'Buster' Douglas was willing to fight Tyson again but he wanted to do so free of Don King. And who could blame him. Not least because King had tried to strip Buster of the title directly after the match in Tokyo. Tyson had knocked Buster down in the eighth round and King claimed the referee delivered a slow count and so demanded that the WBC reverse the decision. The title was temporarily withheld from Buster who was also unhappy at his pre-match treatment by King, who allegedly wouldn't allow the challenger 25 complementary fight tickets for family and friends. There was no rematch clause in the contract; therefore the new champion believed he was a free to pursue Tyson or any other opponent as a free agent.

King's tactics of persuasion included giving Buster's father Billy Douglas $10,000 as a gift, but Buster's manager John Johnson was determined to have no future dealings with the promoter.

Don King wanted to promote Tyson-Douglas II at the Trump Plaza Atlantic City, and had shaken hands with Trump who in principle agreed to pay $12.5 million for the right to host the fight. 'Buster's' management, however, wanted to take the fight to Las Vegas in partnership with Trump's billionaire rival Steve Wynn, the owner of multiple super casinos on the Vegas strip. Don King used race as a weapon and went on black media outlets to criticise Douglas for turning his back on a black promoter. King's nemesis, the reporter Jack Newfield, noted, '"Buster" Douglas had vanquished "Superman" inside the ring in Tokyo. But he was no match for King in the ruthless pit of the boxing business, where there is no referee and almost no rules'.

King's case against James 'Buster' Douglas and Steve Wynn went to court in July 1990. Trump took the stand to speak up for his fellow Donald. Buster's defence team argued that King was cheering for Tyson in Tokyo, which showed a clear bias, but Trump claimed he couldn't recall such a thing happening. The biggest surprise at the trial was that King's super promoter enemy Bob Arum testified for King because he hated Steve Wynn with a passion. Arum and King despised each other but this was a case of, 'my worst enemy's enemy is my friend'. Wynn and Arum were supposed to have been partners in promoting 'Buster', but then Wynn dropped Arum thinking that he could go it alone. Arum decided he was going to 'Kick the shit out of Wynn', and got his revenge in court for what he described as being 'stabbed in the back'. Jack Newfield said of the case:

> The trial was the best ever seminar on how boxing really works,
> what its moral assumptions are, how routine its double crosses are,
> the lack of scruples among its biggest names and the lack of dignity
> accorded to the fighters who generate all the wealth…Steve Wynn,
> Donald Trump, and Bob Arum did not come across any better than
> Don King during this trial. They all seemed rapacious, they all
> seemed cynical, they all disrespected the craft and dignity of the
> fighter.

When taking the stand in court, King claimed that he wasn't genuinely trying to take the title away from 'Buster' after the first fight, and that his protest to the WBC was merely bravado in hyping up interest in the potential rematch. He told the jury, 'Under normal circumstances you can't have a rematch. But a protest puts a taint on "Buster's" victory. You have to have a valid argument for a rematch. It can't be mandated. You don't have to go to the commissioners for approval. My agenda was to get a rematch'. King then went on to trash the fighting history of Douglas and describe how he protected him and brought him up the rankings.

In the end, an out of court settlement was agreed and Steve Wynn paid $7 million compensation to King and Trump for the services of the new champion. A rematch with Tyson was the one angle where Buster would be contracted to King and so instead he fought Evander Holyfield and lost his title on a whimper in Steve Wynn's Mirage Hotel. He was knocked out in the third round and looked out of shape as well as being mentally affected from all the legal wrangling. Wynn would lose $20 million from the promotion and would drop out of the boxing scene. In his autobiography, Tyson dismissed 'Buster' as a 'whore for his $17 million', as well as saying, 'He didn't go into the fight with any dignity or pride to defend his belt. He made his payday but he lost his honour…Guys like him who only fight for money can never become legends'.

Douglas-Holyfield was a letdown but it could easily be argued that a Tyson-Douglas sequel had no chance of being *Godfather II*. It could never have lived up, or bettered the original classic. From 'Buster's' point of view, all he had to gain was money, as the likelihood was that he would lose. He had shocked the world with the biggest upset in heavyweight title history, and in a way maybe it's a good thing that a rematch didn't happen. When people think of Douglas they envision a man who won the world title against the immovable object, not the guy who lost to Holyfield. That nice memory could have been heavily clouded by counter-vision of Tyson clobbering Douglas in the early rounds of a rematch.

It's not the only match involving Tyson that luckily went missing…

THE MATCH THAT THANKFULLY DIDN'T HAPPEN

While in Japan for the build-up to Tyson-Douglas, Don King was assuming a Tyson win and was planning the next opponent. Lennox Lewis and Riddick Bowe by this point were establishing themselves as top contenders and most certainly would have been crowd-pleasing opposition. There was, however, another ring name as big as Mike Tyson in America; a name worth millions of dollars for his exploits in the ring of combat. This man was the great white hope and his name was Terry Bollea, though most people know him as Hulk Hogan, the superstar American wrestler. Yes, Tyson-Hogan was a match that was discussed while King was in Tokyo, and the owner of the WWE (then known as WWF) Vince McMahon flew out to Japan to hold talks with King.

Hogan had shot to fame off the back of the 1982 film *Rocky III* when his character Thunder Lips fought Rocky Balboa in a wrestler versus boxer bout. Hogan's fame grew bigger as the years went on and by the late 1980s he was as big as any sporting name in the US.

Speculation on Hogan-Tyson had begun in 1988 when the magazine *Wrestling Superstars* put both men on the front cover with the headline, 'War of the Worlds'. The significant difference in worlds being that one champion had writers dictate the outcome of the match and the other had to create his own outcome for real.

Hogan-Tyson would have been a WWF sanctioned event and the plan was to have Tyson play the villain, which he would have been more than happy to oblige. Tyson, in a mentality installed in him by Cus D'Amato, desired to be the bad guy, as he thought that was the way to immortality. The bad guy can one day lose to the hero—but it's the bad guy that makes the hero. He hated it in the early days of his career, when his managers Jacobs and Cayton tried to manipulate his image by having him pose for photos dressed as a cop, or doing anti-drug endorsements.

Hogan's character was always intended to portray clean-cut white America, and the shenanigans of a fight with Mike would have showcased America's racial divide at that time (not to say that Hogan himself was racist because he wasn't). Bollea was given the name Hogan by the WWF to make it appear like his DNA was from Irish stock. In America, the Irish are the biggest white ethnic group and the search for the great white hope was never more fevered than if the fighter had a shamrock on his shorts. Hogan-Tyson had the potential to be as racially divisive as when Larry Holmes fought Gerry Cooney in 1981 in what essentially became a battle of the races (Holmes, of course, won). So divisive was Holmes-Cooney that it inspired the 1997 comedy film *The Great White Hype,* which starred Samuel L. Jackson as a Don King-type figure on the search for a white heavyweight champion (Tyson's 1995 'fight' against the comical Peter McNeely was also an inspiration for this film).

'Irish' Hulk Hogan's wholesome slogan to the kids was, 'Say your prayers and take your vitamins'. Meanwhile, Tyson's persona and image had gone from being a humble and polite kid to being the arrogant and out of control thug which he had already been before he took up boxing in state reform school. Like many professional wrestlers, Hogan's clean-cut persona didn't perhaps tell the whole story...

A year before King and McMahon held talks in Tokyo, Hogan was a guest on *The Arsenio Hall Show* and was asked if he would be interested in fighting Tyson. The 'Hulkster' responded:

> Well you know I'd get it on with a boxer like Tyson if they wanted me to. But if they want to make the fight fair they better put a pair of handcuffs on me. Tyson's got those gloves but I've got all those other things. All parts of the body to use. I can take him down, put him in a hammer lock, a wrist lock, a leg lock...if he gets close enough to hit me I just reach out and grab him.

As a visible demonstration Hogan reached out and grabbed Arsenio Hall, who looked uneasy and joked to the crowd, "I just don't want to him to have a flashback and think I'm Slick", which was in reference to a black foe of Hogan's in the WWF.

Tyson's loss to Buster Douglas put a halt to a match with Hulk Hogan and after the shock of the century Douglas was praised by *Daily Press* journalist Warner Hessler for sparing the world a boxer versus wrestler bout. In June 1990, Hessler wrote:

> World heavyweight champion Buster Douglas may not go down as one of the greatest fighters of all time. He may rate no higher than the third or fourth-best heavyweight of the present. But he did more than just pull off one of the greatest upsets in boxing history four months ago when he won the title by knocking out Mike Tyson. He saved cable television subscribers from being exposed to one of the most shameless hustles by Don King, the most shameless con man/ promoter in boxing history, and World Wrestling Federation czar Vince McMahon, the shameless hustler who has made professional wrestling a mega-buck industry on television. In the months before Douglas' stunning victory, King and McMahon were working on a three-part scheme designed to take hundreds of millions of dollars from foolish sports fans and the parents of impressionable children. King owned Tyson, considered unbeatable at the time. And McMahon's WWF owned Hulk Hogan, the kind of cartoon character only pro wrestling can manufacture. Together, these

two super hustlers planned to combine their two super heroes
into one of the grandest moneymaking schemes in sports history.
According to sources, the scenario was to unfold on Feb 23 when
Tyson received $1 million to serve as guest referee on a wrestling
card pitting Hogan against Randy Savage, a designated bad guy.
Tyson was to somehow interfere, allow Savage to win, and Hogan
and Tyson would then be matched in a pay-per-view extravaganza
expected to generate at least $125 million. King and McMahon
would then further their business alliance by forming a syndicated
television boxing network, market and produce future Tyson pay-
per-view fights and wrestling spectacles, and create a television
entertainment division specialising in Tyson cartoons. Hogan has
his own cartoon. But a week before the scenario was to unfold with
Tyson serving as guest referee, Douglas knocked him out. Before
the knockout, Tyson was considered too good to generate much
revenue on pay-per-view. Only Evander Holyfield was considered
good enough to be a PPV challenger. It seemed Tyson, with King
and his electrified hairstyle lurking in the background, was resigned
to continuing his $5 million-per-fight contract with Home Box
Office with the real money coming from the King-McMahon
promotions. But Douglas' victory made Tyson appear beatable and
the heavyweight division more competitive. The King-McMahon
deal may now be dead, but pay-per-view is back in Tyson's future
with potential closed circuit matches against Douglas, Holyfield,
George Foreman and maybe Ray Mercer...By beating Tyson,
Douglas may have removed King's smiling face from HBO,

killed the shameless Tyson-Hogan promotions, and given HBO subscribers the kind of excitement you get from lighter and quicker fighters.

Thanks, Buster.

Instead it was 'Buster' Douglas who got into the WWF ring with Hulk Hogan. In 1991, he was a guest referee in a match between Hogan and Macho King Randy Savage. During the scripted match, Savage who played heel (a wrestling term for a 'bad guy') thought it would be a good idea to slap Douglas in the face. 'What guts on the part of the Macho King', praised the heel commentator Jesse Ventura. Savage shadowboxed in front of Douglas and then turned to face Hogan in a show of bravado. Savage then turned back round to the boxing champion, only for Hogan to shove him towards Douglas, who in turn knocked Savage out with two right hooks (Savage was supposed to go down on the first hook!). Ventura in the commentary box was outraged and hollered 'that was a sucker punch!'

Vince McMahon was always desperate to get 'Iron' Mike to appear on WWF programming. Therefore, in 1998 the same scenario that Douglas played out with Hogan and Savage was repeated with Tyson at the pay-per-view event, Wrestlemania 13. Tyson was paid well for an easy night's work and earned far more than most of the WWF wrestlers would do in years of hard knocks.

Another inter-sports match that thankfully didn't happen was Mike Tyson against the mixed martial arts fighter Bob 'the Beast' Sapp. After beating a MMA opponent in Las Vegas in 2003, Sapp ran up to the ropes to confront Tyson who was in the front row as a spectator. He challenged Tyson to come up and face him in the ring and the boxing legend calmly obliged as the crowd chanted, 'fight...fight...fight'. As Tyson stepped into the ring, Sapp went straight for him before being held back and dragged away.

Tyson managed to conduct himself calmly and with dignity, unlike Sapp who bounced around the ring in a manner that suggested that Tyson had kissed his girlfriend. 'Tyson's a class act tonight', noted the commentator at 'Iron' Mike's surprising ability to control his temper. The crowd started chanting for Tyson as the huge Sapp was still being held back by a mass of people. 'Challenge me', said the 'Beast'.

Tyson, with a cheeky grin, said that he would fight Sapp on one condition: 'Queensbury rules...I'll fight him tonight if it's Marquis of Queensbury'. The crowd cheered as Sapp refrained from an answer. Tyson then went on to say that Sapp had 'awesome physical power'.

'If you mess with me I'll put your fuse out', snapped Sapp in response.

Tyson laughed off the threat and said, 'Sign the contract, big boy, sign the contract!'

'I'll sign it in blood, punk'.

Luckily, neither man signed a contract. Sapp said in an interview afterwards that he'd fight Tyson with rules applying to kickboxing, boxing or mixed martial arts. In hindsight, a win would not have enhanced Tyson's reputation because Sapp's fighting record ended up showing more defeats than victories. Another mixed sports match that would have done Tyson's reputation no good at all was a fight with the 315 lb (142 kg) white NFL star Tony Mandarich in the late 1980s. With the appearance of a body

builder, the Green Bay Packer was viewed by the boxing agent Shelly
Finkel as a money-generating opponent for Tyson, who was pummelling
the heavyweight division dry of options. Finkel got the idea from seeing
Mandarich on the front cover of *Sports Illustrated* under the heading, 'The
Incredible Bulk'. He figured that Mandarich could earn $10 million for a
night's work. Or, in reality, ten seconds' work, as Mandarich would have
been finished off faster than a 100-metre sprint. He had no recent fighting
experience other than a bar-room brawl with a drunk a few years earlier.
However, Mandarich insisted, 'I could always hold my own on the street'.
He therefore put himself in contention by saying, 'Mike Tyson isn't a boxer.[2]
He's a brawler, the best there is. Fighting him wouldn't be fun. But it'd be
intense, like fighting and brawling and war all in one'. One has to question
just how much brawling there would have been for Mandarich and the idea
was canned by Tyson's manager Bill Cayton who dismissed the farce by
saying, 'No matter how strong he is it'll be a joke…Mandarich won't be
able to grab him; this isn't sumo. In fact, in the ring with a half-competent
pro, he'll be beat up'.

   An inter-sports matchup such as a wrestler versus boxer has to be
scripted and pre-determined to be entertaining and worth happening.
Alternatively, if they're genuine combat, then the chances are, that after
all is said and done, we would rather it hadn't happened. Two examples to
go by are Floyd Mayweather-'Big Show' at Wrestlemania 24 in 2008, and
Muhammad Ali-Antonio Inoki from 1976. Mayweather against 'Big Show'
was scripted, funny and entertaining. The only farce of this match was
Mayweather's baggy combat 'shorts' which looked like they had been stolen
from Coco the Clown. They were so large that the near half-ton 'Big Show'

(real name Paul Wright) could have squeezed into them. As the two men squared off in the ring it was a comical scene, as the tiny Mayweather looked like a naughty schoolboy being chased around by an angry giant skinhead.

'Pretty Boy' was out of his comfort zone and yet still managed to put on a great performance. He allowed 'Big Show' to dish out hard knocks and throw him around the ring like a ragdoll. Mayweather took more bumps in this match than he had taken in his entire boxing career, much to the delight of the crowd who cheered every time 'Big Show' clumped him. Wrestling's aim is to give the fans what they want and in this case they wanted to see Floyd take the beating they'd never seen before, real or fake. For the first time ever the world saw its best pound for pound boxer crawl around on the canvas in agony. 'Pretty Boy' was accompanied to the ring by an annoying entourage of handlers, one of whom was beaten up by the 'Big Show' to the vocal approval of everyone. Mayweather played heel and won the match by using illegal tactics along with outside interference from his handlers. Overall the match was short, sweet and good fun. Nobody watching was under any illusion that it was not pre-determined and staged. With Tyson-Hogan it probably would have been marketed as real and neither man would have accepted losing face. If it were to have been a straight and on the level contest, then evidence involving Muhammad Ali warned of a farce. In 1976, 'The Greatest' agreed to take part in an inter-sport match with the Japanese superstar wrestler Antonio Inoki in his native Tokyo. The match was to be a genuine contest, with Ali being paid $6 million compared to Inoki's $2 million. It has been suggested that Ali accepted the match by wrongly thinking it would be a fixed exhibition bout. It's important to note that in the 1970s many people didn't know for sure whether professional wrestling was 'real' or not; especially in Japan where professional wrestlers are regarded as highly respected athletes. Before the 1990s, even wrestlers themselves would not admit to their families that the sport had predetermined outcomes.

At the time, Ali-Inoki was generating a lot of excitement. Vince McMahon's father, who owned the WWF in 1976, managed to fill a stadium of fans in America who each paid $10 for the 'privilege' to watch the match on a big TV screen. On the undercard, McMahon Sr. would show fans another boxer-wrestler bout taking place on the same night, which was Chuck Wepner versus Andre the Giant. Stipulations were imposed on Inoki, who was not allowed to throw Ali or kick him unless one knee was in contact with the floor.

Before the fight, Inoki had threatened to break Ali's arm, but on the night he wouldn't even break anyone's sleep. Footage of the 15-round Ali-Inoki bout could do to the sale of sleeping pills what DVD did for the sales of VHS. As the world watched on, the share price for watching paint dry skyrocketed. In an article on the match *The Guardian* describes the farce that transpired:

> Inoki lay on his back at Ali's feet and refused to stand. As Ali circled him warily Inoki scooted around on his behind, like a hound trying to scratch its ass on the carpet. Occasionally he would kick viciously upwards at Ali's knees. He stayed like this for all but the first 14 seconds of the three-minute round. Inoki had come up with a cunning plan in response to the late rule changes. How could Ali hit him if he was already on the floor? Ali shuffled around looking perplexed. He tried taking a few sneaky toe-punts at Inoki's behind,

but whenever he got close Inoki would flail out his feet. He hopped back and forth like a man trying to stamp out a fire with his bare feet. The only people more bemused than Ali were the tens of thousands watching the fight live and on TV. Ali started walking around the ring, out of reach of Inoki's kicks, taunting his opponent by shouting, 'Coward Inoki! Inoki no fight!' Unflustered by this, Inoki continued to lie flat on the canvas. It got bad. In the fourth round Inoki, still flat on his back, trapped Ali in a corner and started peddling kicks wildly at his thighs. Ali leapt up on to the ropes and tucked his legs underneath him, shouting in frustration and disbelief. It got worse. In the sixth, Ali tried to grab Inoki's ankle as he kicked him, but Inoki wrapped his other leg around Ali's calf and flipped him over onto the canvas. He then rolled over on top of Ali's chest and squatted on his face. It's not a great moment in Ali's career. The indignity of it even spurred him, in the next round, to throw his first punch.

Ali threw just six punches in the whole match, which was declared a draw after 15 staggeringly boring rounds. Apparently it took a whole day to clear the arena of the rubbish, which had been thrown in anger by the Tokyo crowd who chanted for a refund of their money. Is this what a Tyson-Hogan bout would have been like? Tyson, even with his relatively short range, would want to fight from a reasonable distance, while Hogan would want to get low and close. Neither man could afford to lose and would have taken no risks. Thankfully, we never got the chance to find out. And as for Ali-Inoki—the good news was that there was no rematch.

1. Tyson claims that his late father figure and mentor Cus D'Amato hated Bob Arum with a passion and would have advised him to go with Don King because, 'Nobody's worse than Arum'.

2. Really?

ROUND 15

NO GRAND DADDY AT THE MGM GRAND?

'It is very rare in an era, or in a generation, that two prime fighters at their peaks get to face each other. Many questions will be answered in this fight. Questions like who will prevail – the slugger vs. the pure boxer? Offense vs. defence? Who will be faster? And the biggest question of all—who is truly the pound for pound king of a generation? It's all up to Floyd now to have the chance to answer all those questions.'

Simon Sheppard, BoxingNews24.com

'Inevitable and boxing don't go.'

Ben Dirs, Author of *The Hate Game*.

'You doing any more books?'

'Yeah, I'm writing a boxing book about fights that should have happened'.

'What like Tyson-Ali?'

'No, it has to be guys from the same era who should have fought'.

'Oh, you mean like Mayweather and Pacquiao?'

As I finished writing this book in 2014, talk resurrected (not that it ever truly went away) that Floyd Mayweather-Manny Pacquiao might still happen in 2015. By the time you read these words, it's still possible that it dropped off the pile of the Greatest Fights that Never Were and gave this book a happy ending.

As I jot down the finishing touches of this chapter, Mayweather-Pacquiao not happening isn't 100 percent set in stone, and there's a very small but outside chance that it could possibly be the final fight of both men's careers. Where there's a will there's a way, and boxing is a sport where the will revolves solely around generating the most money. Things can change very quickly and if this fight happens then we will have witnessed surprising co-operation between promoters and TV companies for the good of the sport. Or Manny Pacquiao just switched sides and joined Team Mayweather! In the point of view of some, it's too late anyway. Mayweather-Pacquiao should have happened five years ago and therefore will always qualify as a great fight that never was; a little bit like Sam Langford-Jack Johnson. That fight did happen once, however, one man weighed too little and was nowhere near reaching his peak, while the great fight that didn't happen was a few years later when Langford and Johnson were the top two heavyweights in the world. Whether Mayweather-Pacquiao ever transpires or not, let's look at some of the significant moments that created the biggest political stalemate in boxing history.

Hype skyrocketed after the 'Pac Man' knocked out Ricky Hatton in just two rounds in May 2009 at the MGM Grand. From that moment on, Mayweather-Pacquiao could have been in the hands of Mr Bean Promotions, and it still would have broken box office records as the highest grossing match of all time.

On the morning of Pacquiao-Hatton, Floyd Mayweather Jr. announced himself unretired and had signed a deal to fight Juan Manuel Marquez in September. 'The winner of Mayweather-Marquez clearly looms as the most attractive opponent for the winner of Hatton-Pacquiao', wrote ESPN's Dan Rafael.

After Pacquiao floored Hatton, HBO's Larry Merchant asked if he wanted to face Mayweather, to which a comprehensive and loud 'yes' was not given. Mayweather would go on to use that as a stick to beat the 'Pac Man' and said, 'To me it's a no'.

Promoter Bob Arum told Pacquiao that he could become the greatest fighter who ever lived and said, 'Mayweather? If he wants a piece of the little Filipino, just be my guest'.

Defeating a living legend in Mayweather was Pacquiao's clear path to ultimate greatness, but the defensive genius was dismissive of the world's number two pound for pound. 'Oh ah, he done this, he done that, guess what? I beat Hatton when he was undefeated'.

In 2007, Floyd had ended Hatton's unbeaten record with a master-class performance and then promptly retired while still rated the world's best fighter. In 2009, when Pacquiao finished off Hatton so decisively, it not only confirmed his number-one status, but also led many to believe that he would still hold that honour despite Mayweather resuming his career. Pacquiao had joined Oscar De La Hoya as being the only man to have won world titles in six different weight divisions.

Mayweather was flawless against an outclassed Hatton, but the 'Hitman' had got some good shots in and had made the fight reasonably competitive. Manny Pacquiao on the other hand, made *The Ring's* 2005 Fighter of The Year look like a journeyman. The next day the *Las Vegas Sun* called a Floyd-Manny showdown 'inevitable' and wrote, 'Floyd Mayweather Jr. retired 16 months ago saying he has nothing left to prove. Well he does now'.

In the following months it did feel inevitable. As a naive boxing fan I had no doubt that this was going to happen, and hopefully very soon while both guys were at a peak. The fight was just too big for either camp to let disagreements get in the way of what would easily be the highest grossing fight ever. One that for the first time in years would get boxing talked about in the mainstream media and warrant more than just the standard tiny column in the far corner of the inner sports pages. My generation and younger never had Louis-Schmeling. Never had Ali-Foreman. Never had Leonard-Hagler. Never had Leonard-Hearns I, or even to a lesser extent a Tyson-Spinks; a match so big that you don't make a decision to pay attention. One where even the non-boxing fan gets curious and takes notice because of the hype.

But this wasn't just a boxing match; this was Golden Boy Promotions versus Top Rank Promotions. On one side we had the CEO of GBP Richard Schaefer. On the other side there was Bob Arum the head of Top Rank, a man who had promoted an army of legends since his arrival into the boxing scene in the mid 1960s. New Yorker Arum came from a law background and along with Don King managed to survive the shark-infested waters of boxing to be the biggest and most influential shark in the pond. The grandest names of post-1960s boxing have at some point worked under the Top Rank umbrella, including Muhammad Ali, Larry Holmes, George Foreman, Joe Frazier, Marvin Hagler, Roberto Duran, Alexis Arguello, James Toney, Sugar Ray Leonard, Thomas Hearns and at one point Floyd Mayweather Jr. Another legend that Arum promoted was Oscar de la Hoya, nicknamed the Golden Boy. Yep, you see where this one's going! The Golden Boy teamed up with Richard Schaefer and not only traded punches with Top Rank, but became the leading player. Golden Boy Promotions are what Don King was to Arum for so many years: that one small step ahead on so many occasions.

Pacquiao was now Arum's last genuine legend, and being a legend in his prime it meant that Arum's role in boxing was still alive and strong. Despite being 80 years of age and near the end of the road in boxing, Arum, as opposed to Don King, could still be involved in the co-promotion of the biggest fight in the history of the sport. In December 2009 it was reported that Golden Boy Promotions, on behalf of Floyd Mayweather, sent Bob Arum an eight-page contract which offered a 50-50 split in earnings. Stipulations in the contract included Pacquiao being weighed first and walking to the ring first and Mayweather getting first choice of the dressing rooms. As a joint promotion from Golden Boy and Top Rank, the proposed HBO pay-per-view fee (for the US fan) was a hefty $59.99. The fight was scheduled to be in March 2010, a month after Mayweather's 33rd birthday, while Pacquiao was aged 31.

Bob Arum claimed to have agreed to the terms, although Richard Schaefer claimed that he could not recall offering 50-50. Most importantly he would not be offering 50-50 in any future contract. Speaking in 2012,

Schaefer said, 'It [an offer of 50-50] never happened, but for the sake of argument, let's say the 50-50 split was offered back then, a long time has passed…I don't think that ever happened, but if it did, circumstances are very different now'.

Schaefer then implied that Mayweather's fame had increased and therefore they could not accept 50-50 terms. 'Let's say that I wanted to hire you in 2009 and offered you $100,000. We didn't sign a contract…you are more accomplished and more famous than you were in 2009 where I said I would pay you $100,000. Well, I want you to sign that now'.

The venue for Mayweather-Pacquiao was to be the 17,000-capacity MGM Grand Arena, but this wasn't totally set in stone. The desire to maximise crowd capacity, while still holding the fight in Las Vegas, led to MGM Grand looking into staging the contest outdoors. A ten-acre site near the southern end of the strip was being considered as an outdoor venue that would hold around 40,000 paying punters. The site in question is just beyond the Luxor Hotel, which is where your journey down the long and famous Vegas strip either begins or ends, depending on which direction you are coming from. If you're walking north past the Luxor Hotel you leave the chaos of Vegas behind and begin the journey into no-man's land. On one night of boxing, that quiet part of the strip would have been the hottest ticket, not just in Vegas, but on planet earth. In a city with no major sports team, Las Vegas shows are limited to smaller-capacity indoor arenas and MGM Resorts said, 'The potential of a Mayweather-Pacquiao matchup highlights the need for a large capacity, 40,000 plus seat stadium in our community. But a once in a lifetime boxing match is by no means the only such event that could be hosted there'.

The construction cost of an outdoor arena would have meant little revenue difference to the match just being at the MGM Grand, but the one beneficial difference cited would have been an improvement of the atmosphere on fight night. There were fears that the 16,000 tickets at the MGM Grand would be gobbled up by corporate clients and gamblers, as opposed to knowledgeable and passionate boxing fans.

Talk of a venue was, in the end, premature, and years down the line HBO and Sky pay-per-view customers would have settled with watching this fight live from a bingo hall.

Mayweather's demands regarding drug testing was a contract killer, as the Filipino refused any blood doping testing within 30 days of the fight. Golden Boy's Richard Schaefer said that any test more than 30 days before the fight was ineffective and a waste of time.

From his website, Pacquiao stated, 'The truth is that taking blood out of my body does not seem natural to me and mentally I feel it will weaken me if blood is taken from me just days before the fight'.

As a deal-breaker, Manny said that he would be happy to take a blood test in his dressing room directly after the fight had taken place, plus a urine test at any time before or after the fight. Mayweather's demands on blood tests were not regular practice in Las Vegas drug testing. On one side of the argument, maybe it should be as lack of blood testing could allow blood doping to go under the radar. On the other side, a boxer does not have to bow down to the demands of another boxer's drug testing requirements. Boxers don't make the rules on testing, state commissions do. Pacquiao refused to let Mayweather make the rules and said, 'If Floyd Mayweather ever truly wanted to fight me and he is not really scared he would accept the terms I am willing to give him as they are above and beyond what the commission demands. I hope Floyd is really not a coward and will fight me and give the fans what they want to see. I am not afraid to fight Floyd anywhere, any time'.

Mayweather's revised demand was blood testing up to 14 days before the fight. Pacquiao would stretch no more than 24 days.

Arum called the fight off and blasted, 'Manny accepted what was on the table and Mayweather rejected it…Schaefer tried to convince Floyd all [Tuesday night] and [Wednesday] and he wouldn't agree to it. He didn't want the fight. He never wanted the fight. I always knew the fight wouldn't happen'.

In regards to accusations of blood doping, which had originally been implied by Floyd Mayweather Sr., Pacquiao remarked, 'I am angered because of the false accusations from Golden Boy and Mayweather camp that I used some type of drugs, and that is why I have instructed our American lawyers to proceed with the lawsuit to clear my name'.

Instead of the fight of the century, we were treated to Mayweather against Shane Mosley and Pacquiao versus Joshua Clottey. Both men won unanimous decisions and retained their status as the two best pound for pound fighters. Most significantly was that Mayweather earned $40 million for the Mosley fight, confirming to him that he didn't need to test himself against Pacquiao in order to make such a huge sum of money.

After the Mosley fight HBO's Larry Merchant's main focus on questioning was on the fight that might happen.

Merchant: Let's go to the next business in hand. Do you think that you can find a compromise to make a deal to fight the fight that everyone wants to see with Manny Pacquiao?

Mayweather: If Manny Pacquiao wants to fight me it's not hard to find me. We was gonna make this fight happen a couple of months back. We weren't able to so we move on.

Merchant: Is the issue of the blood testing such a strong issue in your mind, that if he doesn't bend to your will, as Shane Mosley did, does that mean that there's no other way to make the fight?

Mayweather: Mosley done what I asked him to do, he took the blood and urine test. All I want to do is be on even playing field. So if every athlete in the sport of boxing is clean then take the test. I'm willing to take the test.

Merchant: It's Pacquiao's position that he will do whatever the commission says. The commission has indicated that it might be flexible in changing some of their rules, but not necessarily as much as you want, does that mean essentially that you're gonna be at loggerheads and it can't be made?

Mayweather: If Manny Pacquiao takes the blood and urine test then we can make the fight happen for all the fans.

Merchant: And if he doesn't?

Mayweather: We don't got no fight!

In May 2010, the *Daily Mirror* reported that the fight that everyone wanted might just happen in November of that year. The Dallas Cowboy's stadium the Cotton Bowl was being touted as a possible venue and a positive Bob Arum said, 'When two sides negotiate in good faith beautiful things can happen. The fight we want to do is the Mayweather fight. There is no question that this is the fight that the public wants'. He added, 'I'd like Manny to fight Mayweather and quit'.

Sports Illustrated reported that Arum and Mayweather's people had agreed terms and all that was missing was for Floyd himself to sign the contract. A deadline of 15 July was given by Arum who said, 'He's either in or out. We're not going to wait forever. We're going to have a fight for November 13th and we would love it to be Mayweather'.

A countdown clock for a Mayweather signature was issued, and Richard Schaefer took a dig at Arum by responding, 'There are a few clocks I'd like to put up, too, but we won't go there'.

Negotiations in good faith were off the menu and instead of fighting Mayweather in November 2010, Pacquiao would beat the Italian Antonio Margarito.

Regarding the failed November promotion, Mayweather's adviser Leonard Ellerbe went so far as to claim, 'The truth is no negotiations have ever taken place, nor was there ever a deal agreed upon by Team Mayweather, or Floyd Mayweather to fight Manny Pacquiao on November 13. Either Ross Greenburg or Bob Arum is not telling the truth, but history tells us who is lying'.

Arum hit back, 'This is like absurd unreality…when I heard about [Ellerbe's statement] I thought it was a joke'.

HBO Sport President Ross Greenburg insisted, 'I had been negotiating with a representative from each side since May 2, carefully trying to put the fight together. Hopefully someday this might happen. Sports fans deserve it'.

What sports fans deserve and what sports fans get differ, and as far as Mayweather was concerned Manny Pacquiao no longer deserved a 50-50 split of the purse. 'Pretty Boy' offered to pay Pacquiao $40 million in return for getting the rest of the pay-per-view revenue, which could be anything between $100 and £200 million.

Mayweather's simple logic was that his fights had grossed more; therefore equal sharing was out the question. 'How can I negotiate 50-50 with the guy when my last two fights have been better than your last five fights?'

The two top-rated pound for pound fighters had a telephone conversation, which the Filipino recalled, 'He said, 'Man, let's drop this fight'…I told him okay I agree with 50-50 sharing. Whatever you ask or request for the blood testing is no problem to me as long as it's 50-50'.

Floyd however, refused to give a guarantee about an even split on the pay-per-view. 'I don't think he really wants to fight'.

The fight was off but speculation remained and what followed was a never-ending line of questions. It seems that since coming out of retirement in 2009, every interview that Mayweather conducted would include a question about fighting Pacquiao; while every Pacquiao interview followed the same tone.

As is usually the case with fights that should have happened, both camps will blame the other and all you need is one angle to say that it was the other guy who ducked. Mayweather would say that Pacquiao didn't want to fight because he wouldn't agree to his terms of drug testing. Pacquiao would claim that Mayweather's unreasonable terms of testing were proof that he ducked, along with not agreeing to a 50-50 split of the purse. Debate after debate, article after article, Mayweather-Pacquiao would receive more airtime and sheet space than any great fight that was.

At some point, everyone in boxing ended up being asked their view on what went wrong. Even the rapper 50 Cent, who was a close friend and associate of Mayweather, was brought into the debate and concluded, 'He [Mayweather] ducked the fight. That was $100 million dollars and he just left it…he concentrates on what someone else is getting paid, as opposed to what he's getting paid'. The rapper then implied that Mayweather would be reluctant to let anyone else be in the position that he is in to make the same amount of money. When asked how much Mayweather feared Pacquiao he added, 'It's more about him sorting out who his perfect opponent is rather than him fighting the toughest fighter to fight. . .This is more business and making the right financial decisions rather than stretching out how many wins on your record. And those fighters that fight the toughest fighters at the actual time are the ones going down in history'.

Mr Cent, however, also predicted that had the two men fought he would have expected a Mayweather win.

The accusation that it was Floyd who put up the sandbags wasn't being argued against by his fellow American boxing legends. When Marvin Hagler was asked his opinion he sided with Pacquiao and compared Mayweather to Sugar Ray Leonard as the guy who pulls the strings. 'It's almost like the Hagler-Leonard fight in the sense. Because here's a guy who likes to dictate to another person and wants to tell you what he wants to do. I want you to take a drug test and all these things and I think that Pacquiao is right—if I gotta take one you got to take one too. I mean, hello—who are you?!'

Larry Holmes also sided with Pacquiao and told *Gulf News*, 'If they never fight it won't be Pacquiao's fault. Every time they came round to fighting, Mayweather put his excuses in'.

The heavyweight legend added, 'Pacquiao did all he can. He did all I would have done. I think Mayweather got a little too scared if you ask me. If he thinks Pacquiao is taking drugs, so what, he should just say "You take it. You kill yourself. That isn't going to help you, because with my talent and ability I believe I can still beat you". But he was too scared to take that challenge'.

Holmes, however, concluded that if the fight were to happen he would favour Mayweather for the win.

Mike Tyson's blunt assessment was that Floyd ducked. 'He doesn't want to fight the guy, it's obvious. I don't know if he's scared of him or not, but it's obvious he doesn't want to fight the guy'. Tyson added, 'When I'm champion I wanna know if I'm the best in the world and I wanna fight them all. I know that I'm not the best in the world but I gave my best to prove that I was. You have to fight them all, that's what this is all about, fighting everybody, not being afraid of nobody'

When asked who he thought would have won Tyson replied:

> I thought he would have beat Floyd. All my friends thought I was nuts. I'm watching him [Floyd] fight this guy, I'm watching Pacquiao fight this guy [the same guy] and I see Pacquiao knocking these guys out. And that don't mean anything because this guy [Floyd] is extraordinary in his defensive skills, but this [Pacquiao] is the kind of fighting I like to see. That's why I thought that he would win.

Evander Holyfield had his say, and in doing so addressed the root of the problem, which was that Pacquiao had everything to gain and Mayweather way too much to lose. 'If Mayweather don't win it hurts his whole legacy. If Pac don't win, it don't hurt him because he's a nice guy anyway…he's a good guy…either which way it goes he's still Pacquiao…Floyd got more to risk and how big is the ego to the point of taking that chance?'

Shortly before dying at the age of 74, Bert Sugar implied the same worry for Mayweather and said, 'He views himself as the greatest fighter of all time because he's never lost. He cites Sugar Ray Robinson, he lost. It's he [Mayweather] versus Sugar Ray. Sugar Ray lost once in his first 123 fights, against Jake LaMotta, then he reversed that loss 6 weeks later'.

After criticising the Mayweather camp for throwing unfounded drug accusations towards Pacquiao, Sugar added, 'He's not afraid of Pacquiao. What Floyd is afraid of is losing and here was a chance, that's his whole résumé [gone]'.

Losing his unbeaten legacy will take away any claim Mayweather has on being the greatest of all time. Not that an unbeaten record is totally unique, as Rocky Marciano and Joe Calzaghe were world champions who both retired undefeated. Combine both men's records and the two Italians were undefeated in 95 fights. But that alone is not enough to claim to be the best. At one stage in his career, Willie Pep was undefeated in 134 fights. He would finish his career with 11 losses, but whose record is better: the guy who retires undefeated on 50 fights? Or the guy like Pep who lost 11 times, but won 229? The great Mexican Julio Cesar Chavez was undefeated up to his 89th contest. Does that loss in his 90th fight mean that he's less of a fighter than Mayweather, who at the time of writing is 46-0?

In 2010, Pacquiao didn't have an unbeaten legacy to lose and had already registered a defeat to Erik Morales (points decision in 2005), as well as defeats against the little-known Far Eastern fighters Medgoen Singsurat (KO in 1999) and Rustico Torrecampo (KO in 1996).

Those three losses would be continually used by Mayweather as reasons why there should be no 50-50 purse.

Instead of being a burden, the three career defeats proved that Pacquiao could lose to Mayweather and still retain his selling point as one of the most exciting, attacking and dangerous fighters in the world. 'Pac Man' could lose and people would still respect him, not least because he has a polite and humble personality, which is a complete contrast to the wealth-spouting Mayweather.

When interviewed, Pacquiao always comes across well and seems genuinely polite and respectful. Meanwhile Mayweather seems to get flustered and argumentative with every reporter who asks him a mildly challenging question. While Manny built up an image of helping the poor in the Philippines, Floyd got filmed burning $100 bills in a nightclub. In his day, Muhammad Ali earned more than anyone, but there's no footage of him boasting about his wealth. In contrast, Ali built up an image of fighting for the little guy, and the 'Pac Man' follows the same lead. When Ali fought with reporters it was entertaining and on many occasions extremely thought provoking. When Mayweather gets into spats with the media very little transpires other than schoolboy spite. If Mayweather's unlikeable image is a clever ploy to get people to pay to see him lose then it's worked a treat. The contrast in personalities of Mayweather-Pacquiao had clear transparency and certainly would have made for an interesting twist in regards to who the

American public got behind and supported. Normally, if an American fights a foreigner in the US, then home support would be expected, but for this fight there would have been a fascinating split in the American crowd.

After Floyd Mayweather beat Victor Ortiz in October 2011, he told the post-fight press conference, 'The only thing that Floyd Mayweather wanna do is give the fans the fights that they want to see…we only wanna fight the biggest and the best out there and, yes, Pacquiao, you're next'.

It was unusual to hear Mayweather so clear in his intention to get this fight on, and with good reason—because giving us the fight that we wanted might have slightly diverted attention away from the farce that had just happened in the MGM Grand. Those who had purchased the pay-per-view of Mayweather-Ortiz got as much value for their money as those who bought a ticket to see Michael Jackson's *This Is It* at the O2 Arena. Mayweather won the first three rounds. Then in the fourth Ortiz went on the attack and forced Mayweather into the corner. Ortiz got carried away and stupidly went in with a blatant butt to the head. The bullish challenger was taken aside by the referee and docked a point. The two boxers then embraced in the ring as Ortiz hugged Mayweather in apology. As they moved away from the hug, Mayweather saw his chance and knocked out an unguarded opponent with a swift left hook and right hand. The knockout was legal in the eyes of the law, but it was against the spirit of the sport and a cheap form of victory. The HBO commentary team were not hugely impressed. Jim Lampley said, 'If you're the best fighter in the world and you like to claim that you're the best fighter in history, you shouldn't have to do that'. His co-commentator Emanuel Steward was too disgusted to make a comment and the hate-hate relationship between Mayweather and veteran broadcaster Larry Merchant sunk to a new low. 'HBO need to fire you. You ain't shit', blasted the champ to Merchant, who replied, 'I wish I was fifty years younger and I'd kick your ass'.[1]

The HBO team wouldn't be working with Floyd much longer anyway, as he would soon be off to work with the rival broadcaster, Showtime. If the prospects for getting the Pacquiao fight on were bad before, now it looked well and truly doomed, with the biggest rivalry in boxing being HBO/Top Rank Promotions versus Showtime/Golden Boy Promotions.

Not long after beating Ortiz and challenging Pacquiao, Mayweather got the spanner back out by saying that the fight has lost much of its grandeur and would not gross as much as it would have done before.

The status of this super-fight was born when Pacquiao stood over a sparked-out Ricky Hatton in May 2009. Any genuine awe still left was seemingly killed off in December 2012 when Juan Manuel Marquez stood over a sparked-out Manny Pacquiao at the MGM Grand. The 'Pac Man' lay on his face totally motionless. It was as if Ricky Hatton had been rolled over on his front three and a half years earlier. Like Hatton's girlfriend in 2009, Pacquiao's wife cried in distress at ringside, in an invasion of privacy and trauma that the viewer had no wish to intrude upon.

In the build-up to Pacquiao-Marquez, talk still revolved around the fight that went missing. In a studio debate with both boxers round the table, Marquez was asked who he thought would win, considering that he had faced both men. The Mexican said that Pacquiao hit harder, but was insistent that Mayweather would win. The 'Pac Man' laughed off the prediction in a good-natured manner, which would have been in total contrast to how Mayweather would have reacted to hearing someone predict against him.

The most telling moment in this studio debate was that Pacquiao said that he needed to be more aggressive than he had been recently, which indicated that he was slipping from his best.

Earlier in the year, Pacquiao had lost a points decision to Timothy Bradley, but in real terms that was brushed aside, as it was one of the most scandalous and disgraceful decisions ever. Pacquiao, in reality, beat Bradley, but the knockout from Marquez was enough to confirm what everyone suspected, which was that he was now past his prime.

The rumours and suggestions were still lingering but the original majesty of the fight had gone. In September 2013, Floyd fought Canelo Alvarez in the biggest fight of that year and one of the highest grossing fights of all time. Mayweather proved that he was still in his prime and put on a master-class performance. The young Mexican tried and tried but could not break the walls of the best boxing defence on the planet. Despite the hype and interest of the Alvarez fight, Mayweather was still being flooded by his usual tirade of Pacquiao questions and responded:

> I wanted to fight Pacquiao at one particular time, but I wanted to fight him when he was at the top. I'm not going to speak on another man's finance business, but like I said before, I left Top Rank for a reason. He's with Top Rank, so I want him to be happy with Top Rank. Everybody's like, 'Aw, Pacquiao', but I'm just letting you know he's not getting a fight with me.

He added:

> The only way he's getting the fight with me is if he signs
> with Mayweather Promotions. He's got to give me fights with
> Mayweather Promotions. If he don't give me no fights under
> Mayweather Promotions, then he's not getting the fight. That's
> how it is working now, because the ball is in my court. The ball
> has been in my court. I have been the A side. I went to Pacquiao at
> one particular time and I offered him $40 million and I told him, 'I
> will wire you $20 million within 48 hours'. He told me he wanted
> 50-50 and he got off the phone. Some guy named Michael Koncz
> [Pacquiao's adviser] came down here. I don't know who he is.
> He looks like a little weasel. He came down here, was in my gym
> and talked to me. He said, 'If you want the Pacquiao fight, you
> talk to me'. I said, 'What about Top Rank?' He said, 'I run all his
> business'. That's what he told me. I've got everything recorded,
> everything on film.

By now, the argument for the fight happening had gone beyond the
original point of why it was so intriguing in the first place. On the ESPN
boxing show First Take, the pundit and Mayweather cheerleader Stephen
A. Smith was calling for the fight to happen so that the issue could be
put to bed. He pleaded, 'Can we get this over with Floyd? Make the fight
happen. Find a way to get Bob Arum out of the way and make the fight with
Pacquiao. That's what I want because I'm tired of this. Floyd will pick him
apart'.

The fight happening just for the sake of it isn't the boxing event of a generation. We wanted it to happen years earlier because it was a showdown of the two best pound for pound fighters. Not the best pound for pound versus the guy who just passed his prime. The conversation changed from 'they need to get this on', to, 'I don't care anymore'.

But that's not to say that matching the two together would still not have been worthy scheduling. In 2014, *Boxing News* still ranked it as number eight in fights that we want to see in 2014 and said, 'While it is a travesty that the superstar pair have not crossed paths already, a fight between the two premier icons in boxing would transcend the sport and grab the world's attention...Even though it would be four years too late, nothing would make casual observers (and for that matter hardcore fans) sit up and take notice of a sport, to such an extent. It could still be the biggest fight of all time, but the sand is running out on the timer'.

Boxing News laid down 19 other fights that should, for the good of the sport, happen in 2014. Of all 20 fights, less than half carried a prediction of being likely to happen. The editor, Tris Dixon, wrote:

> One thing stands out. From the 20 fights on our list, around five are straightforward enough to make given the current splits between TV networks and promoters and the difference of opinions between fighters. For example, feuding promoters will ensure we won't see the clash of welterweight big hitters Marcos Maidana—who fights for Golden Boy—and Top Rank's Ruslan Provodnikov, and the same thing prevents any talk of a fight between the unbeaten pair of Danny Garcia and Timothy Bradley. Guillermo Rigondeaux and

Leo Santa Cruz are divided by TV networks in the USA, ditto Scott
Quigg and Carl Frampton in the UK. And who knows exactly why
the fight we've wanted for almost half a decade hasn't happened
after just about everyone has been blamed at one point or another
for Floyd Mayweather-Manny Pacquiao imploding. It is easy to
find stumbling blocks and reasons not to work together. It seems
far harder to find common ground, to partner up for mutual benefit.
When you consider that the 20 bouts listed would all, in some
way, benefit the sport, it shows how much the rivalries are hurting
boxing.

In April 2014, Pacquiao avenged Timothy Bradley on points and looked
on good form, leading to calls from the media to finally, once and for all
get this super-fight on and also disrupt the narrative for the final chapter
of the book *The Greatest Fights that Never Were*. Pacquiao informed
Mayweather's camp that, 'The line is open 24 hours, 7 days a week'. *The
Guardian* predicted, 'it may be impossible for either side to turn their back
on it any longer'.

Dan Jones in the *Evening Standard* wrote, 'There is still time for these
ageing titans to collide, the impact showering the world from Las Vegas to
Manila with pay-per-view greenbacks. Any other sport would make this
match. Only boxing could be so dumb and stubborn as to let the biggest fight
of the age disappear into the realm of a historical parlour game. What if?'

A few weeks after Pacquiao-Bradley II, Mayweather beat Golden Boy's
Marcos Maidana on points, in a tough contest in which the Argentinean had
looked good in the early rounds. Mayweather had not looked on prime form,

leading to a speculation that at the age of 37 he could be starting to slip from his peak.

Once again, the most telling nail in the Mayweather-Pacquiao coffin was that Floyd, without Manny, could draw big bucks, and Mr Money tweeted, '$32 million for 36 minutes. I'm waiting for the PPV numbers to come in so I can make another $38 million on the back-end. Making it a grand total of $70 million'.

Mayweather was now listed by *Forbes* as the highest earning athlete in the world, and this despite having never signed a contract with Manchester City. Fighting Pacquiao would still bring in more revenue for Mayweather than any other opponent, but $70 million for a handpicked opponent certainly isn't chicken feed.

A rematch with Maidana was being lined up in September, to be followed possibly by Mayweather-Khan in May 2015. Then Mayweather would have one final fight on his Showtime contract remaining. He insists that it will be his last ever fight and hopes to end on 49-0. The question is: do you take the most money-drawing opponent, or do you handpick one that maintains your unbeaten legacy?

The issue of the damaging impact on boxing is not to be taken lightly in this day and age of other combat sports. When Jack Johnson dodged Sam Langford in the early 20th century there was no other real competition to turn to if you wanted to see two guys fight it out. When Lennox Lewis and Riddick Bowe failed to agree terms in the early 1990s it hurt the sport, but who else was there to turn to, Hulk Hogan and 'Gladiators'? A couple of decades down the line and there is competition; One that is structured and has scheduling and league tables. Mixed martial arts in the form of the organisation UFC is now a major rival to boxing and has grown in fan base and media coverage. Many kids now favour going to an MMA school rather than a boxing gym and that more than anything is a time bomb for the sport. Boxing fans will always be there, but losing talent is catastrophic. One way to encourage a young fighter to go to a boxing gym is to inspire them with greatness.

Barry McGuigan once summed up the paradox of boxing by saying, 'It's artistic and beautiful and it's also disastrous and tragic'. Its artistry was the inspiration of the Pierce Egan phrase when he described the sport as the 'Sweet Science of Bruising'.

Even those who hate boxing, and have every right to, can't deny the grace and movement of the likes of Ali, Leonard and Robinson. I once recall watching a UFC show on TV and trying really hard to like it. I wanted to be a fan and I thought the presentation and structure of the show was brilliant. Instead, it made me understand what it was I liked and preferred about boxing: the footwork, the dancing, the ducking, the hooks, the jabs, the tactics, the cussing, the rhyming, the knock-downs, the ten counts. It made me appreciate the fact that boxers are allowed to get up from the canvas and given a chance to get back in the fight. In MMA once a fighter is down we see him jumped upon and pummelled to a defeat. There's a thuggish reality to MMA that just seems all too real, familiar and depressing in a culture of street brawls and pub fights. At the home of Cus D'Amato in 1980, a 13-year-old Mike Tyson watched his first boxing match on TV, which was Leonard-Duran I. Up to that point extreme violence in Tyson's young life had been part of day-to-day life in the bleak streets of Brownsville. On watching Leonard-Duran, the young Tyson saw something mesmerising and a style of artistic fighting which was far removed from the world that he was from. 'They were both so stylish and deadly, throwing punches so fast. It looked choreographed, like the two of them were acting. I was just amazed. I've never felt that feeling again'.

Mixed martial arts fighters are hugely talented, tough and courageous, but UFC is not the sweet science. It's not to say that UFC doesn't have flickers of class and style, but will we ever see a UFC knockout to rival the grace of Ali's knockout of George Foreman in the Rumble in the Jungle? The way Ali pulled back from one last punch as Foreman was already falling to the canvas was pure poetry. In 1981, Sugar Ray Leonard staggered Tommy Hearns with a right hand in round 14—and the 'Hitman' fell backwards to the ropes and then on towards the corner post. As Leonard moved towards him for more punishment he raised both fists in the air in a show of incredible cockiness and bravado that could only come from the sweet science of bruising. That cockiness, poetry and style does, in the eyes of many of us, beat the spectacle of two barefoot men rolling around on the floor in a steel cage while trying to kick and punch each other. But it has to be on show and at a peak of excellence, otherwise it won't provide that inspiration for fans and potential young fighters.

The paradox in boxing is clear. On one hand it's a sport that outside the ring has been dominated by ruthless characters and criminals who have destroyed people both physically and financially. Yet, on the other hand, because of the heart and sacrifice of the fighters, it's also awe-inspiringly soulful and moving. Because of the staggering amount of immorality in boxing, it has to maintain enough magical, meaningful, monumental and soulful moments to keep the interest of the fan. The boxing writer Jack

Newfield said in his book *The Life and Crimes of Don King* that he could handle the days of corruption in boxing when there was the counterbalance of the and skill and class of Sugar Ray Robinson. To be followed in the 1960s and 1970s by Muhammad Ali, whose soul and magic were irresistible enough to tolerate following a violent sport run by scoundrels. Without greatness to counterbalance the political bullshit, eventually we'll just turn away. Boxing is losing young fans to MMA and will continue to do so if one sport provides the best matches and the other one doesn't.

When Mayweather was asked if boxing needed a match like Mayweather-Pacquiao to keep the sport at a higher pinnacle he responded, 'When you're talking boxing you're talking me. Boxing needs me'.

The heat between Mayweather and UFC has been as big a feud as 'Pretty Boy' as ever had, and when asked about MMA's rivalry with boxing he replied, 'They keep telling me about all these different sports that's stealing our blueprint...Everybody wants to have weigh ins now, first it was freestyle, now they want to put gloves on their hands, they want to have cut men, come on man—everybody wants the boxing blueprint. Boxing has been here for hundreds of years, the rest of this shit that's going on is just a fad'.

Before fighting Juan Manuel Marquez in 2009, Mayweather took another swipe at MMA and said:

> It takes true skills to be in the sport of boxing. And mixed martial arts is for beer drinkers. You can't take my shoes off and take my shirt off and just throw me in a cage, you do that with animals, you don't do that with humans. In boxing we know who's dominating – black fighters and Hispanic fighters and this is not

a racial statement but – there's no white fighters in boxing that's dominating so they had to go to something else and start something new.

In the same interview Mayweather said that the fight that everyone wanted would not happen while Pacquiao had a manager and was not his own boss. So in two statements in the same interview Mayweather summed up what many of us don't like about UFC, but also what we admire about it. Yes, great point about humans fighting in cages, but then in the next breath we had a sportsmen tell us about how he dictates his own schedule. In UFC the boss is Dana White and he calls the shots, not his fighters. 'When we purchased the UFC one of the big problems was that the fights couldn't be made but now we have everybody. Not Arum has this guy, and Golden Boy has this guy, King has this guy. Everybody is under one roof and the best always fight the best. And the fans get to see the fights that the fans want to see'.

On the comparison between his sport and boxing, White said, 'This is a league, it's run different than boxing is…we've put all our time our energy and our money into building this sport and creating more revenue and creating more opportunity for fighters'. White then took a swipe at Mayweather: 'You guys have done nothing but destroy a sport. That's what you've done. This will be the biggest fight in the history of boxing when it comes, the thing will probably do 2.6 million buys and it will be huge and yet these guys sit on the fence'.

White then took a shot at the boxing superstar for his personal issues regarding domestic violence: 'You're lucky that you live in city that cares more about money than it does about justice, or your ass would be sitting in jail right now'.

Dana White was more than happy to turn the screw on those he deemed responsible for ruining boxing and he called Bob Arum a scumbag who never gave back to the sport. Arum responded:

> I never said anything bad about Dana, but he has to realise that because of the monopoly that UFC has, they pay their fighters maybe 20 percent of the proceeds that come on a UFC fight — and we pay fighters over 80 percent. So that's the difference. I mean talk about giving back to the sport — when you pay your talent 20 percent and boxing promoters like myself pay 80 percent who's giving back to whom?

White responded:

> Bob Arum's an idiot, he's a moron. I can't stand him. But I'm a Manny Pacquiao fan...and the biggest non-Bob Arum fan...Bob Arum has no clue what we pay our fighters, he couldn't be any more wrong. Bob Arum's got one guy and he'll take other guys and fight that guy. Bob Arum doesn't have a roster as big as mine where he's employing these guys and they're fighting three to four times a year. He's not bringing up any new talent the way that we are. He doesn't even have a gym anymore.

White went on to call called Mayweather a 'knuckle head' for what he perceived as racist comments against an Asian basketball player, as well as his comments on Pacquiao eating sushi:

> Sushi's from Japan! He's from the Philippines, dummy…what you should worry about is getting in there and making the fight that all the boxing fans want to see. Get in there and fight Manny Pacquiao. You don't deserve more of the purse. If there was ever a fight in history that should be split 50-50 it's the Pacquiao-Mayweather fight. Shut up, both of you split the money up and put on the fight that everybody including me wants to see. Yes I run the UFC but I'm a boxing fan and I wanna see this fight and I know that I speak for millions of other people. Shut up and make the fight, Floyd.

So desperate were people to see this fight, that a bog standard and boring homemade computer game version of the match has as many as one million hits on YouTube! One million views (mine included but I plead research) to watch a computer Pacquiao knock Mayweather out cold with a single left hook that was more unconvincing than a Bill Clinton blow job denial. Even Stevie Wonder would have seen that punch coming, and yet something so staggeringly pointless gets one million hits because the real thing hasn't happened. On the comments section below, one viewer made the point, 'Who the fuck puts this fictional bullshit up, Bob Arum?'

In July 1969, a state of the art computer predicted that Rocky Marciano would beat Muhammad Ali had the two men from different eras met. So to make a quick buck from the hype, both men put their boxing gear on and agreed to take part in a fictional fight film to make 'real' the impossible. It was Ali's forced exile from boxing that made him agree to participate in the film, as his income was limited. My advice for those who have not seen this unique video is to go to YouTube, because it's fascinating to see the two men on screen together in such a way. Despite looking good, it had a crazy ending as Marciano, with blood (tomato ketchup) coming from his nose, floored 'The Greatest' in round 10 with a flurry of punches and the famous Suzie Q.

A beaten Ali crawled on the canvas and got counted out, which was something that would never happen once in real life. The computer, which came to that conclusion, had been fed data by 250 boxing experts and Ali accused the machine of racism by saying that it must have been made in Mississippi! For the benefit of the film, Ali accepted the result and played out the computer's outcome with the long-retired, 45-year-old, wig-wearing Rocky. At one point, the wig was knocked off the head, during a rare occasion when a punch connected, but they edited that moment out of the final cut. After the movie was aired in cinemas Ali would claim that he was ashamed and that he had let his people down. One consideration that the 250 experts obviously didn't factor was Ali's punch resilience, as by this point in time he hadn't been tested by the demon hitters of the 1970s. 1969 was before Ali had sucked up and survived the best punches of Frazier, Norton, Foreman and Shavers, which creates a huge doubt that Marciano would have KO'd him, if he was even able to get near him. On the set of the film the two men formed a friendship, but they would only have the chance to be friends for a month, as in August 1969 Rocky's life ended in a plane crash.

One obvious conclusion to the film's outcome is that conservative America would not have been receptive to a computer Ali beating Marciano during a time when he was banned from boxing and putting up a resistance against the Vietnam War. The accuracy of the computer was tested for real when it predicted that Bob Foster would knockout Joe Frazier in 1970. The reverse happened. Foster got splattered in two rounds and the credibility of the concept fizzled away.

Creating a well-made computer version fight of legends from different eras is something that has merit, but how sad that ones have to be made for great fights that should have happened.

1. Merchant said a few minutes later, 'I don't think I could have kicked his ass fifty years ago but I would have tried it!'

SOURCES

BOOKS

Andre, Sam and Nat Fleischer, *A Pictorial History of Boxing*, Castle, 1987.

Benn, Nigel, *The Dark Destroyer*, Blake Publishing, 2001.

Bruno, Frank, *Frank*, Yellow Jersey Press, 2006.

Calzaghe, Joe, *No Ordinary Joe*, Arrow Books, 2007.

Delsa, Michael C., *Cinderella Man*, Milo, 2005.

Dirs, Ben, *The Hate Game*, Simon & Schuster, 2013.

Eubank, Chris, *Chris Eubank: The Autobiography*, Collins Willow, 2013

Foreman, George, *By George*, A Touchstone Book, 1995.

Froch, Carl, *The Cobra*, Ebury Press, 2011.

Hatton, Ricky, *War and Peace: My Story*, Ricky Hatton, MacMillan, 2013

Hogan, Hulk, *Hollywood Hulk Hogan* (WWE), Simon and Schuster, 2002.

Holmes, Larry, *Against All Odds*, Robson Books, 2010.

Hughes, Damian, and Brian Hughes, Hit Man, Milo, 2010.

Marvellous: The Marvin Hagler Story, Pitch Publishing, 2014.

Kimball, George, *Four Kings*, Mainstream Publishing, 2009.

LaMotta, Jake, *Raging Bull*, Da Capo, 1997.

Newfield, Jack, *The Life and Crimes of Don King*, New York, HEP, 2003.

Margolick, David, *Beyond Glory*, Bloomsbury Publishing, 2005.

McGuigan, Barry, *Cyclone: My Story*, Virgin Books.

McRea, Donald, *Dark Trade*, Mainstream Publishing, 2005.

Moyle, Clay, *Sam Langford: Boxing's Greatest Uncrowned Champion*, B&H, 2012.

Myler, Thomas, *Boxing's Hall of Shame*, Mainstream Publishing, 2006.

Patterson, Floyd, *The Fighting Life of Boxing's Invincible Champion*, W. K. Stratton, 2012.

Odd, Gilbert, *Encyclopaedia of Boxing*, Hamlyn, 1989.

Otty, Harry, *Charley Burley and the Black Murderers' Row*, Tora Book Publishing, 2010.

Stratton, W. K., *Floyd Patterson: The Fighting Life of Boxing's Invincible Champion*, Mainstream Publishing, 2012.

Sugar, Bert and Teddy Atlas, *The Ultimate Book of Boxing Lists*, Running Press, 2011.

Sullivan, Russell, *The Rock of His Times*, University of Illinois Press, 2005.

Tyson, Mike, *Tyson: The Undisputed Truth*, Harper Sports, 2013.

Ward, Geoffrey C., *Unforgivable Blackness*, Pimlico, 2006.

Watson, Michael, *My Biggest Fight*, Sphere, 2011.

X, Malcolm, *The Autobiography of Malcolm*, Penguin, 1987.

OTHER MEDIA OUTLETS

ABC News
Augusta Chronicle
BBC 2 – *Clash of the Titans*
Boxing 24
Boxing News
Boxingrec.com
BBC – *Fighting For Castro*
BBC News and Sports
Chicago Tribune
Daily Mirror
Daily Press
ESPN – *All Time Top 25 Knockouts*
ESPN – *Assault in the Ring*
ESPN – *First Take*
ESPN – *Ringside*
ESPN – *Sport's Classics*
ESPN – *The Thrilla in Manila*
ESPN – *Tyson*
ESPN – *When Larry met Muhammad*
Forbes
Gulf News
HBO
ITV Sports
ITV – *The Fight of Their Lives*
Las Vegas Sun
Momentum – *Boxing In and Out of the ring*
Mr. Bongo – *Sons of Cuba*
National Geographic – *The Cinderella Man*
Setanta Sports
Showtime
Sky Sports
The Guardian
The Independent
The Times
Tolendo Blade
Universal – *Beyond the Mat*
Universal – *Klitschko*
The Evening Standard
The Independent
The Metro
The Ring
Wikipedia
Yahoo News